MONTH IN REVIEW

# KEY GOVERNMENT REPORTS

## VOLUME 17

## INFORMATION SECURITY AND TECHNOLOGY – APRIL 2019

# MONTH IN REVIEW

Additional books and e-books in this series can be found
on Nova's website under the Series tab.

MONTH IN REVIEW

# KEY GOVERNMENT REPORTS

## VOLUME 17

### INFORMATION SECURITY AND TECHNOLOGY – APRIL 2019

ERNEST CLARK
EDITOR

Copyright © 2019 by Nova Science Publishers, Inc.

**All rights reserved.** No part of this book may be reproduced, stored in a retrieval system or transmitted in any form or by any means: electronic, electrostatic, magnetic, tape, mechanical photocopying, recording or otherwise without the written permission of the Publisher.

We have partnered with Copyright Clearance Center to make it easy for you to obtain permissions to reuse content from this publication. Simply navigate to this publication's page on Nova's website and locate the "Get Permission" button below the title description. This button is linked directly to the title's permission page on copyright.com. Alternatively, you can visit copyright.com and search by title, ISBN, or ISSN.

For further questions about using the service on copyright.com, please contact:
Copyright Clearance Center
Phone: +1-(978) 750-8400     Fax: +1-(978) 750-4470     E-mail: info@copyright.com.

## NOTICE TO THE READER

The Publisher has taken reasonable care in the preparation of this book, but makes no expressed or implied warranty of any kind and assumes no responsibility for any errors or omissions. No liability is assumed for incidental or consequential damages in connection with or arising out of information contained in this book. The Publisher shall not be liable for any special, consequential, or exemplary damages resulting, in whole or in part, from the readers' use of, or reliance upon, this material. Any parts of this book based on government reports are so indicated and copyright is claimed for those parts to the extent applicable to compilations of such works.

Independent verification should be sought for any data, advice or recommendations contained in this book. In addition, no responsibility is assumed by the Publisher for any injury and/or damage to persons or property arising from any methods, products, instructions, ideas or otherwise contained in this publication.

This publication is designed to provide accurate and authoritative information with regard to the subject matter covered herein. It is sold with the clear understanding that the Publisher is not engaged in rendering legal or any other professional services. If legal or any other expert assistance is required, the services of a competent person should be sought. FROM A DECLARATION OF PARTICIPANTS JOINTLY ADOPTED BY A COMMITTEE OF THE AMERICAN BAR ASSOCIATION AND A COMMITTEE OF PUBLISHERS.

Additional color graphics may be available in the e-book version of this book.

## Library of Congress Cataloging-in-Publication Data

ISBN: 978-1-53616-003-1

*Published by Nova Science Publishers, Inc. † New York*

# CONTENTS

| | | |
|---|---|---|
| **Preface** | | **vii** |
| **Chapter 1** | Veterans Affairs: Addressing IT Management Challenges Is Essential to Effectively Supporting the Department's Mission<br>*Carol C. Harris* | **1** |
| **Chapter 2** | FEMA Grants Modernization: Improvements Needed to Strengthen Program Management and Cybersecurity<br>*United States Government Accountability Office* | **33** |
| **Chapter 3** | Data Center Optimization: Additional Agency Actions Needed to Meet OMB Goals<br>*United States Government Accountability Office* | **115** |
| **Chapter 4** | Information Technology: Effective Practices Have Improved Agencies' FITARA Implementation<br>*United States Government Accountability Office* | **209** |
| **Contents of Earlier Volumes** | | **241** |
| **Index** | | **247** |

# PREFACE

This book is a comprehensive compilation of all reports, testimony, correspondence and other publications issued by the GAO (Government Accountability Office) during the month of April, grouped according to the topics: Information Security and Technology.

Chapter 1 - The use of IT is crucial to helping VA effectively serve the nation's veterans. Each year the department spends billions of dollars on its information systems and assets. However, VA has experienced challenges in managing its IT programs, raising questions about its ability to deliver intended outcomes needed to help advance the department's mission. To improve federal agencies' IT acquisitions, in December 2014 Congress enacted FITARA. GAO has previously reported on IT management challenges at VA, as well as its progress in implementing FITARA and cybersecurity requirements. GAO was asked to summarize key results and recommendations from its work at VA that examined systems modernization efforts, FITARA implementation, and cybersecurity efforts. To do so, GAO reviewed its recently issued reports and incorporated information on the department's actions in response to GAO's recommendations.

Chapter 2 - FEMA, a component of DHS, annually awards billions of dollars in grants to help communities prepare for, mitigate the effects of, and recover from major disasters. However, FEMA's complex IT environment supporting grants management consists of many disparate systems. In 2008, the agency attempted to modernize these systems but experienced significant challenges. In 2015, FEMA initiated a new endeavor (the GMM program) aimed at streamlining and modernizing the grants management IT environment. GAO was asked to review the GMM program. GAO's objectives were to (1) determine the extent to which FEMA is implementing leading practices for reengineering its grants management processes and incorporating needs into IT requirements; (2) assess the reliability of the program's estimated costs and schedule; and (3) determine the extent to which FEMA is addressing key cybersecurity practices. GAO compared program documentation to leading practices for process reengineering and requirements management, cost and schedule estimation, and cybersecurity risk management, as established by the Software Engineering Institute, National Institute of Standards and Technology, and GAO.

Chapter 3 - In December 2014, Congress enacted federal IT acquisition reform legislation that included provisions related to ongoing federal data center consolidation efforts. OMB's Federal Chief Information Officer launched DCOI to build on prior data center consolidation efforts; improve federal data centers' performance; and establish goals for inventory closures, cost savings and avoidances, and optimizing performance. The 2014 legislation included a provision for GAO to annually review agencies' data center inventories and strategies. Accordingly, GAO's objectives were to (1) evaluate agencies' progress and plans for data center closures and cost savings; (2) assess agencies' progress against OMB's data center optimization targets; (3) and identify effective agency practices for achieving data center closures, cost savings, and optimization progress. To do so, GAO assessed the 24 DCOI agencies' data center inventories as of August 2018; reviewed their reported cost savings documentation; evaluated their data center optimization strategic plans; and assessed their progress against OMB's established optimization targets. GAO also solicited practices that selected agencies reported to be effective in meeting DCOI goals.

*Preface*

Chapter 4 - Congress has long recognized that IT has the potential to enable federal agencies to accomplish their missions more quickly, effectively, and economically. However, fully exploiting this potential has presented challenges to covered agencies, and the federal government's management of IT has produced mixed results. As part of its effort to reform the government-wide management of IT, in December 2014 Congress enacted FITARA. The law included specific requirements related to enhancing Chief Information Officers' (CIO) authorities, improving the risk management of IT investments, reviewing agencies' portfolio of IT investments, consolidating federal data centers, and purchasing software licenses. GAO has reported numerous times on agencies' effectiveness in implementing the provisions of the law and highlighted agencies that have had success in implementing selected provisions. In this chapter, GAO identifies practices that agencies have used to effectively implement FITARA. GAO selected five provisions of FITARA to review: (1) CIO authority enhancements; (2) enhanced transparency and improved risk management; (3) portfolio review; (4) data center consolidation; and (5) software purchasing. GAO then selected nine agencies that had success in implementing at least one of the five provisions. GAO compiled practices where at least one agency was better positioned to implement a provision or realized an IT management improvement or cost savings.

In: Key Government Reports. Volume 17   ISBN: 978-1-53616-003-1
Editor: Ernest Clark   © 2019 Nova Science Publishers, Inc.

*Chapter 1*

# VETERANS AFFAIRS: ADDRESSING IT MANAGEMENT CHALLENGES IS ESSENTIAL TO EFFECTIVELY SUPPORTING THE DEPARTMENT'S MISSION*

## *Carol C. Harris*

### WHY GAO DID THIS STUDY

The use of IT is crucial to helping VA effectively serve the nation's veterans. Each year the department spends billions of dollars on its information systems and assets. However, VA has experienced challenges in managing its IT programs, raising questions about its ability to deliver intended outcomes needed to help advance the department's mission. To improve federal agencies' IT acquisitions, in December 2014 Congress

---

* This is an edited, reformatted and augmented version of United States Government Accountability Office; Testimony before the Subcommittee on Technology Modernization, Committee on Veterans' Affairs, House of Representatives, Accessible Version, Publication No. GAO-19-476T, dated April 2, 2019.

enacted FITARA. GAO has previously reported on IT management challenges at VA, as well as its progress in implementing FITARA and cybersecurity requirements.

GAO was asked to summarize key results and recommendations from its work at VA that examined systems modernization efforts, FITARA implementation, and cybersecurity efforts.

To do so, GAO reviewed its recently issued reports and incorporated information on the department's actions in response to GAO's recommendations.

## WHAT GAO RECOMMENDS

GAO has made numerous recent recommendations to VA aimed at improving the department's IT management. VA has generally agreed with the recommendations and has taken steps to address them; however, the department has fully implemented less than half of them. Fully implementing all of GAO's recommendations would help VA ensure that its IT effectively supports the department's mission.

## WHAT GAO FOUND

The Department of Veterans Affairs (VA) has made limited progress toward addressing information technology (IT) system modernization challenges.

- From 2001 through 2018, VA pursued three efforts to modernize its health information system—the Veterans Health Information Systems and Technology Architecture (VistA). However, these efforts experienced high costs, challenges to ensuring interoperability of health data, and ultimately did not result in a modernized VistA. Regarding the department's fourth and most recent effort, the Electronic Health Record Modernization, GAO recently reported that the governance plan for this program was not yet defined. VA has not fully implemented GAO's recommendation calling for the department to define the role of a key office in the governance plans.

- The Family Caregiver Program, which was established to support family caregivers of seriously injured post-9/11 veterans, has not been supported by an effective IT system. Specifically, GAO reported that, due to limitations with the system, the program office did not have ready access to the types of workload data that would allow it to routinely monitor workload problems created by the program. GAO recommended that VA expedite the process for identifying and implementing an IT system. Although the department concurred with the recommendation, VA has not yet fully addressed it.
- VA had developed the Veterans Benefits Management System—its system that is used for processing disability benefit claims; however, the system did not fully support disability and pension claims, as well as appeals processing. GAO made five recommendations for VA to improve its efforts to effectively complete the development and implementation of the system. The department concurred with the recommendations but has implemented only one thus far.

VA has demonstrated uneven progress toward fully implementing GAO's recommendations related to key Federal Information Technology Acquisition Reform Act (FITARA) provisions. Specifically, VA has implemented all six recommendations in response to GAO's 2014 report on managing software licenses, leading to, among other things, savings of about $65 million over 3 years. However, the department has not fully addressed two recommendations from GAO's 2016 report on managing the risks of major IT investments. Further, the department has not implemented (1) two of four recommendations related to its effort to consolidate data centers and (2) GAO's four recommendations to increase the authority of its Chief Information Officer.

VA's management of cybersecurity has also lacked key elements. For example, GAO reported in May 2016 that VA had established numerous security controls, but had not effectively implemented key elements of its information security program. In addition, as GAO reported in March 2019, the department had not accurately categorized positions to effectively identify critical staffing needs for its cybersecurity workforce. VA has implemented three of six cybersecurity-related recommendations from these two reports.

Chair Lee, Ranking Member Banks, and Members of the Subcommittee:

Thank you for the opportunity to participate in today's hearing regarding the Department of Veterans Affairs' (VA) Office of Information and Technology (OI&T). As you know, the use of information technology (IT) is crucial to helping VA effectively serve the nation's veterans. The department annually spends billions of dollars on its information systems and assets—VA's budget for IT now exceeds $4 billion annually.

However, over many years, VA has experienced challenges in managing its IT projects and programs, raising questions about the efficiency and effectiveness of OI&T and its ability to deliver intended outcomes needed to help advance the department's mission. These challenges have spanned a number of critical initiatives related to modernizing the department's (1) health information system, the Veterans Health Information Systems and Technology Architecture (VistA); (2) program to support family caregivers; and (3) benefits management system. The department has also experienced challenges in implementing provisions of the Federal Information Technology Acquisition Reform Act (commonly referred to as FITARA),[1] and in appropriately addressing cybersecurity risks.

---

[1] *Carl Levin and Howard P. 'Buck' McKeon National Defense Authorization Act for Fiscal Year 2015*, Pub. L. No. 113-291, division A, title VIII, subtitle D, 128 Stat. 3292, 3438-50 (Dec. 19, 2014).

*Veterans Affairs* 5

We have previously reported on these IT management challenges at VA and have made recommendations aimed at improving the department's system acquisitions and operations.[2] At your request, my testimony today summarizes results and recommendations from our work at the department that examined its system modernization efforts, as well as its efforts toward implementing FITARA and addressing cybersecurity issues.

In developing this testimony, we relied on our recently issued reports that addressed IT management issues at VA and our bi-annual high-risk series.[3] We also incorporated information on the department's actions in response to recommendations we made in our previous reports. The reports cited throughout this statement include detailed information on the scope and methodology of our prior reviews.

We conducted the work on which this statement is based in accordance with generally accepted government auditing standards. Those standards

---

[2] GAO, *Electronic Health Records: VA and DOD Need to Support Cost and Schedule Claims, Develop Interoperability Plans, and Improve Collaboration*, GAO-14-302 (Washington, D.C.: Feb. 27, 2014); *VA Health Care: Actions Needed to Address Higher-Than-Expected Demand for the Family Caregiver Program*, GAO-14-675 (Washington, D.C.: Sept. 18, 2014); *Veterans Benefits Management System: Ongoing Development and Implementation Can Be Improved; Goals Are Needed to Promote Increased User Satisfaction*, GAO-15-582 (Washington, D.C.: Sept. 1, 2015); *IT Dashboard: Agencies Need to Fully Consider Risks When Rating Their Major Investments*, GAO-16-494 (Washington, D.C.: June 2, 2016); *Information Technology Reform: Agencies Need to Improve Certification of Incremental Development*, GAO-18-148 (Washington, D.C.: Nov. 7, 2017); *Data Center Optimization: Continued Agency Actions Needed to Meet Goals and Address Prior Recommendations*, GAO-18-264 (Washington, D.C.: May 23, 2018); *Federal Chief Information Officers: Critical Actions Needed to Address Shortcomings and Challenges in Implementing Responsibilities*, GAO-18-93 (Washington, D.C.: Aug. 2, 2018); *Information Security, Agencies Need to Improve Controls over Selected High-Impact Systems*, GAO-16-501 (Washington, D.C.: May 18, 2016); *Information Security: Agencies Need to Improve Implementation of Federal Approach to Securing Systems and Protecting against Intrusions*, GAO-19-105 (Washington, D.C.: Dec. 18, 2018); and *Cybersecurity Workforce: Agencies Need to Accurately Categorize Positions to Effectively Identify Critical Staffing Needs*, GAO-19-144 (Washington, D.C.: Mar. 12, 2019).

[3] GAO maintains a high-risk program to focus attention on government operations that it identifies as high risk due to their greater vulnerabilities to fraud, waste, abuse, and mismanagement or the need for transformation to address economy, efficiency, or effectiveness challenges. VA's issues were highlighted in our 2015 High-Risk Report, GAO, *High-Risk Series: An Update*, GAO-15-290 (Washington, D.C.: Feb. 11, 2015), 2017 update, GAO, *High-Risk Series: Progress on Many High-Risk Areas, While Substantial Efforts Needed on Others*, GAO-17-317 (Washington, D.C.: Feb. 15, 2017), and 2019 update, GAO, *High-Risk Series, Substantial Efforts Needed to Achieve Greater Progress on High-Risk Areas*, GAO-19-157SP (Washington, D.C.: Mar. 6, 2019).

# 6 Carol C. Harris

require that we plan and perform the audit to obtain sufficient, appropriate evidence to provide a reasonable basis for our findings and conclusions based on our audit objectives. We believe that the evidence obtained provides a reasonable basis for our findings and conclusions based on our audit objectives.

## BACKGROUND

VA's mission is to promote the health, welfare, and dignity of all veterans in recognition of their service to the nation by ensuring that they receive medical care, benefits, social support, and lasting memorials. In carrying out this mission, the department operates one of the largest health care delivery systems in America, providing health care to millions of veterans and their families at more than 1,500 facilities.

The department's three major components—the Veterans Health Administration (VHA), the Veterans Benefits Administration (VBA), and the National Cemetery Administration (NCA)—are primarily responsible for carrying out its mission. More specifically, VHA provides health care services, including primary care and specialized care, and it performs research and development to address veterans' needs. VBA provides a variety of benefits to veterans and their families, including disability compensation, educational opportunities, assistance with home ownership, and life insurance. Further, NCA provides burial and memorial benefits to veterans and their families.

## VA Relies Extensively on IT

The use of IT is critically important to VA's efforts to provide benefits and services to veterans. As such, the department operates and maintains an IT infrastructure that is intended to provide the backbone necessary to meet the day-to-day operational needs of its medical centers, veteran-facing systems, benefits delivery systems, memorial services, and all other

## Veterans Affairs 7

systems supporting the department's mission. The infrastructure is to provide for data storage, transmission, and communications requirements necessary to ensure the delivery of reliable, available, and responsive support to all VA staff offices and administration customers, as well as veterans.

Toward this end, the department operates approximately 240 information systems, manages approximately 314,000 desktop computers and 30,000 laptops, and administers nearly 460,000 network user accounts for employees and contractors to facilitate providing benefits and health care to veterans. These systems are used for the determination of benefits, benefits claims processing, patient admission to hospitals and clinics, and access to health records, among other services.

VHA's systems provide capabilities to establish and maintain electronic health records that health care providers and other clinical staff use to view patient information in inpatient, outpatient, and long-term care settings. The department's health information system—VistA—serves an essential role in helping the department to fulfill its health care delivery mission.

Specifically, VistA is an integrated medical information system that was developed in-house by the department's clinicians and IT personnel, and has been in operation since the early 1980s.[4] The system consists of 104 separate computer applications, including 56 health provider applications; 19 management and financial applications; eight registration, enrollment, and eligibility applications; five health data applications; and three information and education applications. Within VistA, an application called the Computerized Patient Record System enables the department to create and manage an individual electronic health record for each VA patient.

In June 2017, the former VA Secretary announced that the department planned to acquire the same Cerner electronic health record system that the

---

[4] VistA began operation in 1983 as the Decentralized Hospital Computer Program. In 1996, the name of the system was changed to VistA.

8                          *Carol C. Harris*

Department of Defense (DOD) has acquired.[5] VA's effort—the Electronic Health Record Modernization (EHRM) program—calls for the deployment of a new electronic health record system at three initial sites in 2020, with a phased implementation of the remaining sites over the next decade.

In addition, VBA relies on the Veterans Benefits Management System (VBMS) to collect and store information such as military service records, medical examinations, and treatment records from VA, DOD, and private medical service providers. In 2014, VA issued its 6-year strategic plan, which emphasizes the department's goal of increasing veterans' access to benefits and services, eliminating the disability claims backlog, and ending veteran homelessness. According to the plan, the department intends to improve access to benefits and services through the use of enhanced technology to provide veterans with access to more effective care management.

The plan also calls for VA to eliminate the disability claims backlog by fully implementing an electronic claims process that is intended to reduce processing time and increase accuracy. Further, the department has an initiative under way that provides services, such as health care, housing assistance, and job training, to end veteran homelessness. Toward this end, VA is working with other agencies, such as the Department of Health and Human Services, to implement more coordinated data entry systems to streamline and facilitate access to appropriate housing and services.

## VA Manages IT Resources Centrally

Since 2007, VA has been operating a centralized organization, OI&T, in which most key functions intended for effective management of IT are performed. This office is led by the Assistant Secretary for Information and Technology—VA's Chief Information Officer (CIO). The office is

---

[5] In July 2015, DOD awarded a $4.3 billion contract for a commercial electronic health record system developed by Cerner, to be known as MHS GENESIS. The transition to the new system began in February 2017 in the Pacific Northwest region of the United States and is expected to be completed in 2022.

*Veterans Affairs* 9

responsible for providing strategy and technical direction, guidance, and policy related to how IT resources are to be acquired and managed for the department, and for working closely with its business partners—such as VHA—to identify and prioritize business needs and requirements for IT systems. Among other things, OI&T has responsibility for managing the majority of VA's IT-related functions, including the maintenance and modernization of VistA.[6] As of January 2019, OI&T was comprised of about 15,800 staff, with more than half of these positions filled by contractors.

## VA Is Requesting about $5.9 Billion for IT and a New Electronic Health Record System for Fiscal Year 2020

VA's fiscal year 2020 budget request includes about $5.9 billion for OI&T and its new electronic health record system. Of this amount, about $4.3 billion was requested for OI&T, which represents a $240 million increase over the $4.1 billion enacted for 2019. The request seeks the following levels of funding:

- $401 million for new systems development efforts to support current health care systems platforms, and to replace legacy systems, such as the Financial Management System;
- approximately $2.7 billion for the operations and maintenance of existing systems, which includes $327.3 million for infrastructure readiness that is to support the transition to the new electronic health record system; and
- approximately $1.2 billion for administration.

Additionally, the department requested about $1.6 billion for the EHRM program. This amount is an increase of $496 million over the $1.1

---

[6] VistA is a joint program with OI&T and VHA.

billion that was enacted for the program for fiscal year 2019. The request includes the following:

- $1.1 billion for the contract with the Cerner Corporation to acquire the new system,
- $161,800 for program management, and
- $334,700 for infrastructure support.

## VA's Management of IT Has Contributed to High-Risk Designations

In 2015, we designated *VA Health Care* as a high-risk area for the federal government and noted that IT challenges were among the five areas of concern.[7] In part, we identified limitations in the capacity of VA's existing systems, including the outdated, inefficient nature of certain systems and a lack of system interoperability—that is, the ability to exchange and use electronic health information—as contributors to the department's IT challenges related to health care.

Also, in February 2015, we added *Improving the Management of IT Acquisitions and Operations* to our list of high-risk areas.[8] Specifically, federal IT investments were too frequently failing or incurring cost overruns and schedule slippages while contributing little to mission-related outcomes. We have previously reported that the federal government has spent billions of dollars on failed IT investments, including at VA.[9]

---

[7] GAO maintains a high-risk program to focus attention on government operations that it identifies as high risk due to their greater vulnerabilities to fraud, waste, abuse, and mismanagement or the need for transformation to address economy, efficiency, or effectiveness challenges. VA's issues were highlighted in our 2015 High-Risk Report, GAO, *High-Risk Series: An Update*, GAO-15-290 (Washington, D.C.: Feb. 11, 2015) and 2017 update, GAO, *High-Risk Series: Progress on Many High-Risk Areas, While Substantial Efforts Needed on Others*, GAO-17-317 (Washington, D.C.: Feb. 15, 2017).

[8] GAO-15-290.

[9] GAO, *Information Technology: Management Improvements Are Essential to VA's Second Effort to Replace Its Outpatient Scheduling System*, GAO-10-579 (Washington, D.C.: May 27, 2010); *Information Technology: Actions Needed to Fully Establish Program*

*Veterans Affairs*    11

Our 2017 update to the high-risk report noted that VA had partially met our leadership commitment criterion by involving top leadership in addressing the IT challenges portion of the VA Health Care high-risk area; however, it had not met the action plan, monitoring, demonstrated progress, or capacity criteria.

We have also identified VA as being among a handful of departments with one or more archaic legacy systems. Specifically, in our May 2016 report on legacy systems used by federal agencies, we identified two of VA's systems as being over 50 years old—the Personnel and Accounting Integrated Data system and the Benefits Delivery Network system.[10] These systems were among the 10 oldest investments and/or systems that were reported by 12 selected agencies.

Accordingly, we recommended that the department identify and plan to modernize or replace its legacy systems. VA addressed the recommendation in May 2018, when it provided a Comprehensive Information Technology Plan that showed a detailed roadmap for the key programs and systems required for modernization. The plan included time frames, activities to be performed, and functions to be replaced or enhanced. The plan also indicated that the Personnel and Accounting Integrated Data system and the Benefits Delivery Network system are to be decommissioned in quarters 3 and 4 of fiscal year 2019, respectively.

Our March 2019 update to our high-risk series noted that the ratings for leadership commitment criterion regressed, while the action plan criterion improved for the IT Challenges portion of the VA Health Care area.[11] The capacity, monitoring, and demonstrated progress criteria remained unchanged. Our work continued to indicate that VA was not yet able to demonstrate progress in this area.

Since its 2015 high-risk designation, we have made 14 new recommendations in the *VA Health Care* area, 12 of which were made since our 2017 high-risk report was issued. For example, in June 2017, to

---

*Management Capability for VA's Financial and Logistics Initiative*, GAO-10-40 (Washington, D.C.: Oct. 26, 2009).

[10] GAO, *Information Technology: Federal Agencies Need to Address Aging Legacy Systems*, GAO-16-468 (Washington, D.C.: May 25, 2016).

[11] GAO-19-157SP.

address deficiencies we recommended that the department take six actions to provide clinicians and pharmacists with improved tools to support pharmacy services to veterans and reduce risks to patient safety. VA generally concurred with these recommendations; however, all of them remain open.

## FITARA Is Intended to Help VA and Other Agencies Improve Their IT Acquisitions

Congress enacted FITARA in December 2014 to improve agencies' acquisitions of IT and enable Congress to better monitor agencies' progress and hold them accountable for reducing duplication and achieving cost savings. The law applies to VA and other covered agencies.[12] It includes specific requirements related to seven areas, including agency CIO authority, data center consolidation and optimization, risk management of IT investments, and government-wide software purchasing.[13]

- Agency CIO authority enhancements. CIOs at covered agencies are required to (1) approve the IT budget requests of their respective agencies, (2) certify that IT investments are adequately implementing incremental development, as defined in capital

---

[12] The provisions apply to the agencies covered by the Chief Financial Officers Act of 1990, 31 U.S.C. § 901(b). These agencies are the Departments of Agriculture, Commerce, Defense, Education, Energy, Health and Human Services, Homeland Security, Housing and Urban Development, Justice, Labor, State, the Interior, the Treasury, Transportation, and Veterans Affairs; the Environmental Protection Agency, General Services Administration, National Aeronautics and Space Administration, National Science Foundation, Nuclear Regulatory Commission, Office of Personnel Management, Small Business Administration, Social Security Administration, and U.S. Agency for International Development. However, FITARA has generally limited application to the Department of Defense.

[13] FITARA also includes requirements for covered agencies to enhance the transparency and improve risk management of IT investments, annually review IT investment portfolios, expand training and use of IT acquisition cadres, and compare their purchases of services and supplies to what is offered under the federal strategic sourcing initiative that the General Services Administration is to develop. The Federal Strategic Sourcing Initiative is a program established by the General Services Administration and the Department of the Treasury to address government-wide opportunities to strategically source commonly purchased goods and services and eliminate duplication of efforts across agencies.

# Veterans Affairs

planning guidance issued by the Office of Management and Budget (OMB), (3) review and approve contracts for IT, and (4) approve the appointment of other agency employees with the title of CIO.

- Federal data center consolidation initiative. Agencies are required to provide OMB with a data center inventory, a strategy for consolidating and optimizing their data centers (to include planned cost savings), and quarterly updates on progress made. The law also requires OMB to develop a goal for how much is to be saved through this initiative, and provide annual reports on cost savings achieved.[14]

- Enhanced transparency and improved risk management in IT investments. OMB and covered agencies are to make detailed information on federal IT investments publicly available, and department-level CIOs are to categorize their major IT investments by risk.[15] Additionally, in the case of major investments rated as high risk for 4 consecutive quarters,[16] the act required that the department-level CIO and the investment's program manager conduct a review aimed at identifying and addressing the causes of the risk.

- Government-wide software purchasing program. The General Services Administration is to enhance government-wide acquisition and management of software and allow for the purchase of a software license agreement that is available for use by all executive branch agencies as a single user. Additionally, the *Making Electronic Government Accountable by Yielding Tangible*

---

[14] In November 2017, the *FITARA Enhancement Act of 2017* was enacted into law to extend the sunset date for the data center provisions of FITARA. The law's data center consolidation and optimization provisions currently expire on October 1, 2020. Pub. L. No. 115-88 (Nov. 21, 2017).

[15] "Major IT investment" means a system or an acquisition requiring special management attention because it has significant importance to the mission or function of the government; significant program or policy implications; high executive visibility; high development, operating, or maintenance costs; an unusual funding mechanism; or is defined as major by the agency's capital planning and investment control process.

[16] The IT Dashboard lists the CIO-reported risk level of all major IT investments at federal agencies on a quarterly basis.

14                         *Carol C. Harris*

*Efficiencies Act of 2016*, or the "MEGABYTE Act," further enhanced CIOs' management of software licenses by requiring agency CIOs to establish an agency software licensing policy and a comprehensive software license inventory to track and maintain licenses, among other requirements.[17]

In June 2015, OMB released guidance describing how agencies are to implement FITARA.[18] This guidance is intended to, among other things:

- assist agencies in aligning their IT resources with statutory requirements;
- establish government-wide IT management controls that will meet the law's requirements, while providing agencies with flexibility to adapt to unique agency processes and requirements;
- clarify the CIO's role and strengthen the relationship between agency CIOs and bureau CIOs; and
- strengthen CIO accountability for IT costs, schedules, performance, and security.

## VA and Other Agencies Face Cybersecurity Risks

The federal approach and strategy for securing information systems is prescribed by federal law and policy. The Federal Information Security Modernization Act (FISMA) provides a comprehensive framework for ensuring the effectiveness of information security controls over information resources that support federal operations and assets.[19] In

---

[17] Pub. L. No. 114-210 130 Stat. 824 (July 29, 2016).

[18] OMB, *Management and Oversight of Federal Information Technology*, Memorandum M15-14 (Washington, D.C.: June 10, 2015).

[19] The *Federal Information Security Modernization Act of 2014* (FISMA 2014) (Pub. L. No. 113-283, Dec. 18, 2014) largely superseded the *Federal Information Security Management Act of 2002* (FISMA 2002), enacted as *Title III, E-Government Act of 2002*, Pub. L. No. 107-347, 116 Stat. 2899, 2946 (Dec. 17, 2002). As used in this chapter, FISMA refers both to FISMA 2014 and to those provisions of FISMA 2002 that were either incorporated into FISMA 2014 or were unchanged and continue in full force and effect.

*Veterans Affairs* 15

addition, the *Federal Cybersecurity Enhancement Act of 2015* requires protecting federal networks through the use of federal intrusion prevention and detection capabilities. Further, Executive Order 13800, *Strengthening the Cybersecurity of Federal Networks and Critical Infrastructure*,[20] directs agencies to manage cybersecurity risks to the federal enterprise by, among other things, using the National Institute of Standards and Technology *Framework for Improving Critical Infrastructure Cybersecurity*[21] (cybersecurity framework).

Federal agencies, including VA, and our nation's critical infrastructures— such as energy, transportation systems, communications, and financial services—are dependent on IT systems and electronic data to carry out operations and to process, maintain, and report essential information. The security of these systems and data is vital to public confidence and national security, prosperity, and well-being.

Because many of these systems contain vast amounts of personally identifiable information, agencies must protect the confidentiality, integrity, and availability of this information. In addition, they must effectively respond to data breaches and security incidents when they occur.

The risks to IT systems supporting the federal government and the nation's critical infrastructure are increasing, including insider threats from witting or unwitting employees, escalating and emerging threats from around the globe, and the emergence of new and more destructive attacks. Cybersecurity incidents continue to impact federal entities and the information they maintain. According to OMB's 2018 annual FISMA report to Congress, agencies reported 35,277 information security incidents to DHS's U.S. Computer Emergency Readiness Team[22] in fiscal year 2017.

---

[20] The White House, *Strengthening the Cybersecurity of Federal Networks and Critical Infrastructure*, Executive Order 13800 (Washington, D.C.: May 11, 2017), 82 Fed. Reg. 22391 (May 16, 2017).

[21] National Institute of Standards and Technology, *Framework for Improving Critical Infrastructure Cybersecurity*, Version 1.1 (Gaithersburg, MD: Apr. 16, 2018).

[22] Within DHS, the U.S. Computer Emergency Readiness Team is a component of the National Cybersecurity and Communications Integration Center. It serves as the central federal information security incident center specified by FISMA.

## VA HAS MADE LIMITED PROGRESS TOWARD ADDRESSING IT SYSTEM MODERNIZATION CHALLENGES

VA has made limited progress toward addressing the IT management challenges for three critical initiatives: VistA, the Family Caregiver Program, and VBMS. Specifically, the department has recently initiated its fourth effort to modernize VistA, but uncertainty remains regarding the program's governance. In addition, although VA has taken steps to address our recommendations for the Family Caregiver Program and VBMS, the department has not fully implemented most of them.

### VA Recently Initiated Its Fourth Effort to Modernize VistA

VA has pursued four efforts over nearly 2 decades to modernize VistA.[23] These efforts—HealtheVet, the integrated Electronic Health Record (iEHR), VistA Evolution, and EHRM—reflect varying approaches that the department has considered to achieve a modernized health care system. Figure 1 shows a timeline of the four efforts that VA has pursued to modernize VistA since 2001.

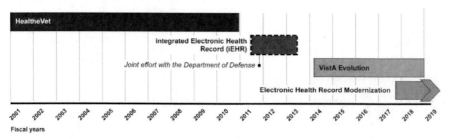

Source: GAO analysis of Department of Veterans Affairs data. | GAO-19-476T.

Figure 1. Timeline of the Department of Veterans Affairs Four Efforts to Modernize the Veterans Health Information Systems and Technology Architecture (VistA) Since 2001.

---

[23] GAO, *VA Health IT Modernization: Historical Perspective on Prior Contracts and Update on Plans for New Initiative*, GAO-18-208 (Washington, D.C.: Jan. 18, 2018).

## *HealtheVet*

In 2001, VA undertook its first VistA modernization project, the HealtheVet initiative, with the goals of standardizing the department's health care system and eliminating the approximately 130 different systems used by its field locations at that time. HealtheVet was scheduled to be fully implemented by 2018 at a total estimated development and deployment cost of about $11 billion. As part of the effort, the department had planned to develop or enhance specific areas of system functionality through six projects, which were to be completed between 2006 and 2012.

In June 2008, we reported that the department had made progress on the HealtheVet initiative, but noted concerns with its project planning and governance.[24] In June 2009, the Secretary of Veterans Affairs announced that VA would stop financing failed projects and improve the management of its IT development projects. Subsequently in August 2010, the department reported that it had terminated the HealtheVet initiative.

## *iEHR*

In February 2011, VA began its second VistA modernization initiative, the iEHR program, in conjunction with DOD. The program was intended to replace the two separate electronic health record systems used by the two departments with a single, shared system. In addition, because both departments would be using the same system, this approach was expected to largely sidestep the challenges that had been encountered in trying to achieve interoperability between their two separate systems.

Initial plans called for the development of a single, joint iEHR system consisting of 54 clinical capabilities to be delivered in six increments between 2014 and 2017. Among the agreed-upon capabilities to be delivered were those supporting laboratory, anatomic pathology, pharmacy, and immunizations. According to VA and DOD, the single system had an estimated life cycle cost of $29 billion through the end of fiscal year 2029.

---

[24] GAO-08-805.

However, in February 2013, the Secretaries of VA and DOD announced that they would not continue with their joint development of a single electronic health record system. This decision resulted from an assessment of the iEHR program that the secretaries had requested in December 2012 because of their concerns about the program facing challenges in meeting deadlines, costing too much, and taking too long to deliver capabilities. In 2013, the departments abandoned their plan to develop the integrated system and stated that they would again pursue separate modernization efforts.

### VistA Evolution

In December 2013, VA initiated its VistA Evolution program as a joint effort of VHA and OI&T. The program was to be comprised of a collection of projects and efforts focused on improving the efficiency and quality of veterans' health care, modernizing the department's health information systems, increasing the department's data exchange and interoperability with DOD and private sector health care partners, and reducing the time it takes to deploy new health information management capabilities. Further, the program was intended to result in lower costs for system upgrades, maintenance, and sustainment. However, VA ended the VistA Evolution program in December 2018 to focus on its new electronic health record system acquisition.

### EHRM

In June 2017, VA's Secretary announced a significant shift in the department's approach to modernizing VistA. Specifically, rather than continue to use VistA, the Secretary stated that the department would acquire the same electronic health record system that DOD is implementing. In this regard, DOD awarded a contract to acquire a new integrated electronic health record system developed by the Cerner Corporation. According to the Secretary, VA decided to acquire this same product because it would allow all of VA's and DOD's patient data to reside in one system, thus enabling seamless care between the department and DOD without the manual and electronic exchange and reconciliation of data between two separate systems.

According to the Secretary, this fourth VistA modernization initiative is intended to minimize customization and system differences that currently exist within the department's medical facilities, and ensure the consistency of processes and practices within VA and DOD. When fully operational, the system is intended to be a single source for patients to access their medical history and for clinicians to use that history in real time at any VA or DOD medical facility, which may result in improved health care outcomes. According to VA's Chief Technology Officer, Cerner is expected to provide integration, configuration, testing, deployment, hosting, organizational change management, training, sustainment, and licenses necessary to deploy the system in a manner that meets the department's needs.

To expedite the acquisition, in June 2017, the Secretary signed a "Determination and Findings," for a public interest exception[25] to the requirement for full and open competition, and authorized VA to issue a solicitation directly to Cerner. Accordingly, the department awarded a contract to Cerner in May 2018 for a maximum of $10 billion over 10 years. Cerner is to replace VistA with a commercial electronic health record system. This new system is to support a broad range of health care functions that include, for example, acute care, clinical decision support, dental care, and emergency medicine. When implemented, the new system will be expected to provide access to authoritative clinical data sources and become the authoritative source of clinical data to support improved health, patient safety, and quality of care provided by VA.

Further, the department has estimated that, as of November 2018, an additional $6.1 billion in funding, above the Cerner contract amount, will be needed to fund additional project management support supplied by outside contractors, government labor costs, and infrastructure improvements over a 10-year implementation period.

---

[25] FAR, 48 C.F.R. § 6.302-7.

# 20                                 *Carol C. Harris*

Deployment of the new electronic health record system at three initial sites is planned for March 2020,[26] with a phased implementation of the remaining sites over the next decade. Each VA medical facility is expected to continue using VistA until the new system has been deployed at that location.

After VA announced in June 2017 that it planned to acquire the Cerner electronic health record system, we testified in June 2018 that a governance structure had been proposed that would be expected to leverage existing joint governance facilitated by the Interagency Program Office.[27] At that time, VA's program officials had stated that the department's governance plans for the new program were expected to be finalized in October 2018. However, the officials had not indicated what role, if any, the Interagency Program Office was to have in the governance process. This office has been involved in various approaches to increase health information interoperability since it was established by the National Defense Authorization Act for Fiscal Year 2008 to function as the single point of accountability for DOD's and VA's electronic health record system interoperability efforts.

In September 2018, we recommended that VA clearly define the role and responsibilities of the Interagency Program Office in the governance plans for acquisition of the department's new electronic health record system.[28] The department concurred with our recommendation and stated that the Joint Executive Committee, a joint governance body comprised of leadership from DOD and VA, had approved a role for the Interagency Program Office that included providing expertise, guidance, and support for DOD, VA, and joint governance bodies as the departments continue to acquire and implement interoperable electronic health record systems.

However, the department has not yet provided documentation supporting these actions and how they relate to VA's governance structure

---

[26] The three initial deployment sites are the Mann-Grandstaff, American Lake, and Seattle VA Medical Centers.

[27] GAO, *VA IT Modernization: Preparations for Transitioning to a New Electronic Health Record System Are Ongoing*, GAO-18-636T (Washington, D.C.: June 26, 2018).

[28] GAO, *Electronic Health Records: Clear Definition of the Interagency Program Office's Role in VA's New Modernization Effort Would Strengthen Accountability*, GAO-18-696T (Washington, D.C.: Sept. 13, 2018).

for the new acquisition. In addition, the role described does not appear to position the office to be the single point of accountability originally identified in the National Defense Authorization Act for Fiscal Year 2008. We continue to monitor the department's governance plans for the acquisition of the new electronic health record system and its relationship with the Interagency Program Office.

## The Family Caregiver Program Has Not Been Supported by an Effective IT System

In May 2010, VA was required by statute to establish a program to support family caregivers of seriously injured post-9/11 veterans. In May 2011, VHA implemented its Family Caregiver Program at all VA medical centers across the country, offering caregivers an array of services, including a monthly stipend, training, counseling, referral services, and expanded access to mental health and respite care. In fiscal year 2014, VHA obligated over $263 million for the program.

In September 2014, we reported that the Caregiver Support Program office, which manages the program, did not have ready access to the types of workload data that would allow it to routinely monitor the effects of the Family Caregiver Program on VA medical centers' resources due to limitations with the program's IT system—the Caregiver Application Tracker.[29] Program officials explained that this system was designed to manage a much smaller program and, as a result, the system has limited capabilities. Outside of obtaining basic aggregate program statistics, the program office was not able to readily retrieve data from the system that would allow it to better assess the scope and extent of workload problems at VA medical centers.

Program officials also expressed concern about the reliability of the system's data. The lack of ready access to comprehensive workload data impeded the program office's ability to monitor the program and identify

---

[29] GAO-14-675.

workload problems or make modifications as needed. This runs counter to federal standards for internal control which state that agencies should monitor their performance over time and use the results to correct identified deficiencies and make improvements.

We also noted in our report that program officials told us that they had taken initial steps to obtain another IT system to support the Family Caregiver Program, but they were not sure how long it would take to implement. Accordingly, we recommended that VA expedite the process for identifying and implementing a system that would fully support the Family Caregiver Program. VA concurred with our recommendation and subsequently began taking steps to implement a replacement system. However, the department has encountered challenges related to the system implementation efforts. We have ongoing work to evaluate VA's effort to acquire a new IT system to support the Family Caregiver Program.

## Additional Actions Can Improve Efforts to Develop and Use the Veterans Benefits Management System

In September 2015, we reported that VBA had made progress in developing and implementing VBMS—its system for processing disability benefit claims—but also noted that additional actions could improve efforts to develop and use the system.[30] Specifically, VBA had deployed the initial version of the system to all of its regional offices as of June 2013. Further, after initial deployment, it continued developing and implementing additional system functionality and enhancements to support the electronic processing of disability compensation claims.

Nevertheless, we pointed out that VBMS was not able to fully support disability and pension claims, as well as appeals processing. While the Under Secretary for Benefits stated in March 2013 that the development of the system was expected to be completed in 2015, implementation of functionality to fully support electronic claims processing was delayed

---

[30] GAO-15-582.

beyond 2015. In addition, VBA had not produced a plan that identified when the system would be completed. Accordingly, holding VBA management accountable for meeting a time frame and demonstrating progress was difficult.

Our report further noted that, even as VBA continued its efforts to complete the development and implementation of VBMS, three areas were in need of increased management attention: cost estimating, system availability, and system defects. We also noted in our report that VBA had not conducted a customer satisfaction survey that would allow the department to compile data on how users viewed the system's performance and, ultimately, to develop goals for improving the system.

We made five recommendations to improve VA's efforts to effectively complete the development and implementation of VBMS. VA agreed with four of the recommendations. In addition, the department has addressed one of the recommendations—that it establish goals for system response time and use the goals as the basis for reporting system performance.

However, the department has not yet fully addressed our remaining recommendations to (1) develop a plan with a time frame and a reliable cost estimate for completing VBMS, (2) reduce the incidence of system defects present in new releases, (3) assess user satisfaction, and (4) establish satisfaction goals to promote improvement. Continued attention to these important areas can improve VA's efforts to effectively complete the development and implementation of VBMS and, in turn, more effectively support the department's processing of disability benefit claims.

# VA HAS DEMONSTRATED UNEVEN PROGRESS TOWARD IMPLEMENTING KEY FITARA PROVISIONS

FITARA included provisions for federal agencies to, among other things, enhance government-wide acquisition and management of software, improve the risk management of IT investments, consolidate data centers, and enhance CIOs' authorities. Since its enactment, we have reported numerous times on VA's efforts toward implementing FITARA.[31]

VA's progress toward implementing key FITARA provisions has been uneven. Specifically, VA issued a software licensing policy and has generated an inventory of its software licenses to inform future investment decisions. However, the department did not fully address requirements related to IT investment risk, data center consolidation, or CIO authority enhancement.

## Software Licensing

VA has made progress in addressing federal software licensing requirements. In May 2014, we reported on federal agencies' management of software licenses and stressed that better management was needed to achieve significant savings government-wide.[32] Specifically regarding VA, we noted that the department did not have comprehensive policies that included the establishment of clear roles and central oversight authority for managing enterprise software license agreements, among other things. We also noted that it had not established a comprehensive software license inventory, a leading practice that would help the department to adequately manage its software licenses.

The inadequate implementation of these and other leading practices in software license management was partially due to weaknesses in the department's policies related to licensing management. Thus, we made six recommendations to VA to improve its policies and practices for managing licenses. For example, we recommended that the department regularly track and maintain a comprehensive inventory of software licenses and analyze the inventory to identify opportunities to reduce costs and better inform investment decision making.

---

[31] GAO-16-494, GAO-16-469, GAO-18-148, GAO-18-264, GAO-18-93.
[32] GAO, *Federal Software Licenses: Better Management Needed to Achieve Significant Savings Government-Wide*, GAO-14-413 (Washington, D.C.: May 22, 2014).

*Veterans Affairs* 25

Since our 2014 report, VA has taken actions to implement all six recommendations. For example, the department implemented a solution to generate and maintain a comprehensive inventory of software licenses using automated tools for the majority of agency software license spending and/or enterprise-wide licenses. Additionally, the department implemented a solution to analyze agency-wide software license data, including usage and costs; and it subsequently identified approximately $65 million in cost savings over 3 years due to analyzing one of its software licenses.

### Risk Management

VA has made limited progress in addressing the FITARA requirements related to managing the risks associated with IT investments. In June 2016, we reported on risk ratings assigned to investments by CIOs.[33] We noted that the department had reviewed compliance with risk management practices, but had not assessed active risks when developing its risk ratings.

VA determined its ratings by quantifying and combining inputs such as cost and schedule variances, risk exposure values, and compliance with agency processes. Metrics for compliance with agency processes included those related to program and project management, project execution, the quality of investment documentation, and whether the investment was regularly updating risk management plans and logs.

When developing CIO ratings, VA chose to focus on investments' risk management processes, such as whether a process was in place or whether a risk log was current. Such approaches did not consider individual risks, such as funding cuts or staffing changes, which detail the probability and impact of pending threats to success. Instead, VA's CIO rating process considered several specific risk management criteria: whether an investment (1) had a risk management strategy, (2) kept the risk register current and complete, (3) clearly prioritized risks, and (4) put mitigation plans in place to address risks. As a result, we recommended that VA factor active risks into its CIO ratings. We also recommended that the

---

[33] GAO-16-494.

26                *Carol C. Harris*

department ensure that these ratings reflect the level of risk facing an investment relative to that investment's ability to accomplish its goals. VA concurred with the recommendations and cited actions it planned to take to address them.

## Data Center Consolidation

VA has reported progress on consolidating and optimizing its data centers, although this progress has fallen short of targets set by OMB.[34] Specifically, VA reported a total inventory of 415 data centers, of which 39 had been closed as of August 2017.[35] While the department anticipated another 10 data centers would be closed by the end of fiscal year 2018, these closures fell short of the targets set by OMB. Further, while VA reported $23.61 million in data center-related cost savings and avoidances from 2012 through August 2017, the department did not realize further savings from the additional 10 data center closures.[36]

In addition, as of February 2017, VA reported meeting one of OMB's five data center optimization metrics related to power usage effectiveness. Also, the department's data center optimization strategic plan indicated that VA planned to meet three of the five metrics by the end of fiscal year 2018. Further, while OMB directed agencies to replace manual collection and reporting of metrics with automated tools no later than fiscal year 2018, the department had only implemented automated tools at 6 percent of its data centers.

---

[34] GAO-18-264.

[35] VA reported this data in its August 2017 inventory update to OMB.

[36] For additional information, see Department of Veterans Affairs, Office of Inspector General, *Lost Opportunities for Efficiencies and Savings During Data Center Consolidation*, 16-04396-44 (Washington, D.C.: Jan. 30, 2019). In January 2019, the VA Office of the Inspector General released a report that concluded VA had not reported a projected 860 facilities as data centers, due to incorrect internal agency guidance on what should be classified as a data center. The department agreed with the report's associated recommendations to develop additional guidance on determining what facilities were subject to OMB's data center optimization initiative and to establish a process for conducting a VA-wide inventory of data centers. The VA Office of Inspector General reports the status of these recommendations as closed, based on actions taken by the department.

## Veterans Affairs

We have recommended that VA take actions to address data center savings goals and optimization performance targets identified by OMB.[37] The department has taken actions to address these recommendations, including reporting data center consolidation savings and avoidance costs to OMB and updating its data center optimization strategic plan. However, the department has yet to address recommendations related to areas that we reported as not meeting OMB's established targets, including implementing automated monitoring tools at its data centers.

### CIO Authorities

VA has made limited progress in addressing the CIO authority requirements of FITARA. Specifically, in November 2017, we reported on agencies' efforts to utilize incremental development practices for selected major investments.[38] We noted that VA's CIO had certified the use of adequate incremental development for all 10 of the department's major IT investments. However, VA had not updated the department's policy and process for the CIO's certification of major IT investments' adequate use of incremental development, in accordance with OMB's guidance on the implementation of FITARA, as we had recommended. As of October 2018, a VA official stated that the department was working to draft a policy to address our recommendation, but did not identify time frames for when all activities would be completed.

In January 2018, we reported on the need for agencies to involve CIOs in reviewing IT acquisition plans and strategies.[39] We noted that VA's CIO did not review IT acquisition plans or strategies and that the Chief

---

[37] For other reports on data center consolidation, see GAO, *Data Center Consolidation: Reporting Can Be Improved to Reflect Substantial Planned Savings*, GAO-14-713 (Washington, D.C.: Sept. 25, 2014); *Data Center Consolidation: Agencies Making Progress, but Planned Savings Goals Need to Be Established* [Reissued on March 4, 2016], GAO-16-323 (Washington, D.C.: Mar. 3, 2016); *Data Center Optimization: Agencies Need to Complete Plans to Address Inconsistencies in Reported Savings*, GAO-17-388 (Washington, D.C.: May 18, 2017); and *Data Center Optimization: Agencies Need to Address Challenges and Improve Progress to Achieve Cost Savings Goal*, GAO-17-448 (Washington, D.C.: Aug. 15, 2017).

[38] GAO-18-148.

[39] GAO-18-42.

Acquisition Officer was not involved in the process of identifying IT acquisitions.

Accordingly, we recommended that the VA Secretary ensure that the office of the Chief Acquisition Officer is involved in the process to identify IT acquisitions. We also recommended that the Secretary ensure that the acquisition plans or strategies are reviewed and approved in accordance with OMB guidance. The department concurred with the recommendations and, in a May 2018 update, provided a draft process map that depicted its forthcoming acquisition process. However, as of March 2019, this process had not yet been finalized and implemented.

In August 2018, we reported that the department had only fully addressed two of the six key areas that we identified—IT Leadership and Accountability and Information Security.[40] The department had partially addressed IT Budgeting, minimally addressed IT Investment Management, and had not at all addressed IT Strategic Planning or IT Workforce. Thus, we recommended that the VA Secretary ensure that the department's IT management policies address the role of the CIO for key responsibilities in the four areas we identified. The department concurred with the recommendation and acknowledged that many of the responsibilities provided to the CIO were not explicitly formalized by VA policy.

# VA's Cybersecurity Management Lacks Key Elements

In December 2018, we reported on the effectiveness of the government's approach and strategy for securing its systems.[41] The federal approach and strategy for securing information systems is prescribed by federal law and policy, including FISMA and the presidential executive

---

[40] Based on our reviews of FITARA and other relevant laws and guidance, we identified 35 key CIO IT management responsibilities and categorized them in six management areas for this chapter. GAO-18-93.

[41] GAO-19-105.

order on Strengthening the Cybersecurity of Federal Networks and Critical Infrastructure.[42]

Accordingly, federal reports describing agency implementation of this law and policy, and reports of related agency information security activities, indicated VA's lack of effectiveness in its efforts to implement the federal approach and strategy. Our December 2018 report identified that the department was deficient or had material weaknesses in all four indicators of departments' effectiveness in implementing the federal approach and strategy for securing information systems. Specifically, VA was not effective in the Inspector General Information Security Program Ratings, was found to have material weaknesses in the Inspector General Internal Control Deficiencies over Financial Reporting, did not meet CIO Cybersecurity Cross-Agency Priority Goal Targets, and had enterprises that were at risk according to OMB Management Assessment Ratings.

### *High-Impact Systems*

We reported on federal high-impact systems—those that hold sensitive information, the loss of which could cause individuals, the government, or the nation catastrophic harm—in May 2016.[43] We noted that VA had implemented numerous controls, such as completion of risk assessments, over selected systems. However, the department had not always effectively implemented access controls, patch management, and contingency planning to protect the confidentiality, integrity and availability of these high-impact systems. These weaknesses existed in part because the department had not effectively implemented elements of its information security program.

We made five recommendations to VA to improve its information security program. The department concurred with the recommendations and, as of March 2019, had implemented three of the five recommendations.

---

[42] The White House, *Strengthening the Cybersecurity of Federal Networks and Critical Infrastructure*, Executive Order 13800 (Washington, D.C.: May 11, 2017), 82 Fed. Reg. 22391 (May 16, 2017).
[43] GAO-16-501.

## Cybersecurity Workforce

Our March 2019 report on the federal cybersecurity workforce indicated that VA was not accurately categorizing positions to effectively identify critical staffing needs.[44] The Federal Cybersecurity Workforce Assessment Act of 2015 required agencies to assign the appropriate work role codes to each position with cybersecurity, cyber-related, and IT functions. Agencies were to assign a code of "000" only to positions that did not perform IT, cybersecurity, or cyber-related functions.

As we reported, VA had assigned a "000" code to 3,008 (45 percent) of its 6,636 IT positions. Human resources and IT officials from the department stated that they may have assigned the "000" code in error and that they had not completed the process to validate the accuracy of their codes.

We recommended that VA take steps to review the assignment of the "000" code to any of the department's positions in the IT management occupational series and assign the appropriate work role codes. VA concurred with the recommendation and indicated that it was in the process of conducting a cyber coding review.

In conclusion, VA has long struggled to overcome IT management challenges, which have resulted in a lack of system capabilities needed to successfully implement critical initiatives. In this regard, VA is set to begin deploying its new electronic health record system in less than 1 year and questions remain regarding the governance structure for the program. Thus, it is more important than ever for the department to ensure that it is managing its IT budget in a way that addresses the challenges we have identified in our previous reports and high-risk updates. If the department continues to experience the challenges that we have previously identified, it may jeopardize its fourth attempt to modernize its electronic health record system.

Additionally, the department has been challenged in fully implementing provisions of FITARA, which has limited its ability to improve its management of IT acquisitions. Until the department

---

[44] GAO-19-144.

implements the act's provisions, Congress will be unable to effectively monitor VA's progress and hold it accountable for reducing duplication and achieving cost savings. Further, the lack of key cybersecurity management elements at VA is concerning given that agencies' systems are increasingly susceptible to the multitude of cyber-related threats that exist. As VA continues to pursue modernization efforts, it is critical that the department take steps to adequately secure its systems.

Chair Lee, Ranking Member Banks, and Members of the Subcommittee, this completes my prepared statement. I would be pleased to respond to any questions that you may have.

In: Key Government Reports. Volume 17　　ISBN: 978-1-53616-003-1
Editor: Ernest Clark　　© 2019 Nova Science Publishers, Inc.

*Chapter 2*

# FEMA GRANTS MODERNIZATION: IMPROVEMENTS NEEDED TO STRENGTHEN PROGRAM MANAGEMENT AND CYBERSECURITY[*]

## *United States Government Accountability Office*

### ABBREVIATIONS

| | |
|---|---|
| AFG | Assistance to Firefighters Grants |
| DHS | Department of Homeland Security |
| EMMIE | Emergency Management Mission Integrated Environment |
| FEMA | Federal Emergency Management Agency |
| FISMA | Federal Information Security Modernization Act of 2014 and Federal Information Security Management Act of 2002 |

---

[*] This is an edited, reformatted and augmented version of United States Government Accountability Office; Report to Congressional Requesters, Publication No. GAO-19-164, dated April 2019.

34      *United States Government Accountability Office*

GMM      Grants Management Modernization
IT      information technology
NIST      National Institute of Standards and Technology
OCIO      Office of the Chief Information Officer
OIG      Office of Inspector General

## WHY GAO DID THIS STUDY

FEMA, a component of DHS, annually awards billions of dollars in grants to help communities prepare for, mitigate the effects of, and recover from major disasters. However, FEMA's complex IT environment supporting grants management consists of many disparate systems. In 2008, the agency attempted to modernize these systems but experienced significant challenges. In 2015, FEMA initiated a new endeavor (the GMM program) aimed at streamlining and modernizing the grants management IT environment.

GAO was asked to review the GMM program. GAO's objectives were to (1) determine the extent to which FEMA is implementing leading practices for reengineering its grants management processes and incorporating needs into IT requirements; (2) assess the reliability of the program's estimated costs and schedule; and (3) determine the extent to which FEMA is addressing key cybersecurity practices. GAO compared program documentation to leading practices for process reengineering and requirements management, cost and schedule estimation, and cybersecurity risk management, as established by the Software Engineering Institute, National Institute of Standards and Technology, and GAO.

## WHAT GAO RECOMMENDS

GAO is making eight recommendations to FEMA to implement leading practices related to reengineering processes, managing

# FEMA Grants Modernization

requirements, scheduling, and implementing cybersecurity. DHS concurred with all recommendations and provided estimated dates for implementing each of them.

## WHAT GAO FOUND

Of six important leading practices for effective business process reengineering and information technology (IT) requirements management, the Federal Emergency Management Agency (FEMA) fully implemented four and partially implemented two for the Grants Management Modernization (GMM) program (see table). Specifically, FEMA ensured senior leadership commitment, took steps to assess its business environment and performance goals, took recent actions to track progress in delivering IT requirements, and incorporated input from end user stakeholders. However, FEMA has not yet fully established plans for implementing new business processes or established complete traceability of IT requirements.

**Extent to Which the Federal Emergency Management Agency Implemented Selected Leading Practices for Business Process Reengineering and Information Technology (IT) Requirements Management for the Grants Management Modernization Program**

| Leading practice | Overall area rating |
|---|---|
| Ensure executive leadership support for process reengineering | ● |
| Assess the current and target business environment and business performance goals | ● |
| Establish plans for implementing new business processes | ◑ |
| Establish clear, prioritized, and traceable IT requirements | ◑ |
| Track progress in delivering IT requirements | ● |
| Incorporate input from end user stakeholders | ● |

Legend: ● = Fully implemented, ◑ = Partially implemented, o = Not implemented.
Source: GAO analysis of Federal Emergency Management Agency documentation. | GAO-19-164

36     *United States Government Accountability Office*

Until FEMA fully implements the remaining two practices, it risks delivering an IT solution that does not fully modernize FEMA's grants management systems.

While GMM's initial May 2017 cost estimate of about $251 million was generally consistent with leading practices for a reliable, high-quality estimate, it no longer reflects current assumptions about the program. FEMA officials stated in December 2018 that they had completed a revised cost estimate, but it was undergoing departmental approval. GMM's program schedule was inconsistent with leading practices; of particular concern was that the program's final delivery date of September 2020 was not informed by a realistic assessment of GMM development activities, and rather was determined by imposing an unsubstantiated delivery date. Developing sound cost and schedule estimates is necessary to ensure that FEMA has a clear understanding of program risks.

Of five key cybersecurity practices, FEMA fully addressed three and partially addressed two for GMM. Specifically, it categorized GMM's system based on security risk, selected and implemented security controls, and monitored security controls on an ongoing basis. However, the program had not initially established corrective action plans for 13 medium- and low-risk vulnerabilities. This conflicts with the Department of Homeland Security's (DHS) guidance that specifies that corrective action plans must be developed for every weakness identified. Until FEMA, among other things, ensures that the program consistently follows the department's guidance on preparing corrective action plans for all security vulnerabilities, GMM's system will remain at increased risk of exploits.

April 9, 2019

The Honorable Donald M. Payne, Jr.
Chairman
Subcommittee on Emergency Preparedness, Response, and Recovery
Committee on Homeland Security
House of Representatives

Dear Mr. Chairman:

The Federal Emergency Management Agency (FEMA), a component of the Department of Homeland Security (DHS), leads the federal effort to mitigate, respond to, and recover from disasters. FEMA is responsible for saving lives and protecting property, public health, and safety in a natural disaster, act of terrorism, or other manmade disaster.

FEMA accomplishes a large part of its mission through awarding grants to state, local, and tribal governments and nongovernmental entities to help communities prevent, prepare for, protect against, mitigate the effects of, respond to, and recover from disasters and terrorist attacks. According to the agency, these grants represent about 70 percent of its annual budget—FEMA's annual budget averaged about $15 billion per year for the past 3 fiscal years (2016, 2017, and 2018).

The federal government, including FEMA, obligates billions of dollars in grants each year for disaster assistance, and the increases in the number and severity of disasters has become a key source of federal fiscal exposure.[1] We reported in September 2016 that the federal government had obligated at least $277.6 billion in disaster assistance grants during fiscal years 2005 through 2014. Of this amount, FEMA had obligated about $104.5 billion in disaster assistance grants.[2]

FEMA relies heavily on the use of information technology (IT) to support its grant award processes. According to its IT investment portfolio for fiscal year 2018, the agency reported spending about $405 million on these investments.

However, the agency has long reported that its grants management IT environment is highly complex and consists of many disparate systems and labor-intensive manual processes. This has led to poor information sharing

---

[1] The term fiscal exposure refers to the responsibilities, programs, and activities that may either legally commit the federal government to future spending or create the expectation for future spending. See GAO, *Fiscal Exposures: Improving Cost Recognition in the Federal Budget*, GAO-14-28 (Washington, D.C.: Oct. 29, 2013). Also, see GAO's Federal Fiscal Outlook web page: http://www.gao.gov/americas_fiscal_future.

[2] GAO, *Federal Disaster Assistance: Federal Departments and Agencies Obligated at Least $277.6 Billion during Fiscal Years 2005 through 2014*, GAO-16-797 (Washington, D.C.: Sept. 22, 2016).

38 *United States Government Accountability Office*

and reporting capabilities, difficulties in reconciling financial data, and an increased burden on grant recipients.

In 2008, FEMA attempted to develop and implement a single grants processing solution, referred to as the Emergency Management Mission Integrated Environment (EMMIE), to address these IT concerns and modernize its legacy grants management systems. However, as we have previously reported, the program experienced significant implementation challenges, which resulted in a solution that was missing important capabilities.[3] Subsequently, in 2015, FEMA initiated a new endeavor to modernize and streamline the agency's grants management IT environment. This most recent initiative is referred to as the Grants Management Modernization (GMM) program.

Given the importance of having modernized grants management systems and FEMA's past system implementation challenges, you asked us to review the GMM program. Our specific objectives were to (1) determine the extent to which FEMA is implementing leading practices for reengineering its grants management business processes and incorporating business needs into IT requirements for GMM; (2) assess the reliability of the GMM program's estimated costs and schedule; and (3) determine the extent to which FEMA is addressing key cybersecurity practices for GMM.

To address the first objective, we reviewed leading practices and guidance that GAO and the Software Engineering Institute have developed,[4] and from these sources, identified six practice areas associated with business process reengineering and IT requirements management. These selected areas, in our professional judgment, represented foundational practices that were of particular importance to the successful

---

[3] GAO, *Information Technology: FEMA Needs to Address Management Weaknesses to Improve Its Systems*, GAO-16-306 (Washington, D.C.: Apr. 5, 2016) and *Disaster Assistance: Opportunities to Enhance Implementation of the Redesigned Public Assistance Grant Program*, GAO-18-30 (Washington, D.C.: Nov. 8, 2017).

[4] GAO, *Business Process Reengineering Assessment Guide*, Version 3, GAO/AIMD-10.1.15 (Washington, D.C.: May 1997); Software Engineering Institute, *Capability Maturity Model® Integration for Development*, Version 1.3 (Pittsburgh, Pa.: November 2010); and draft *GAO Agile Assessment Guide*, Version 6A. To develop the draft Agile guide, we have worked closely with Agile experts in the public and private sector and some chapters of the guide are considered more mature because they were reviewed by the expert panel. For our assessment, we used these chapters of the draft guide.

implementation of an IT modernization effort that is using incremental software development processes.

We then reviewed relevant GMM program documentation, such as grants management business processes, the acquisition program baseline, IT requirements documents, and a concept of operations. We assessed the program documentation against the six selected practice areas and made determinations on the extent to which the agency had

- fully implemented the practice area (FEMA provided complete evidence showing that it fully implemented the practice area);
- partially implemented the practice area (FEMA provided evidence showing that it partially implemented the practice area); or
- not implemented the practice area (FEMA did not provide evidence showing that it implemented any of the practice area).

We also observed the program's incremental software development activities and a demonstration of the program's automated requirements management tool at GMM facilities in Washington, D.C. Further, we interviewed FEMA officials regarding their efforts to streamline grants management business processes, collect and incorporate stakeholder input, and manage GMM's IT requirements.

To assess the reliability of data from the program's automated IT requirements management tool, we interviewed knowledgeable officials about the quality control procedures used by the program to ensure accuracy and completeness of the data. In addition, we assessed the data against other relevant program documentation on GMM's requirements. We determined that the data used were sufficiently reliable for the purpose of evaluating GMM's practices for managing IT requirements.

For the second objective, we reviewed documentation supporting GMM's lifecycle cost estimate and schedule. Specifically, we evaluated documentation regarding the program's May 2017 lifecycle cost estimate against the leading practices for developing a comprehensive, accurate,

40    *United States Government Accountability Office*

well-documented, and credible cost estimate identified in GAO's Cost Estimating and Assessment Guide.[5]

Additionally, we evaluated documentation regarding GMM's integrated master schedule, dated May 2018, against the leading practices for developing a comprehensive, well-constructed, credible, and controlled schedule identified in GAO's Schedule Assessment Guide.[6] We also interviewed responsible GMM program officials to understand their practices for developing and maintaining the program cost estimate and schedule. We found that the cost data were sufficiently reliable and we noted in our report the instances where the quality of the schedule data impacted the reliability of the program's schedule.

To address the third objective, we reviewed the National Institute of Standards and Technology's (NIST) risk management framework and identified key cybersecurity practices.[7] Next, we reviewed DHS's and FEMA's cybersecurity policies and guidance, as well as documentation on FEMA's authorization to operate[8] for GMM's engineering and test environment. This environment went live in February 2018 and had obtained authorization to operate at the time that we began our review.[9] We assessed FEMA's cybersecurity documentation against the NIST framework's five key cybersecurity practices[10] and assessed the extent to which the agency had

- fully addressed the practice area (FEMA provided complete evidence which showed that it fully implemented the practice area),

---

[5] GAO, *Cost Estimating and Assessment Guide: Best Practices for Developing and Managing Capital Program Costs,* GAO-09-3SP (Washington, D.C.: March 2009).

[6] GAO, *Schedule Assessment Guide: Best Practices for Project Schedules,* GAO-16-89G (Washington, D.C.: December 2015).

[7] NIST, *Guide for Applying the Risk Management Framework to Federal Information Systems: A Security Life Cycle Approach,* SP 800-37, Revision 1 (Gaithersburg, Md.: February 2010).

[8] According to NIST, an authorization to operate is an official management decision, made after all cybersecurity assessment activities have been performed, stating that the system is authorized for use and explicitly accepting the risk to the organization.

[9] Subsequent to the start of our review, GMM conducted a separate authorization to operate process for the GMM production environment, in July 2018.

[10] The framework identifies six total practices, but for reporting purposes we combined two interrelated practices into one practice, thus resulting in five key cybersecurity practices.

- partially addressed the practice area (FEMA provided evidence which showed that it partially implemented the practice area), or
- not addressed the practice area (FEMA did not provide evidence which showed that it implemented any of the practice area).

We also interviewed cognizant officials in the GMM program office and FEMA's Office of the Chief Information Officer (OCIO). We obtained information from these officials about their efforts to assess, document, and review cybersecurity controls for GMM.

To assess the reliability of data from the program's automated security controls management tool, we interviewed knowledgeable officials about the quality control procedures used by the program to assure accuracy and completeness of the data. We also compared the data to other relevant program documentation on GMM security controls for the engineering and test environment. We found that some of the security controls data we examined were sufficiently reliable for the purpose of evaluating FEMA's cybersecurity practices for GMM, and we noted in our report the instances where the accuracy of the data impacted the program's ability to address key cybersecurity practices. Additional details on our objectives, scope, and methodology can be found in appendix I.

We conducted this performance audit from December 2017 to April 2019 in accordance with generally accepted government auditing standards. Those standards require that we plan and perform the audit to obtain sufficient, appropriate evidence to provide a reasonable basis for our findings and conclusions based on our audit objectives. We believe that the evidence obtained provides a reasonable basis for our findings and conclusions based on our audit objectives.

## BACKGROUND

FEMA's mission is to help people before, during, and after disasters. It provides assistance to those affected by emergencies and disasters by supplying immediate needs (e.g., ice, water, food, and temporary housing)

42     *United States Government Accountability Office*

and providing financial assistance grants for damage to personal or public property. FEMA also provides non-disaster assistance grants to improve the nation's preparedness, readiness, and resilience to all hazards.

FEMA accomplishes a large part of its mission through awarding grants to state, local, and tribal governments and nongovernmental entities to help communities prevent, prepare for, protect against, mitigate the effects of, respond to, and recover from disasters and terrorist attacks. As previously mentioned, for fiscal years 2005 through 2014, the agency obligated about $104.5 billion in disaster relief grants.[11] In addition, as of April 2018, the four major disasters in 2017—hurricanes Harvey, Irma, and Maria; and the California wildfires—had resulted in over $22 billion in FEMA grants.[12]

## Overview of FEMA's Grants Management Programs and Administration

The current FEMA grants management environment is highly complex with many stakeholders, IT systems, and users. Specifically, this environment is comprised of 45 active disaster and non-disaster grant programs, which are grouped into 12 distinct grant categories.[13]

For example, one program in the Preparedness: Fire category is the Assistance to Firefighters Grants (AFG) program, which provides grants to fire departments, nonaffiliated emergency medical service organizations, and state fire training academies to support firefighting and emergency response needs. As another example, the Housing Assistance grant

---

[11] GAO-16-797.

[12] GAO, *2017 Hurricanes and Wildfires: Initial Observations on the Federal Response and Key Recovery Challenges,* GAO-18-472 (Washington, D.C.: Sept. 4, 2018). The $22 billion in obligated FEMA grants for the four major disasters in 2017 are in addition to the $104.5 billion that FEMA obligated for disaster assistance during fiscal years 2005 through 2014.

[13] The number of active grant programs varies based on programs being authorized or discontinued and how "grant programs" are defined. In 2018, FEMA Office of Chief Counsel officials identified 37 programs, whereas GMM program officials identified 45 programs because they defined "grant programs" more broadly and further decomposed the programs to facilitate the development of the GMM solution. For this chapter, we use GMM's 45 grant programs (listed in appendix II).

program is in the Recovery Assistance for Individuals category and provides financial assistance to individuals and households in geographical areas that have been declared an emergency or major disaster by the President.

Table 1 lists FEMA's non-disaster and disaster-based grant categories.

According to FEMA, the processes for managing these different types of grants vary because the grant programs were developed independently by at least 18 separate authorizing laws that were enacted over a 62-year period (from 1947 through 2009). The various laws call for different administrative and reporting requirements.

For example, the Robert T. Stafford Disaster Relief and Emergency Assistance Act, as amended,[14] established the statutory authority for 11 of the grant programs, such as the administration of Public Assistance and Individual Assistance grant programs after a presidentially declared disaster.[15] The act also requires the FEMA Administrator to submit an annual report to the President and Congress covering FEMA's expenditures, contributions, work, and accomplishments, pursuant to the act.[16] As another example, the National Dam Safety Program Act established one of the grant programs aimed at providing financial assistance to improve dam safety.[17]

Key stakeholders in modernizing the IT grants management environment include the internal FEMA officials that review, approve, and monitor the grants awarded, such as grant specialists, program analysts, and supervisors. FEMA has estimated that it will need to support about 5,000 simultaneous internal users of its grants management systems.

Other users include the grant recipients that apply for, receive, and submit reports on their grant awards; these are considered the external system users. These grant recipients can include individuals, states, local governments, Indian tribes, institutions of higher education, and nonprofit organizations. FEMA has estimated that there are hundreds of thousands of external users of its grants systems.

---

[14] 42 U.S.C. §§ 5121-5207.
[15] 42 U.S.C. §§ 5170a, 5170b, 5172, 5173, 5192(a).
[16] 42 U.S.C. § 5197c.
[17] 33 U.S.C. § 467f.

# 44    *United States Government Accountability Office*

**Table 1. Federal Emergency Management Agency's Grant Categories**

| Grant category | Disaster | Non-disaster | Both |
|---|---|---|---|
| Preparedness: Fire | | X | |
| Preparedness: Chemical | | X | |
| Preparedness: Homeland Security | | X | |
| Preparedness: Standards | | X | |
| Preparedness: Training | | X | |
| Mitigation: Hazards | | | X |
| Mitigation: Community Assistance | | X | |
| Mitigation: Earthquake | | X | |
| Mitigation: Risk Management | | X | |
| Recovery (Assistance for Individuals) | X | | |
| Recovery (Assistance for Organizations/Government) | X | | |
| Response: Urban Search and Rescue | | | X |

Source: Federal Emergency Management Agency documentation. | GAO-19-164

The administration of the many different grant programs is distributed across four divisions within FEMA's organizational structure. Figure 1 provides an overview of FEMA's organizational structure and the divisions that are responsible for administering grants.

Within three of the four divisions—Resilience, United States Fire Administration, and Office of Response and Recovery—16 different grant program offices are collectively responsible for administering the 45 grant programs. The fourth division consists of 10 regional offices that help administer grants within their designated geographical regions. For example, the Office of Response and Recovery division oversees three different offices that administer 13 grant programs that are largely related to providing assistance in response to presidentially declared disasters.

Figure 2 shows the number of grant programs administered by each of the four divisions' grant program and regional offices. In addition, appendix II lists the names of the 45 grant programs.

FEMA's OCIO is responsible for developing, enhancing, and maintaining the agency's IT systems, and for increasing efficiencies and cooperation across the entire organization. However, we and the DHS Office of Inspector General (OIG) have previously reported that the grant programs and regional offices develop information systems independent of the OCIO and that this has contributed to the agency's disparate IT environment.

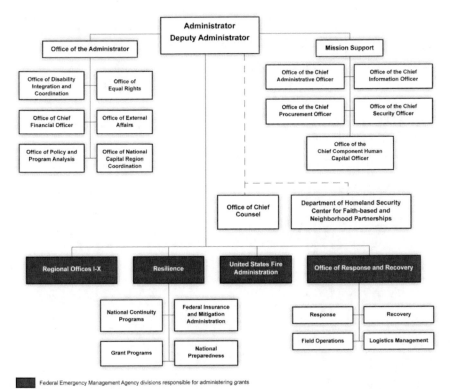

Source: GAO analysis of Federal Emergency Management Agency documentation. | GAO-19-164

Figure 1 Federal Emergency Management Agency's Organizational Structure and the Divisions That Are Responsible for Administering Grants.

We and the DHS OIG have reported that this disparate IT environment was due, in part, to FEMA's decentralized IT budget and acquisition practices. For example, from fiscal years 2010 through 2015, the OCIO's budget represented about one-third of the agency's IT budget, with the grant program offices accounting for the remaining two-thirds of that budget.[18]

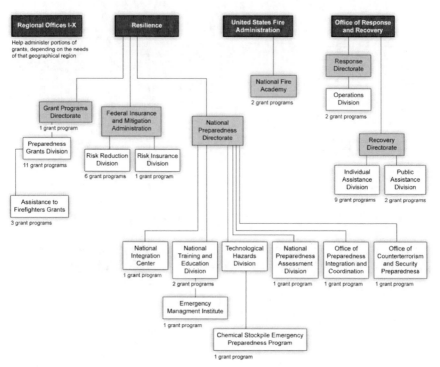

Source: GAO analysis of Federal Emergency Management documentation. | GAO-19-164

Note: The number of active grant programs varies based on programs being authorized or discontinued and how "grant programs" are defined. In 2018, FEMA Office of Chief Counsel officials identified 37 programs, whereas GMM program officials identified 45 programs because they defined "grant programs" more broadly and further decomposed the programs to facilitate the development of the GMM solution.

Figure 2. Federal Emergency Management Agency's (FEMA) Structure of Grant Programs Identified by the Grants Management Modernization (GMM) Program, as of August 2018.

---

[18] GAO-16-306; DHS OIG, *FEMA Faces Challenges in Managing Information Technology*, OIG-16-10 (Washington, D.C.: Nov. 20, 2015); and *Federal Emergency Management Agency Faces Challenges in Modernizing Information Technology*, OIG-11-69 (Washington, D.C.: Apr. 1, 2011).

In February 2018, the OIG found that FEMA had shown limited progress in improving its IT management and that many of the issues reported in prior audits remained unchanged. As such, the OIG initiated a more comprehensive audit of the agency's IT management that is ongoing.[19]

## Overview of FEMA's Legacy Grants Management Systems

FEMA has identified 10 primary legacy IT systems that support its grants management activities. According to the agency, most of these systems were developed to support specific grant programs or grant categories. Table 2 summarizes the 10 primary legacy systems.

According to FEMA officials, the 10 primary grant systems are all in operation (several have been for decades) and are not interoperable. As a result, individual grant programs and regional offices have independently developed work arounds intended to address existing capability gaps with the primary systems.

FEMA officials stated that while these work arounds have helped the agency partially address capability gaps with its primary systems, they are often nonstandardized processes, and introduce the potential for information security risks and errors. This environment has contributed to labor-intensive manual processes and an increased burden for grant recipients. The disparate systems have also led to poor information sharing and reporting capabilities, as well as difficulty reconciling financial data.

The DHS OIG and we have previously highlighted challenges with FEMA's past attempts to modernize its grant management systems. For example,

---

[19] DHS OIG, *Management Alert – Inadequate FEMA Progress in Addressing Open Recommendations from our 2015 Report, "FEMA Faces Challenges in Managing Information Technology" (OIG-16-10)*, OIG-18-54 (Washington, D.C.: Feb. 26, 2018).

48            *United States Government Accountability Office*

## Table 2. Federal Emergency Management Agency's Primary Grants Management Legacy Systems

| System | Description | Initial deployment of system |
|---|---|---|
| Assistance to Firefighters eGrant Portal | Web-based system that processes applications for the Assistance to Firefighters Grants program. | 2002 |
| Emergency Management Mission Integrated Environment (EMMIE) | Web-based system that supports the management of public assistance recovery grants throughout the entire grant lifecycle, using a standardized web-based interface. | 2008 |
| Environmental and Historic Preservation Management Information System | Web-based system that supports environmental and historic preservation reviews to ensure regulatory compliance with federal laws and Executive Orders for disaster and non-disaster grants. | 2007 |
| FEMA Applicant Case Tracker | Web-based system that was developed to supplement the EMMIE system and supports project tracking and case management functionality for pre-award activities. | 2016 |
| Grants Reporting Tool | Custom-developed web application that allows grant recipients from states, territories, and tribes to report on the allocation of their grant awards for several preparedness/homeland security grant programs. | 2003 |
| Individual Assistance | System that supports the processing of Individual Assistance grants, such as housing assistance, other needs assistance, and disaster housing operations. | 1997 |
| Mitigation eGrants | Web-based grants system that processes applications for the Flood Mitigation Assistance and Pre-Disaster Mitigation grant programs. | 2003 |
| National Emergency Management Information System – Hazard Mitigation Grant Program | Server-based application that processes mitigation grants and manages approvals on a state's mitigation plan. | 1998 |
| National Emergency Management Information System – Public Assistance | System that supports the processing of legacy public assistance grants. As of October 2018, FEMA officials stated they had mostly decommissioned the system. | 1998 |
| Non-Disaster Grants | Web-based system that supports the application, award, and administration of non-disaster-based preparedness and mitigation grants. | 2011 |

Source: GAO analysis of Federal Emergency Management Agency documentation. | GAO-19-164

- In December 2006, the DHS OIG reported that EMMIE, an effort to modernize its grants management systems and provide a single grants processing solution, was being developed without a clear understanding and definition of the future solution. The report also identified the need to ensure crosscutting participation from headquarters, regions, and states in developing and maintaining a

FEMA Grants Modernization    49

complete, documented set of FEMA business and system requirements.[20]

- In April 2016, we found weaknesses in FEMA's development of the EMMIE system.[21] For example, we noted that the system was implemented without sufficient documentation of system requirements, an acquisition strategy, up-to-date cost estimate and schedule, total amount spent to develop the system, or a systems integration plan. In response to our findings and related recommendations, FEMA took action to address these issues. For example, the agency implemented a requirements management process that, among other things, provided guidance to programs on analyzing requirements to ensure that they are complete and verifiable.

- We reported in November 2017 that EMMIE lacked the ability to collect information on all pre-award activities and, as a result, agency officials said that they and applicants used ad hoc reports and personal tracking documents to manage and monitor the progress of grant applications. FEMA officials added that applicants often struggled to access the system and that the system was not user friendly.[22] Due to EMMIE's shortfalls, the agency had to develop another system in 2017 to supplement EMMIE with additional grant tracking and case management capabilities.

## GMM Is to Address FEMA's Shortcomings with Grants Management

FEMA initiated GMM in 2015, in part, due to EMMIE's failed attempt to modernize the agency's grants management environment. The program

---

[20] DHS OIG, *FEMA's Progress in Addressing Information Technology Management Weaknesses*, OIG-07-17 (Washington, D.C.: Dec. 8, 2006).
[21] GAO-16-306.
[22] GAO-18-30.

## 50 *United States Government Accountability Office*

is intended to modernize and streamline the agency's grants management environment.

To help streamline the agency's grants management processes, the program established a standard framework intended to represent a common grants management lifecycle. The framework consists of five sequential phases—pre-award, award, post-award, closeout, and post- closeout—along with a sixth phase dedicated to continuous grant program management activities, such as analyzing data and producing reports on grant awards and managing IT systems.

FEMA also established 43 distinct business functions associated with these six lifecycle phases. Figure 3 provides the general activities that may occur in each of the grant lifecycle phases, but specific activities would depend on the type of grant being administered (i.e., disaster versus non-disaster).

GMM is expected to be implemented within the complex IT environment that currently exists at FEMA. For example, the program is intended to replace the 10 legacy grants management systems, and potentially many additional subsystems, with a single IT system. Each of the 10 legacy systems was developed with its own database(s) and with no standardization of the grants management data and, according to FEMA officials, this legacy data has grown significantly over time.

Accordingly, FEMA will need to migrate, analyze, and standardize the grants management data before transitioning it to GMM. The agency awarded a contract in June 2016 to support the data migration efforts for GMM. The agency also implemented a data staging environment in October 2017 to migrate the legacy data and identify opportunities to improve the quality of the data.

Further, the GMM system is expected to interface with a total of 38 other systems. These include 19 systems external to DHS (e.g., those provided by commercial entities or other federal government agencies) and 19 systems internal to DHS or FEMA. Some of the internal FEMA systems are undergoing their own modernization efforts and will need to be coordinated with GMM, such as the agency's financial management systems, national flood insurance systems, and enterprise data warehouses.

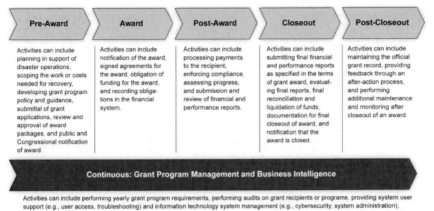

Source: GAO analysis of Federal Emergency Management Agency Documentation. | GAO-19-164

Figure 3. Federal Emergency Management Agency's Planned Grants Management Lifecycle.

For example, FEMA's Financial Systems Modernization Program was originally expected to deliver a new financial system in time to interface with GMM. However, the financial modernization has been delayed until after GMM is to be fully implemented; thus, GMM will instead need to interface with the legacy financial system. As a result, GMM is in the process of removing one of its key performance parameters in the acquisition program baseline related to financial systems interoperability and timeliness of data exchanged.

In May 2017, DHS approved the acquisition program baseline for GMM. The baseline estimated the total lifecycle costs to be about $251 million, initial operational capability to be achieved by September 2019, and full operational capability to be achieved by September 2020.

## GMM's Agile Software Development and Acquisition Approach

FEMA intends to develop and deploy its own software applications for GMM using a combination of commercial-off-the-shelf software, open

# 52 *United States Government Accountability Office*

source software, and custom developed code.[23] The agency plans to rely on an Agile software development approach. According to FEMA planning documentation, the agency plans to fully deliver GMM by September 2020 over eight Agile development increments.[24]

Agile development is a type of incremental development, which calls for the rapid delivery of software in small, short increments. Many organizations, especially in the federal government, are accustomed to using a waterfall software development model. This type of model typically consists of long, sequential phases, and differs significantly from the Agile development approach. We have previously reported that DHS has sought to establish Agile software development as the preferred method for acquiring and delivering IT capabilities.[25] However, the department has not yet completed critical actions necessary to update its guidance, policies, and practices for Agile programs, in areas such as, developing lifecycle cost estimates, managing IT requirements, testing and evaluation, oversight at key decision points, and ensuring cybersecurity.[26] (See appendix III for more details on the Agile software development approach.)

FEMA's acquisition approach includes using contract support to assist with the development and deployment efforts. The agency selected a public cloud environment to host the computing infrastructure.[27] In addition, from March through July 2017, the agency used a short-term contract aimed at developing prototypes of GMM functionality for grant tracking and monitoring, case management of disaster survivors, grant reporting, and grant closeout. The agency planned to award a second

---

[23] Open source software is publicly available for use, study, reuse, modification, enhancement, and redistribution by the software's users.

[24] Agile development programs may use different terminology to describe their software development processes. The Agile terms used in this chapter (e.g., increment, sprint, epics, etc.) are specific to the GMM program.

[25] GAO, *TSA Modernization: Use of Sound Program Management and Oversight Practices Is Needed to Avoid Repeating Past Problems,* GAO-18-46 (Washington, D.C.: Oct. 17, 2017).

[26] We have an ongoing review evaluating DHS's Agile adoption.

[27] According to NIST, cloud computing is a means for enabling convenient, on-demand network access to a shared pool of configurable computing resources that can be rapidly provisioned and released with minimal management effort or service provider interaction. A public cloud is a type of deployment model for providing cloud services that is available to the general public and is owned and operated by the service provider.

development contract by December 2017 to complete the GMM system (beyond the prototypes) and to begin this work in September 2018.

However, due to delays in awarding the second contract to develop the complete GMM system, in January 2018, the program extended the scope and time frames of the initial short-term prototype contract for an additional year to develop the first increment of the GMM system—referred to as the AFG pilot.

On August 31, 2018, FEMA awarded the second development contract, which is intended to deliver the remaining functionality beyond the AFG pilot (i.e., increments 2 through 8). FEMA officials subsequently issued a 90-day planning task order for the Agile development contractor to define the work that needs to be done to deliver GMM and the level of effort needed to accomplish that work. However, the planning task order was paused after a bid protest was filed with GAO in September 2018.[28] According to FEMA officials, they resumed work on the planning task order after the bid protest was withdrawn by the protester on November 20, 2018, and then the work was paused again during the partial government shutdown from December 22, 2018, through January 25, 2019.

## Assistance to Firefighters Grants Pilot

FEMA began working on the AFG pilot—GMM's first increment—in January 2018. This increment was intended to pilot GMM's use of Agile development methods to replace core functionality for the AFG system (i.e., one of the 10 legacy systems).This system supports three preparedness/fire-related grant programs—Assistance to Firefighters Grants Program, Fire Prevention and Safety Grant Program, and Staffing for Adequate Fire and Emergency Response Grant Program. According to FEMA officials, the AFG system was selected as the first system to be

---

[28] GAO's statutory bid protest function is separate from its audit mission.

replaced because it is costly to maintain and the DHS OIG had identified cybersecurity concerns with the system.[29]

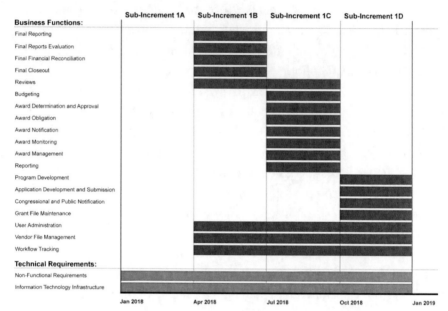

Source: GAO analysis of Federal Emergency Management Agency documentation. | GAO-19-164

Figure 4. Planned Functionality for the Federal Emergency Management Agency's Assistance to Firefights Grants Pilot, as of August 2018.

Among the 43 GMM business functions discussed earlier in this chapter, FEMA officials specified 19 functions to be delivered in the AFG pilot. Figure 4 shows the planned time frames for delivering the AFG pilot in increment 1 (which consisted of four 3-month Agile development sub-increments), as of August 2018.

As of August 2018, the program was working on sub-increment 1C of the pilot.[30] In September 2018, GMM deployed its first set of functionality

---

[29] See for example, DHS OIG, *Security Concerns with Federal Emergency Management Agency's eGrants Grant Management System*, OIG-16-11 (Washington, D.C.: Nov. 19, 2015).

[30] These increments consist of many shorter iterations that are referred to as sprints, during which development teams build a small iteration of working software. As of August 2018, the

to a total of 19 AFG users—which included seven of 169 total internal AFG users, and 12 of more than 153,000 external AFG users. The functionality supported four of the 19 business functions that are related to the closeout of grants (i.e., the process by which all applicable administrative actions and all required work to award a grant have been completed). This functionality included tasks such as evaluation of final financial reports submitted by grant recipients and final reconciliation of finances (e.g., final disbursement to recipients and return of unobligated federal funds).

According to FEMA officials, closeout functionality was selected first for deployment because it was the most costly component of the legacy AFG system to maintain, as it is an entirely manual and labor-intensive process. The remaining AFG functionality and remaining AFG users are to be deployed by the end of the AFG pilot.

## GMM Oversight Structure

The GMM program is executed by a program management office, which is overseen by a program manager and program executive. This office is responsible for directing the day-to-day operations and ensuring completion of GMM program goals and objectives. The program office resides within the Office of Response and Recovery, which is headed by an Associate Administrator who reports to the FEMA Administrator. In addition, the GMM program executive (who is also the Regional Administrator for FEMA Region IX) reports directly to the FEMA Administrator.

GMM is designated as a level 2 major acquisition,[31] which means that it is subject to oversight by the DHS acquisition review board. The board is

---

program had completed 12 sprints. Since Agile programs plan and prioritize requirements iteratively, the total number of sprints to be completed for an entire program is unknown.

[31] According to DHS policy, a level 2 investment has a lifecycle cost estimate that is greater than or equal to $300 million and less than $1 billion, or has been designated to be of special interest, which automatically increases the program to at least a level 2 investment. While GMM's initial cost estimate was below the level 2 threshold, it was considered to be of

# 56    *United States Government Accountability Office*

chaired by the DHS Undersecretary for Management and is made up of executive-level members, such as the DHS Chief Information Officer.

The acquisition review board serves as the departmental executive board that decides whether to approve GMM through key acquisition milestones and reviews the program's progress and its compliance with approved documentation every 6 months. The board approved the acquisition program baseline for GMM in May 2017 (i.e., estimated costs to be about $251 million and full operational capability to be achieved by September 2020).

In addition, the program is reviewed on a monthly basis by FEMA's Grants Management Executive Steering Group. This group is chaired by the Deputy Administrator of FEMA. Further, DHS's Financial Systems Modernization Executive Steering Committee, chaired by the DHS Chief Financial Officer, meets monthly and is to provide guidance, oversight, and support to GMM.

## Cybersecurity Risk Management Framework

For government organizations, including FEMA, cybersecurity is a key element in maintaining the public trust. Inadequately protected systems may be vulnerable to insider threats. Such systems are also vulnerable to the risk of intrusion by individuals or groups with malicious intent who could unlawfully access the systems to obtain sensitive information, disrupt operations, or launch attacks against other computer systems and networks. Moreover, cyber-based threats to federal information systems are evolving and growing. Accordingly, we designated cybersecurity as a government-wide high risk area 22 years ago, in 1997, and it has since remained on our high-risk list.[32]

---

special interest to the DHS Chief Financial Officer because it is a critical element of the department's financial system modernization efforts.

[32] GAO, *High-Risk Series: Information Management and Technology*, GAO/HR-97-9 (Washington, D.C.: Feb. 1, 1997).

*FEMA Grants Modernization* 57

Federal law and guidance specify requirements for protecting federal information and information systems. The Federal Information Security Modernization Act (FISMA) of 2014 requires executive branch agencies to develop, document, and implement an agency-wide cybersecurity program to provide security for the information and information systems that support operations and assets of the agency.[33]

The act also tasks NIST with developing, for systems other than those for national security, standards and guidelines to be used by all agencies to establish minimum cybersecurity requirements for information and information systems based on their level of cybersecurity risk.[34] Accordingly, NIST developed a risk management framework of standards and guidelines for agencies to follow in developing cybersecurity programs.[35]

The framework addresses broad cybersecurity and risk management activities, including categorizing the system's impact level; selecting, implementing, and assessing security controls; authorizing the system to operate (based on progress in remediating control weaknesses and an assessment of residual risk); and monitoring the efficacy of controls on an ongoing basis. Figure 5 provides an overview of this framework.

Prior DHS OIG assessments, such as the annual evaluation of DHS's cybersecurity program, have identified issues with FEMA's cybersecurity practices.[36]

---

[33] The Federal Information Security Modernization Act of 2014 (FISMA 2014) (Pub. L. No. 113-283, Dec. 18, 2014) largely superseded the Federal Information Security Management Act of 2002 (FISMA 2002), enacted as Title III, E-Government Act of 2002, Pub. L. No. 107-347, 116 Stat. 2899, 2946 (Dec. 17, 2002). As used in this chapter, FISMA refers both to FISMA 2014 and to those provisions of FISMA 2002 that were either incorporated into FISMA 2014 or were unchanged and continue in full force and effect.

[34] 40 U.S.C. § 11331(b).

[35] NIST, *Guide for Applying the Risk Management Framework to Federal Information Systems: A Security Life Cycle Approach*, SP 800-37, Revision 1 (Gaithersburg, Md.: February 2010).

[36] See for example, DHS OIG, *Evaluation of DHS's Information Security Program for Fiscal Year 2016*, OIG-17-24 (Washington, D.C.: Jan. 18, 2017); *Evaluation of DHS's Information Security Program for Fiscal Year 2015*, OIG-16-08 (Washington, D.C.: Jan. 5, 2016); and *Evaluation of DHS's Information Security Program for Fiscal Year 2014*, OIG-15-16 (Washington, D.C.: Dec. 12, 2014).

For example, in 2016, the OIG reported that FEMA was operating 111 systems without an authorization to operate. In addition, the agency had not created any corrective action plans for 11 of the systems that were classified as "Secret" or "Top Secret," thus limiting its ability to ensure that all identified cybersecurity weaknesses were mitigated in a timely manner. The OIG further reported that, for several years, FEMA was consistently below DHS's 90 percent target for remediating corrective action plans, with scores ranging from 73 to 84 percent. Further, the OIG reported that FEMA had a significant number of open corrective action plans (18,654) and that most of these plans did not contain sufficient information to address identified weaknesses.

In 2017, the OIG reported that FEMA had made progress in addressing security weaknesses. For example, it reported that the agency had reduced the number of systems it was operating without an authorization to operate from 111 to 15 systems.

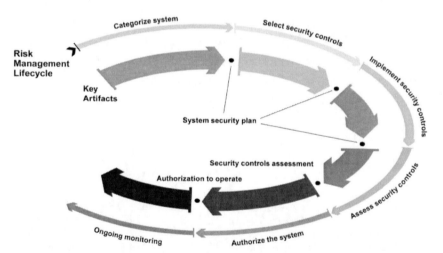

Source: GAO and National Institute of Standards and Technology. | GAO-19-164

Figure 5. Overview of the National Institute of Standards and Technology's Risk Management Framework for a Cybersecurity Program.

## FEMA HAS IMPLEMENTED MOST LEADING PRACTICES FOR REENGINEERING GRANTS MANAGEMENT BUSINESS PROCESSES AND MANAGING IT REQUIREMENTS

According to GAO's Business Process Reengineering Assessment Guide and the Software Engineering Institute's Capability Maturity Model Integration® for Development, successful business process reengineering can enable agencies to replace their inefficient and outmoded processes with streamlined processes that can more effectively serve the needs of the public and significantly reduce costs and improve performance.[37] Many times, new IT systems are implemented to support these improved business processes. Thus, effective management of IT requirements is critical for ensuring the successful design, development, and delivery of such new systems.

These leading practices state that effective business process reengineering and IT requirements management involve, among other things, (1) ensuring strong executive leadership support for process reengineering; (2) assessing the current and target business environment and business performance goals; (3) establishing plans for implementing new business processes; (4) establishing clear, prioritized, and traceable IT requirements; (5) tracking progress in delivering IT requirements; and (6) incorporating input from end user stakeholders.

Among these six selected leading practices for reengineering business processes and managing IT requirements, FEMA fully implemented four and partially implemented two of them for its GMM program. For example, the agency ensured strong senior leadership commitment to changing the way it manages its grants, took steps to assess and document its business environment and performance goals, defined initial IT requirements for GMM, took recent actions to better track progress in

---

[37] GAO, *Business Process Reengineering Assessment Guide*—Version 3, GAO/AIMD-10.1.15 (Washington, D.C.: May 1997); Software Engineering Institute, *Capability Maturity Model® Integration for Development*, Version 1.3 (Pittsburgh, Pa.: November 2010); and draft *GAO Agile Assessment Guide*, Version 6A.

60 *United States Government Accountability Office*

delivering planned IT requirements, and incorporated input from end user stakeholders.

In addition, FEMA had begun planning for business process reengineering; however, it had not finalized plans for transitioning users to the new business processes. Further, while GMM took steps to establish clearly defined and prioritized IT requirements, key requirements were not always traceable. Table 3 summarizes the extent to which FEMA implemented the selected leading practices.

## FEMA Executive Leadership Demonstrated Strong Commitment to Reengineering Grants Management Processes

According to GAO's Business Process Reengineering Assessment Guide,[38] the most critical factor for engaging in a reengineering effort is having strong executive leadership support to establish credibility regarding the seriousness of the effort and to maintain the momentum as the agency faces potentially extensive changes to its organizational structure and values. Without such leadership, even the best process design may fail to be accepted and implemented. Agencies should also ensure that there is ongoing executive support (e.g., executive steering committee meetings headed by the agency leader) to oversee the reengineering effort from start to finish.

FEMA senior leadership consistently demonstrated its commitment and support for streamlining the agency's grants management business processes and provided ongoing executive support. For example, one of the Administrator's top priorities highlighted in FEMA's 2014 through 2022 strategic plans was to strengthen grants management through innovative systems and business processes to rapidly and effectively deliver the agency's mission. In accordance with this strategic priority, FEMA initiated GMM with the intent to streamline and modernize grants management across the agency.

---

[38] GAO/AIMD-10.1.15.

# FEMA Grants Modernization

**Table 3. Extent to Which the Federal Emergency Management Agency Implemented Selected Leading Practices for Business Process Reengineering and Information Technology (IT) Requirements Management for the Grants Management Modernization Program**

| Leading practice | Overall area rating |
|---|---|
| Ensure executive leadership support for process reengineering | ● |
| Assess the current and target business environment and business performance goals | ● |
| Establish plans for implementing new business processes | ◑ |
| Establish clear, prioritized, and traceable IT requirements | ◑ |
| Track progress in delivering IT requirements | ● |
| Incorporate input from end user stakeholders | ● |

Legend: ● = Fully implemented, ◑ = Partially implemented, ○ = Not implemented.
Source: GAO analysis of Federal Emergency Management Agency documentation. | GAO-19-164

In addition, FEMA established the Grants Management Executive Steering Group in September 2015. This group is responsible for transforming the agency's grants management capabilities through its evaluation, prioritization, and oversight of grants management modernization programs, such as GMM.[39] The group's membership consists of FEMA senior leaders from across the agency's program and business support areas, such as FEMA regions, Individual Assistance, Public Assistance, Preparedness, Office of the Chief Financial Officer, Office of Chief Counsel, OCIO, and the Office of Policy and Program Analysis. In this group's ongoing commitment to reengineering grants management processes, it meets monthly to review GMM's updates, risks, and action items, as well as the program's budget, schedule, and acquisition activities. For example, the group reviewed the status of key acquisition activities and program milestones, such as the follow-on award for the pilot contractor and the program's initial operational capability date. The group also reviewed GMM's program risks, such as data migration challenges (discussed later in this chapter) and delays in the

---

[39] According to DHS officials, the Grants Management Executive Steering Group is also intended to address a recommendation from the DHS OIG that FEMA assign the responsibility for central oversight of grants management to one program office to ensure that there is effective management and administration of the grants process, as well as ensuring effective implementation of the provisions of 31 U.S.C. §§ 7501-06 (see for example, DHS OIG-18-16).

# 62 United States Government Accountability Office

Agile development contract award. With this continuous executive involvement, FEMA is better positioned to maintain momentum for reengineering the new grants management business processes that the GMM system is intended to support.

## FEMA Documented Its Current and Target Grants Management Business Processes and Performance Improvement Goals

GAO's Business Process Reengineering Assessment Guide[40] states that agencies undergoing business process reengineering should develop a common understanding of the current environment by documenting existing core business processes to show how the processes work and how they are interconnected. The agencies should then develop a deeper understanding of the target environment by modeling the workflow of each target business process in enough detail to provide a common understanding of exactly what will be changed and who will be affected by a future solution. Agencies should also assess the performance of their current major business processes to identify problem areas that need to be changed or eliminated and to set realistically achievable, customer-oriented, and measurable business performance improvement goals.

FEMA has taken steps to document the current and target grants management business processes. Specifically,

- The agency took steps to develop a common understanding of its grants management processes by documenting each of the 12 grant categories. For example, in 2016 and 2017, the agency conducted several nationwide user outreach sessions with representatives from FEMA headquarters, the 10 regional offices, and state and local grant recipients to discuss the grant categories and the current grants management business environment.

---

[40] GAO/AIMD-10.1.15.

In addition, FEMA's Office of Chief Counsel developed a Grants Management Manual in January 2018 that outlined the authorizing laws, regulations, and agency policies for all of its grant programs. According to the Grants Management Executive Steering Group, the manual is intended to promote standardized grants management procedures across the agency. Additionally, the group expects grant program and regional offices to assess the manual against their own practices, make updates as needed, and ensure that their staff are properly informed and trained.

- FEMA also documented target grants management business process workflows for 18 of the 19 business functions that were notionally planned to be developed and deployed in the AFG pilot by December 2018.[41] However, the program experienced delays in developing the AFG pilot (discussed later in this chapter) and, thus, deferred defining the remaining business function until the program gets closer to developing that function, which is now planned for August 2019.

In addition, FEMA established measurable business performance goals for GMM that are aimed at addressing problem areas and improving grants management processes. Specifically, the agency established 14 business performance goals and associated thresholds in an October 2017 acquisition program baseline addendum, as well as 126 performance metrics for all 43 of the target grants management business functions in its March 2017 test and evaluation master plan.

According to FEMA, the 14 business performance goals are intended to represent essential outcomes that will indicate whether GMM has successfully met critical, business-focused mission needs. GMM performance goals include areas such as improvements in the satisfaction level of users with GMM compared to the legacy systems and

---

[41] While the pilot was originally intended to deliver just the IT infrastructure for GMM, the program later decided that it would also attempt to replace core functionality for AFG. This core functionality consisted of 19 of 33 total GMM business functions that are needed for the AFG program. The remaining 14 business functions are to be delivered to the AFG program sometime after the pilot, based on priorities set by GMM stakeholders.

64  *United States Government Accountability Office*

improvements in the timeliness of grant award processing. For example, one of GMM's goals is to get at least 40 percent of users surveyed to agree or strongly agree that their grants management business processes are easier to accomplish with GMM, compared to the legacy systems.

Program officials stated that they plan to work with the Agile development contractor to refine their performance goals and target thresholds, develop a plan for collecting the data and calculating the metrics, and establish a performance baseline with the legacy systems. Program officials also stated that they plan to complete these steps by September 2019—GMM's initial operational capability date—which is when they are required to begin reporting these metrics to the DHS acquisition review board.

## FEMA has Begun Planning Its Grants Management Business Process Reengineering, but Has Not Finalized Plans for Transition Activities

According to GAO's Business Process Reengineering Assessment Guide,[42] agencies undergoing business process reengineering should (1) establish an overall plan to guide the effort (commonly referred to as an organizational change management plan) and (2) provide a common understanding for stakeholders of what to expect and how to plan for process changes. Agencies should develop the plan at the beginning of the reengineering effort and provide specific details on upcoming process changes, such as critical milestones and deliverables for an orderly transition, roles and responsibilities for change management activities, reengineering goals, skills and resource needs, key barriers to change, communication expectations, training, and any staff redeployments or reductions-in-force. The agency should develop and begin implementing its change management plan ahead of introducing new processes to ensure sufficient support among stakeholders for the reengineered processes.

---

[42] GAO/AIMD-10.1.15.

While FEMA has begun planning its business process reengineering activities, it has not finalized its plans or established time frames for their completion. Specifically, as of September 2018, program officials were in the process of drafting an organizational change management plan that is intended to establish an approach for preparing grants management stakeholders for upcoming changes. According to FEMA, this document is intended to help avoid uncertainty and confusion among stakeholders as changes are made to the agency's grant programs, and ensure successful adoption of new business processes, strategies, and technologies.

As discussed previously in this chapter, the transition to GMM will involve changes to FEMA's disparate grants management processes that are managed by many different stakeholders across the agency. Program officials acknowledged that change management is the biggest challenge they face in implementing GMM and said they had begun taking several actions intended to support the agency's change management activities. For example, program officials reported in October 2018 that they had recently created an executive-level working group intended to address FEMA's policy challenges related to the standardization of grants management processes. Additionally, program officials reported that they planned to: (1) hire additional support staff focused on coordinating grants change management activities; and (2) pursue regional office outreach to encourage broad support among GMM's decentralized stakeholders, such as state, local, and tribal territories.

However, despite these actions, the officials were unable to provide time frames for completing the organizational change management plan or the additional actions. Until the plan and actions are complete, the program lacks assurance that it will have sufficient support among stakeholders for the reengineered processes.

In addition, GMM did not establish plans and time frames for the activities that needed to take place prior to, during, and after the transition from the legacy AFG to GMM. Instead, program officials stated that they had worked collaboratively with the legacy AFG program and planned these details informally by discussing them in various communications, such as emails and meetings. However, this informal planning approach is

66     *United States Government Accountability Office*

not a repeatable process, which is essential to this program as FEMA plans to transition many sets of functionality to many different users during the lifecycle of this program.

Program officials acknowledged that for future transitions they will need more repeatable transition planning and stated that they intend to establish such plans, but did not provide a time frame for when such changes would be made. Until FEMA develops a repeatable process, with established time frames for communicating the transition details to its customers prior to each transition, the agency risks that the transition from the legacy systems to GMM will not occur as intended. It also increases its risk that stakeholders will not support the implementation of reengineered grants management processes.

## GMM Took Steps to Establish Clearly Defined and Prioritized IT Requirements, but Key Requirements Were Not Always Traceable

Leading practices for software development efforts state that IT requirements are to be clearly defined and prioritized.[43] This includes, among other things, maintaining bidirectional traceability as the requirements evolve, to ensure there are no inconsistencies among program plans and requirements.[44] In addition, programs using Agile software development are to maintain a product vision, or roadmap, to guide the planning of major program milestones and provide a high-level view of planned requirements.[45]

---

[43] Software Engineering Institute, *Capability Maturity Model® Integration for Development*, Version 1.3 (Pittsburgh, Pa.: November 2010); and draft *GAO Agile Assessment Guide*, Version 6A.

[44] Bidirectional traceability refers to a discernable association in either direction between different levels of IT requirements, as well as between IT requirements and related work products.

[45] Agile programs may have multiple artifacts depicting the program's milestones and planned requirements. For reporting purposes, we referred to these collectively as GMM's "roadmap."

# FEMA Grants Modernization

Programs should also maintain a prioritized list (referred to as a backlog) of narrowly defined requirements (referred to as lower-level requirements) that are to be delivered. Programs should maintain this backlog with the product owner to ensure the program is always working on the highest priority requirements that will deliver the most value to the users.[46]

The GMM program established clearly defined and prioritized requirements and maintained bidirectional traceability among the various levels of requirements:

- Grant lifecycle phases: In its Concept of Operations document, the program established six grants management lifecycle phases that represent the highest level of GMM's requirements, through which it derives lower-level requirements.

- Business functions: The Concept of Operations document also identifies the next level of GMM requirements—the 43 business functions that describe how FEMA officials, grant recipients, and other stakeholders are to manage grants. According to program officials, the 43 business functions are to be refined, prioritized, and delivered to GMM customers iteratively. Further, for the AFG pilot, the GMM program office prioritized 19 business functions with the product owner and planned the development of these functions in a roadmap.

- Epics: GMM's business functions are decomposed into epics, which represent smaller portions of functionality that can be developed over multiple increments. According to program officials, GMM intends to develop, refine, and prioritize the epics iteratively. As of August 2018, the program had developed 67 epics in the program backlog. An example of one of the epics for the AFG pilot is to prepare and submit grant closeout materials.

---

[46] Product owners represent the end users of the system and they work closely with the Agile development teams to establish priorities based on business needs, clarify the IT requirements, and approve whether completed work meets those requirements.

- User stories: The epics are decomposed into user stories, which convey the customers' requirements at the smallest and most discrete unit of work that must be done within a single sprint to create working software. GMM develops, refines, and prioritizes the user stories iteratively. As of August 2018, the program had developed 1,118 user stories in the backlog. An example of a user story is "As an external user, I can log in with a username and password."

Figure 6 provides an example of how GMM's different levels of requirements are decomposed.

Nevertheless, while we found requirements to be traceable at the sprint- level (i.e., epics and user stories), traceability of requirements at the increment-level (i.e., business functions) were inconsistent among different requirements planning documents.[47] Specifically, the capabilities and constraints document shows that five business functions are planned to be developed within sub-increment 1A, whereas the other key planning document—the roadmap for the AFG pilot—showed one of those five functions as being planned for the sub-increment 1B. In addition, the capabilities and constraints document shows that nine business functions are planned to be developed within sub-increment 1B, but the roadmap showed one of those nine functions as being planned for the sub- increment 1C.

Program officials stated that they decided to defer these functions to later sub-increments due to unexpected technical difficulties encountered when developing functionality and reprioritizing functions with the product owners.[48] While the officials updated the roadmap to reflect the deferred functionality, they did not update the capabilities and constraints document

---

[47] GMM's sprints are shorter periods of time (weeks) and increments are longer periods of time (months), in which the requirements that will be developed within that time period are planned in advance.

[48] Increment 1 was originally intended to deliver just the IT infrastructure for GMM. The program later decided that it would also attempt to replace core functionality for the AFGsystem—which was the functionality that was deferred.

to maintain traceability between these two important requirements planning documents.

Program officials stated that they learned during the AFG pilot that the use of a capabilities and constraints document for increment-level scope planning was not ideal and that they intended to change the process for how they documented planned requirements for future increments. However, program officials did not provide a time frame for when this change would be made. Until the program makes this change and then ensures it maintains traceability of increment-level requirements between requirements planning documents, it will continue to risk confusion among stakeholders about what is to be delivered.

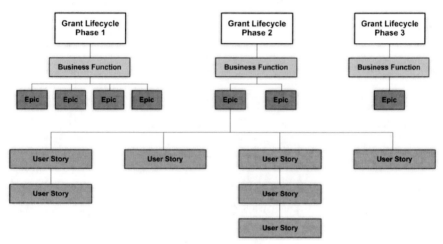

Source: GAO analysis of Federal Emergency Management Agency Documentation. | GAO-19-164

Figure 6. Example of the Decomposition of Information Technology Requirements for the Federal Emergency Management Agency's Grants Management Modernization Program.

In addition, until recently, GMM's planning documents were missing up-to-date information regarding when most of the legacy systems will be transitioned to GMM. Specifically, while the program's planning documents (including the GMM roadmap) provided key milestones for the entire lifecycle of the program and high-level capabilities to be delivered in

70        *United States Government Accountability Office*

the AFG pilot, these documents lacked up-to-date time frames for when FEMA planned to transition the nine remaining legacy systems. For example, in May 2017, GMM drafted notional time frames for transitioning the legacy systems, including plans for AFG to be the seventh system replaced by GMM. However, in December 2017, the program decided to reprioritize the legacy systems so that AFG would be replaced first—yet this major change was not reflected in the program's roadmap.

Moreover, while AFG program officials were informed of the decision to transition the AFG program first, in June 2018 officials from other grant programs told us that they had not been informed on when their systems were to be replaced. As a result, these programs were uncertain about when they should start planning for their respective transitions. In August 2018, GMM program officials acknowledged that they were delayed in deciding the sequencing order for the legacy system transitions. Program officials stated that the delay was due to their need to factor the Agile development contractor's perspective into these decisions; yet, at that time, the contract award had been delayed by approximately 8 months. Subsequently, in October 2018, program officials identified tentative time frames for transitioning the remaining legacy systems.

Program officials stated that they determined the tentative time frames for transitioning the legacy systems based on key factors, such as mission need, cost, security vulnerabilities, and technical obsolescence, and that they had shared these new time frames with grant program officials. The officials also stated that, once the Agile contractor begins contract performance, they expect to be able to validate the contractor's capacity and finalize these time frames by obtaining approval from the Grants Management Executive Steering Group. By taking steps to update and communicate these important time frames, FEMA should be better positioned to ensure that each of the grant programs are prepared for transitioning to GMM.

## GMM Recently Began Tracking Progress in Delivering Planned IT Requirements

According to leading practices,[49] Agile programs should track their progress in delivering planned IT requirements within a sprint (i.e., short iterations that produce working software). Given that sprints are very short cycles of development (e.g., 2 weeks), the efficiency of completing planned work within a sprint relies on a disciplined approach that includes using a fixed pace, referred to as the sprint cadence, that provides a consistent and predictable development routine. A disciplined approach also includes identifying by the start of a sprint which user stories will be developed, developing those stories to completion (e.g., fully tested and demonstrated to, and accepted by, the product owner), and tracking completion progress of those stories. Progress should be communicated to relevant stakeholders and used by the development teams to better understand their capacity to develop stories, continuously improve on their processes, and forecast how long it will take to deliver all remaining capabilities. The GMM program did not effectively track progress in delivering IT requirements during the first nine sprints, which occurred from January to June 2018. These gaps in tracking the progress of requirements, in part, had an impact on the program's progress in delivering the 19 AFG business functions that were originally planned by December 2018 and are now deferred to August 2019. However, beginning in July 2018, in response to our ongoing review, the program took steps to improve in these areas. Specifically,

- The GMM program did not effectively track progress in delivering IT requirements during the first nine sprints, which occurred from January to June 2018. These gaps in tracking the progress of requirements, in part, had an impact on the program's progress in delivering the 19 AFG business functions that were originally

---

[49] Software Engineering Institute, *Capability Maturity Model® Integration for Development*, Version 1.3 (Pittsburgh, Pa.: November 2010); and draft *GAO Agile Assessment Guide*, Version 6A.

planned by December 2018 and are now deferred to August 2019. However, beginning in July 2018, in response to our ongoing review, the program took steps to improve in these areas. Specifically, GMM did not communicate the status of its Agile development progress to program stakeholders, such as the grant programs, the regional offices, and the development teams, during most of the first nine sprints. Program officials acknowledged that they should use metrics to track development progress and, in July 2018, they began reporting metrics to program stakeholders. For example, they began collecting and providing data on the number of stories planned and delivered, estimated capacity for development teams, and the number of days spent working on the sprint, as part of the program's weekly status reports to program stakeholders, such as product owners.

- Rather than using a fixed, predictable sprint cadence, GMM allowed a variable development cadence, meaning that sprint durations varied from 1 to 4 weeks throughout the first nine sprints. Program officials noted that they had experimented with the use of a variable cadence to allow more time to complete complex technical work. Program officials stated that they realized that varying the sprints was not effective and, in July 2018 for sprint 10, they reverted back to a fixed, 2 week cadence.

- GMM added a significant amount of scope during its first nine sprints, after the development work had already begun. For example, the program committed to 28 user stories at the beginning of sprint eight, and then nearly doubled the work by adding 25 additional stories in the middle of the sprint. Program officials cited multiple reasons for adding more stories, including that an insufficient number of stories had been defined in the backlog when the sprint began, the realization that planned stories were too large and needed to be decomposed into smaller stories, and the realization that other work would be needed in addition to what was originally planned. Program officials recognized that, by the start of a sprint, the requirements should be sufficiently

# FEMA Grants Modernization

defined, such that they are ready for development without requiring major changes during the sprint. The program made recent improvements in sprints 11 and 12, which had only five stories added after the start of a sprint.

By taking these steps to establish consistency among sprints, the program has better positioned itself to more effectively monitor and manage the remaining IT development work. In addition, this improvement in consistency should help the program avoid future deferments of functionality.

## GMM is Involving Stakeholders and Incorporating Input

Leading practices state that programs should regularly collaborate with, and collect input from, relevant stakeholders; monitor the status of stakeholder involvement; incorporate stakeholder input; and measure how well stakeholders' needs are being met.[50] For Agile programs, it is especially important to track user satisfaction to determine how well the program has met stakeholders' needs. Consistent stakeholder participation ensures that the program meets its stakeholders' needs.

FEMA implemented its responsibilities in this area through several means, such as stakeholder outreach activities; development of a strategic communications plan; and continuous monitoring, solicitation, and recording of stakeholder involvement and feedback. For example, the agency conducted nationwide outreach sessions from January 2016 through August 2017 and began conducting additional outreach sessions in April 2018. These outreach sessions involved hundreds of representatives from FEMA headquarters, the 10 regional offices, and state and local grant recipients to collect information on the current grants management environment and opportunities for streamlining grants management

---

[50] Software Engineering Institute, *Capability Maturity Model® Integration for Development*, Version 1.3 (Pittsburgh, Pa.: November 2010); and draft *GAO Agile Assessment Guide*, Version 6A.

74 *United States Government Accountability Office*

processes. FEMA also held oversight and stakeholder outreach activities and actively solicited and recorded feedback from its stakeholders on a regular basis. For example, GMM regularly verified with users that the new functionality met their IT requirements, as part of the Agile development cycle. Additionally, we observed several GMM biweekly requirements validation sessions where the program's stakeholders were involved and provided feedback as part of the requirements development and refinement process.

In addition, FEMA identified GMM stakeholders and tracked its engagement with these stakeholders using a stakeholder register. The agency also defined processes for how the GMM program is to collaborate with its stakeholders in a stakeholder communication plan and Agile development team agreement. Also, while several officials from the selected grant program and regional offices that we interviewed indicated that the program could improve in communicating its plans for GMM and incorporating stakeholder input, most of the representatives from these offices stated that GMM is doing well at interacting with its stakeholders.

Finally, in October 2018, program officials reported that they had recently begun measuring user satisfaction by conducting surveys and interviews with users that have utilized the new functionality within GMM. The program's outreach activities, collection of stakeholder input, and measurement of user satisfaction demonstrate that the program is taking the appropriate steps to incorporate stakeholder input.

## FEMA LACKS A CURRENT COST ESTIMATE AND RELIABLE SCHEDULE FOR GMM

### GMM's Initial Cost Estimate Was Reliable, but Is Now Outdated

Reliable cost estimates are critical for successfully delivering IT programs. Such estimates provide the basis for informed decision making,

# FEMA Grants Modernization

realistic budget formulation, meaningful progress measurement, and accountability for results. GAO's Cost Estimating and Assessment Guide defines leading practices related to the following four characteristics of a high-quality, reliable estimate.[51]

- Comprehensive. The estimate accounts for all possible costs associated with a program, is structured in sufficient detail to ensure that costs are neither omitted nor double counted, and documents all cost-influencing assumptions.
- Well-documented. Supporting documentation explains the process, sources, and methods used to create the estimate; contains the underlying data used to develop the estimate; and is adequately reviewed and approved by management.
- Accurate. The estimate is not overly conservative or optimistic, is based on an assessment of the costs most likely to be incurred, and is regularly updated so that it always reflects the program's current status.
- Credible. Discusses any limitations of the analysis because of uncertainty or sensitivity surrounding data or assumptions, the estimate's results are cross-checked, and an independent cost estimate is conducted by a group outside the acquiring organization to determine whether other estimating methods produce similar results.

In May 2017, DHS approved GMM's lifecycle cost estimate of about $251 million for fiscal years 2015 through 2030. We found this initial estimate to be reliable because it fully or substantially addressed all the characteristics associated with a reliable cost estimate. For example, the estimate comprehensively included government and contractor costs, all elements of the program's work breakdown structure, and all phases of the system lifecycle; and was aligned with the program's technical documentation at the time the estimate was developed. GMM also fully

---

[51] GAO-09-3SP.

documented the key assumptions, data sources, estimating methodology, and calculations for the estimate. Further, the program conducted a risk assessment and sensitivity analysis, and DHS conducted an independent assessment of the cost estimate to validate the accuracy and credibility of the cost estimate.

However, key assumptions that FEMA made about the program changed soon after DHS approved the cost estimate in May 2017. Thus, the initial cost estimate no longer reflects the current approach for the program. For example, key assumptions about the program that changed include:

- Change in the technical approach: The initial cost estimate assumed that GMM would implement a software-as-a-service model, meaning that FEMA would rely on a service provider to deliver software applications and the underlying infrastructure to run them. However, in December 2017, the program instead decided to implement an infrastructure-as-a-service model, meaning that FEMA would develop and deploy its own software application and rely on a service provider to deliver and manage the computing infrastructure (e.g., servers, software, storage, and network equipment). According to program officials, this decision was made after learning from the Agile prototypes that the infrastructure-as-a-service model would allow GMM to develop the system in a more flexible environment.

- Increase in the number of system development personnel: A key factor with Agile development is the number of development teams (each consisting of experts in software development, testing, and cybersecurity) that are operating concurrently and producing separate portions of software functionality. Program officials initially assumed that they would need three to four concurrent Agile development teams, but subsequently realized that they would instead need to expend more resources to achieve GMM's original completion date. Specifically, program officials now expect they will need to at least double, and potentially triple, the number of concurrent development teams to meet GMM's original target dates.

- Significant delays and complexities with data migration: In 2016 and 2017, GMM experienced various technical challenges in its effort to transfer legacy system data to a data staging platform. This data transfer effort needed to be done to standardize the data before eventually migrating the data to GMM. These challenges resulted in significant delays and cost increases. Program officials reported that, by February 2018—at least 9 months later than planned—all legacy data had been transferred to a data staging platform so that FEMA officials could begin analyzing and standardizing the data prior to migrating it into GMM.

FEMA officials reported that they anticipated the cost estimate to increase, and for this increase to be high enough to breach the $251 million threshold set in GMM's May 2017 acquisition program baseline. Thus, consistent with DHS's acquisition guidance, the program informed the DHS acquisition review board of this anticipated breach. The board declared that the program was in a cost breach status, as of September 12, 2018. As of October 2018, program officials stated that they were in the process of revising the cost estimate to reflect the changes in the program and to incorporate actual costs. In addition, the officials stated that the program was applying a new cost estimating methodology tailored for Agile programs that DHS's Cost Analysis Division had been developing. In December 2018, program officials stated that they had completed the revised cost estimate but it was still undergoing departmental approval. Establishing an updated cost estimate should help FEMA better understand the expected costs to deliver GMM under the program's current approach and time frames.

## GMM's Schedule is Unreliable

The success of an IT program depends, in part, on having an integrated and reliable master schedule that defines when the program's set of work

# United States Government Accountability Office

activities and milestone events are to occur, how long they will take, and how they are related to one another. Among other things, a reliable schedule provides a roadmap for systematic execution of an IT program and the means by which to gauge progress, identify and address potential problems, and promote accountability.

GAO's Schedule Assessment Guide defines leading practices related to the following four characteristics that are vital to having a reliable integrated master schedule.[52]

- Comprehensive. A comprehensive schedule reflects all activities for both the government and its contractors that are necessary to accomplish a program's objectives, as defined in the program's work breakdown structure. The schedule also includes the labor, materials, and overhead needed to do the work and depicts when those resources are needed and when they will be available. It realistically reflects how long each activity will take and allows for discrete progress measurement.

- Well-constructed. A schedule is well-constructed if all of its activities are logically sequenced with the most straightforward logic possible. Unusual or complicated logic techniques are used judiciously and justified in the schedule documentation. The schedule's critical path represents a true model of the activities that drive the program's earliest completion date and total float[53] accurately depicts schedule flexibility.

- Credible. A schedule that is credible is horizontally traceable—that is, it reflects the order of events necessary to achieve aggregated products or outcomes. It is also vertically traceable—that is, activities in varying levels of the schedule map to one another and key dates presented to management in periodic briefings are consistent with the schedule. Data about risks are used to predict a level of confidence in meeting the program's completion date. The

---

[52] GAO-16-89G.

[53] Total float, or slack, in the schedule is based on the amount of time that activities can be delayed before the delay affects the program's estimated completion date.

# FEMA Grants Modernization

level of necessary schedule contingency and high-priority risks are identified by conducting a robust schedule risk analysis.

- Controlled. A schedule is controlled if it is updated regularly by trained schedulers using actual progress and logic to realistically forecast dates for program activities. It is compared to a designated baseline schedule to measure, monitor, and report the program's progress. The baseline schedule is accompanied by a baseline document that explains the overall approach to the program, defines ground rules and assumptions, and describes the unique features of the schedule. The baseline schedule and current schedule are subject to a configuration management control process.

GMM's schedule was unreliable because it minimally addressed three characteristics—comprehensive, credible, and controlled—and did not address the fourth characteristic of a reliable estimate—well-constructed. One of the most significant issues was that the program's fast approaching, final delivery date of September 2020 was not informed by a realistic assessment of GMM development activities, and rather was determined by imposing an unsubstantiated delivery date. Table 4 summarizes our assessment of GMM's schedule.

In discussing the reasons for the shortfalls in these practices, program officials stated that they had been uncertain about the level of rigor that should be applied to the GMM schedule, given their use of Agile development. However, leading practices state that program schedules should meet all the scheduling practices, regardless of whether a program is using Agile development.[54] As discussed earlier in this chapter, GMM has already experienced significant schedule delays. For example, the legacy data migration effort, the AFG pilot, and the Agile development contract have been delayed.

---

[54] GAO-16-89G and draft *GAO Agile Assessment Guide*, Version 6A.

# 80 *United States Government Accountability Office*

**Table 4. Extent to Which the Federal Emergency Management Agency's (FEMA) Grants Management Modernization (GMM) Program's Schedule Addressed the Characteristics of a Reliable Schedule, as of May 2018**

| Characteristic | Rating | Summary of assessment |
|---|---|---|
| Comprehensive<br>• Captures all activities, as identified in the work breakdown structure, which defines in detail the work for both the government and its contractors necessary to accomplish a program's objectives.<br>• Reflects what resources (e.g., labor, materials, and overhead) are needed to do the work, whether all required resources will be available when needed, and whether any funding or time constraints exist.<br>• Establishes the duration of all activities and has specific start and end dates. | ◑ | The GMM schedule included both government and contractor activities and was aligned at a high level with key milestones established in the acquisition program baseline. However, the schedule's activities did not align with the program's work breakdown structure. Additionally, the schedule contained limited information on the resources needed to complete activities. Program officials stated that they did not include information on resources in the schedule because they did not rely on the schedule to manage its resources. Instead, the officials stated that they planned the work and resources outside of the schedule, as they approached each Agile development cycle sprint. However, sprint-related activities only accounted for about a quarter of the schedule (174 out of 662 days, or approximately 26 percent). Further, the schedule had activities that were missing durations and work that was planned to start or finish on weekends. Finally, the program's final delivery date of September 2020 was not informed by a realistic assessment of GMM development activities. Instead, FEMA's Executive Steering Group decided that GMM would be a 5-year program when it was initiated in 2015. However, schedules that are determined by imposed target completion dates, rather than the work that has to be performed and the dependencies among them, are often infeasible. |
| Well-constructed<br>• Sequences all activities— that is, all activities are sequenced in the order that they are to be implemented with the most straightforward logic possible.<br>• Establishes a valid critical path, which represents the chain of dependent activities with the longest total duration. A valid critical path is necessary to examine the effects of any activity slippage along this path. | ○ | Approximately 82 percent of the activities were not sequenced in the order that they were to be implemented because they were missing dependencies, meaning that they did not identify other activities in the schedule that must occur before or after that activity. As a result, if the program experienced a delay in an activity, the effect of that change on downstream activities could not be automatically reflected in the schedule. Additionally, about 38 percent of remaining activities had unjustified constraints, meaning that the program manually imposed restrictions on when the activity was allowed to start or finish. According to GAO's Schedule Assessment Guide, such constraints should be used only when necessary and only if their justification is documented because they override schedule logic and restrict how planned dates respond to accomplished effort or resource availability. The lack of scheduling logic prevented the schedule from calculating a valid critical path and created |

# FEMA Grants Modernization

| Characteristic | Rating | Summary of assessment |
|---|---|---|
| • Identifies the total float time—the amount of time by which an activity can slip before the delay affects the program's estimated finish date—so that a schedule's flexibility can be determined. | | unreasonable total float values. Without a valid critical path, management cannot focus on activities that could detrimentally affect the key program milestones if they slip. |
| Credible<br>• Verifies that the schedule is (1) horizontally traceable, meaning that it reflects the order of events necessary to achieve aggregated products or outcomes; and (2) vertically traceable, meaning that activities in varying levels of the schedule align with one another and key dates presented to management in periodic briefings are consistent with the schedule.<br>• Conducts a schedule risk analysis to predict a level of confidence in meeting the program's completion date and the level of necessary schedule contingency. | ◑ | While the schedule's high-level dates were consistent with the dates found in other program documents, such as GMM's roadmap and acquisition program baseline, the program had manually imposed restrictions, or constraints, on these activities so that they would start or end at a specific time. However, GAO's Schedule Assessment Guide states that the high-level start and end dates should be automatically derived by the scheduling logic established by lower-level activities in the schedule. Additionally, the schedule was not horizontally or vertically traceable because of the lack of scheduling logic discussed previously in this table. Finally, a formal schedule risk analysis was not completed. Program officials said they were assessing the risks facing the program and mitigating those risks in real time as part of their Agile development process. However, a formal schedule risk analysis focuses on how uncertainty and key risks affect activities in the schedule and uses statistical techniques to predict a level of confidence in meeting the program's completion date. Without such an analysis, FEMA is unable to determine the likelihood of GMM achieving its estimated completion date for the estimated scope, or the paths or activities that are most likely to delay the program. |
| Controlled<br>• Updates schedule regularly using actual progress and logic to realistically forecast dates for program activities.<br>• Maintains a baseline schedule to measure, monitor, and report the program's progress. | ◑ | While GMM program officials cited ways that the status of activities were tracked and updated weekly and daily, such as by examining impediments that slow down Agile development progress, the schedule itself was not being updated as part of these activities. Additionally, the schedule had numerous date anomalies, including activities with planned dates in the past or actual dates in the future. According to GAO's Schedule Assessment Guide, a schedule that has not been appropriately updated will not reflect what is actually occurring on the program and will prevent management from using the schedule to monitor progress. Further, while program officials stated that they considered the milestones in the acquisition program baseline to serve as their schedule baseline, they did not establish a baseline schedule to measure, monitor, and report progress in the schedule management software. |

# 82 *United States Government Accountability Office*

## Table 4. (Continued)

| Characteristic | Rating | Summary of assessment |
|---|---|---|
| | | Without continual monitoring of program performance against the baseline, GMM has limited ability to determine when forecasted completion dates differ from baseline dates and whether schedule variances affect downstream work. |

Legend: ● = Fully addressed, ◕ = Substantially addressed, ◑ = Partially addressed, ◔ = Minimally addressed, ○ = Not addressed.

Source: GAO analysis of Federal Emergency Management Agency data. | GAO-19-164

Program officials also stated that the delay in awarding and starting the Agile contract has delayed other important activities, such as establishing time frames for transitioning legacy systems. A more robust schedule could have helped FEMA predict the impact of delays on remaining activities and identify which activities appeared most critical so that the program could ensure that any risks in delaying those activities were properly mitigated.

In response to our review and findings, program officials recognized the need to continually enhance their schedule practices to improve the management and communication of program activities. As a result, in August 2018, the officials stated that they planned to add a master scheduler to the team to improve the program's schedule practices and ensure that all of the areas of concern we identified are adequately addressed. In October 2018, the officials reported that they had recently added two master schedulers to GMM. According to the statement of objectives, the Agile contractor is expected to develop an integrated master schedule soon after it begins performance.

However, program officials stated that GMM is schedule-driven—due to the Executive Steering Group's expectation that the solution will be delivered by September 2020. The officials added that, if GMM encounters challenges in meeting this time frame, the program plans to seek additional resources to allow it to meet the 2020 target.

GMM's schedule-driven approach has already led to an increase in estimated costs and resources. For example, as previously mentioned, the program has determined that, to meet its original target dates, GMM needs to at least double, and possibly triple, the number of concurrent Agile development teams. In addition, we have previously reported that schedule pressure on federal IT programs can lead to omissions and skipping of key activities, especially system testing.[55]

In August 2018, program officials acknowledged that September 2020 may not be feasible and that the overall completion time frames established in the acquisition program baseline may eventually need to be rebaselined. Without a robust schedule to forecast whether FEMA's aggressive delivery goal for GMM is realistic to achieve, leadership will be limited in its ability to make informed decisions on what additional increases in cost or reductions in scope might be needed to fully deliver the system.

## FEMA FULLY ADDRESSED THREE KEY CYBERSECURITY PRACTICES AND PARTIALLY ADDRESSED TWO OTHERS

NIST's risk management framework establishes standards and guidelines for agencies to follow in developing cybersecurity programs.[56] Agencies are expected to use this framework to achieve more secure information and information systems through the implementation of appropriate risk mitigation strategies and by performing activities that ensure that necessary security controls are integrated into agencies' processes. The framework addresses broad cybersecurity and risk management activities, which include the following:

- Categorize the system: Programs are to categorize systems by identifying the types of information used, selecting a potential impact level (e.g., low, moderate, or high), and assigning a

---

[55] GAO, *2020 Census: Continued Management Attention Needed to Address Challenges and Risks with Developing, Testing, and Securing IT Systems*, GAO-18-655 (Washington, D.C.: Aug. 30, 2018); and *Information Technology: Census Bureau Testing of 2010 Decennial Systems Can Be Strengthened*, GAO-09-262 (Washington, D.C.: Mar. 5, 2009).

[56] NIST, *Guide for Applying the Risk Management Framework to Federal Information Systems: A Security Life Cycle Approach*, SP 800-37, Revision 1 (Gaithersburg, Md.: February 2010).

84        *United States Government Accountability Office*

category based on the highest level of impact to the system's confidentiality, integrity, and availability, if the system was compromised. Programs are also to document a description of the information system and its boundaries and should register the system with appropriate program management offices. System categorization is documented in a system security plan.

- Select and implement security controls: Programs are to determine protective measures, or security controls, to be implemented based on the system categorization results. These security controls are documented in a system security plan. For example, control areas include access controls, incident response, security assessment and authorization, identification and authentication, and configuration management. Once controls are identified, programs are to determine planned implementation actions for each of the designated controls. These implementation actions are also specified in the system security plan.

- Assess security controls: Programs are to develop, review, and approve a security assessment plan. The purpose of the security assessment plan approval is to establish the appropriate expectations for the security control assessment. Programs are to also perform a security control assessment by evaluating the security controls in accordance with the procedures defined in the security assessment plan, in order to determine the extent to which the controls were implemented correctly. The output of this process is intended to produce a security assessment report to document the issues, findings, and recommendations. Programs are to conduct initial remediation actions on security controls and reassess those security controls, as appropriate.[57]

- Obtain an authorization to operate the system: Programs are to obtain security authorization approval in order to operate a system. Resolving weaknesses and vulnerabilities identified during testing

---

[57] Initial remediation should be conducted for vulnerabilities that should be corrected immediately. Remaining vulnerabilities are corrected over time with the use of corrective action plans.

is an important step leading up to achieving an authorization to operate. Programs are to establish corrective action plans to address any deficiencies in cybersecurity policies, procedures, and practices. DHS guidance also states that corrective action plans must be developed for every weakness identified during a security control assessment and within a security assessment report.

- Monitor security controls on an ongoing basis: Programs are to monitor their security controls on an ongoing basis after deployment, including determining the security impact of proposed or actual changes to the information system and assessing the security controls in accordance with a monitoring strategy that determines the frequency of monitoring the controls.

For the GMM program's engineering and test environment, which went live in February 2018,[58] FEMA fully addressed three of the five key cybersecurity practices in NIST's risk management framework and partially addressed two of the practices. Specifically, FEMA categorized GMM's environment based on security risk, implemented select security controls, and monitored security controls on an ongoing basis.

**Table 5. Extent to Which the Federal Emergency Management Agency Addressed Key Cybersecurity Practices for the Grants Management Modernization Program**

| Key practice | Overall area rating |
|---|---|
| Categorize the system based on security risk | ● |
| Select and implement security controls | ● |
| Assess security controls | ◑ |
| Obtain an authorization to operate the system | ◑ |
| Monitor security controls on an ongoing basis | ● |

Legend: ● = Fully addressed, ◑ = Partially addressed, ○ = Not addressed.
Source: GAO analysis of Federal Emergency Management Agency documentation. | GAO-19-164

---

[58] The program's engineering and test environment was intended to mirror the production environment's configuration and security controls. GMM conducted a separate authorization to operate process for the production environment, which went live in July 2018.

86 *United States Government Accountability Office*

However, the agency partially addressed the areas of assessing security controls and obtaining an authorization to operate the system. Table 5 provides a summary of the extent to which FEMA addressed NIST's key cybersecurity practices for GMM's engineering and test environment.

## GMM Categorized the System Based on Security Risk

Consistent with NIST's framework, GMM categorized the security risk of its engineering and test environment and identified it as a moderate-impact environment. A moderate-impact environment is one where the loss of confidentiality, integrity, or availability could be expected to have a serious or adverse effect on organizational operations, organizational assets, or individuals. GMM completed the following steps leading to this categorization:

- The program documented in its System Security Plan the various types of data and information that the environment will collect, process, and store, such as conducting technology research, building or enhancing technology, and maintaining IT networks.
- The program established three information types and assigned security levels of low, moderate, or high impact in the areas of confidentiality, availability, and integrity. A low-impact security level was assigned to two information types: (1) conducting technology research and (2) building or enhancing technology; and a moderate- impact security level was assigned to the third information type: maintaining IT networks.
- The engineering and test environment was categorized as an overall moderate-impact system, based on the highest security impact level assignment.
- GMM documented a description of the environment, including a diagram depicting the system's boundaries, which illustrates, among other things, databases and firewalls.

- GMM properly registered its engineering and test environment with FEMA's Chief Information Officer, Chief Financial Officer, and acting Chief Information Security Officer.

By conducting the security categorization process, GMM has taken steps that should ensure that the appropriate security controls are selected for the program's engineering and test environment.

## GMM Selected and Planned for the Implementation of Controls in Its System Security Plan

Consistent with NIST's framework and the system categorization results, GMM appropriately determined which security controls to implement and planned actions for implementing those controls in its System Security Plan for the engineering and test environment. For example, the program utilized NIST guidance to select standard controls for a system categorized with a moderate-impact security level.[59] These control areas include, for example, access controls, risk assessment, incident response, identification and authentication, and configuration management.

Further, the program documented its planned actions to implement each control in its System Security Plan. For example, GMM documented

that the program plans to implement its Incident Response Testing control by participating in an agency-wide exercise and unannounced vulnerability scans. As another example, GMM documented that the program plans to implement its Contingency Plan Testing control by testing the contingency plan annually, reviewing the test results, and preparing after action reports. By selecting and planning for the implementation of security controls, GMM has taken steps to mitigate its security risks and protect the confidentiality, integrity, and availability of the information system.

---

[59] NIST, *Security and Privacy Controls for Federal Information Systems and Organizations*, SP 800-53, Revision 4 (Gaithersburg, Md.: April 2013).

## GMM Developed a Security Assessment Plan, but It Lacked Essential Details and Approvals

Consistent with NIST's framework, in January 2018, GMM program officials developed a security assessment plan for the engineering and test environment. According to GMM program officials, this plan was reviewed by the security assessment team.

However, the security assessment plan lacked essential details. Specifically, while the plan included the general process for evaluating the environment's security controls, the planned assessment procedures for all 964 security controls were not sufficiently defined. Specifically, GMM program officials copied example assessment procedures from NIST guidance and inserted them into its security assessment documentation for all of its 964 controls, without making further adjustments to explain the steps that should be taken specific to GMM. Table 6 shows an example of a security assessment procedure copied from the NIST guidance that should have been further adjusted for GMM.

In addition, the actual assessment procedures that the GMM assessors used to evaluate the security controls were not documented. Instead, the program only documented whether each control passed or failed each test.

GMM program officials stated that the planned assessment procedures are based on an agency template that was exported from a DHS compliance tool, and that FEMA security officials have been instructed by the DHS OCIO not to tailor or make any adjustments to the template language. However, the assessment procedures outlined in NIST's guidance are to serve as a starting point for organizations preparing their program specific assessments. According to NIST, organizations are expected to select and tailor their assessment procedures for each security control from NIST's list of suggested assessment options (e.g., review, analyze, or inspect policies, procedures, and related documentation options).

DHS OCIO officials stated that, consistent with NIST's guidance, they expect that components will ensure they are in compliance with the minimum standards and will also add details and additional rigor, as

# FEMA Grants Modernization

appropriate, to tailor the planned security assessment procedures to fit their unique missions or needs.

**Table 6. Example of the Federal Emergency Management Agency's Grants Management Modernization (GMM) Program's Assessment Procedures Compared to the National Institute of Standards and Technology (NIST) Guidance**

| | NIST assessment procedure | GMM's assessment procedure |
|---|---|---|
| Security control | IA-4.1, Identifier Management | IA-4.1, Identifier Management |
| Examine (the process of analyzing one or more assessment objects to achieve clarification, the results of which are used to support the determination of security and privacy control completeness, and potential for improvement over time): | Identification and authentication policy; procedures addressing identifier management; procedures addressing account management; security plan; information system design documentation; information system configuration settings and associated documentation; list of information system accounts; list of identifiers generated from physical access control devices; other relevant documents or records | Identification and authentication policy; procedures addressing identifier management; procedures addressing account management; security plan; information system design documentation; information system configuration settings and associated documentation; list of information system accounts; list of identifiers generated from physical access control devices; other relevant documents or records. |
| Interview (the process of conducting discussions with individuals or groups within an organization to achieve clarification, or lead to the location of evidence, the results of which are used to support the determination of security and privacy control completeness, and potential for improvement over time): | Organizational personnel with identifier management responsibilities; organizational personnel with information security responsibilities; system/network administrators; system developers | Organizational personnel with identifier management responsibilities. |

Source: GAO analysis of Federal Emergency Management Agency documentation. | GAO-19-164.

In November 2018, in response to our audit, DHS OCIO officials stated that they were meeting with FEMA OCIO officials to understand why they did not document the planned and actual assessment procedures performed by the assessors for GMM. Until FEMA ensures that detailed planned evaluation methods and actual evaluation procedures specific to GMM are defined, the program risks assessing security controls

# 90 *United States Government Accountability Office*

incorrectly, having controls that do not work as intended, and producing undesirable outcomes with respect to meeting the security requirements.

In addition, the security assessment plan was not approved by FEMA's OCIO before proceeding with the security assessment. Program officials stated that approval was not required for the security assessment plan prior to the development of the security assessment report. However, NIST guidance states that the purpose of the security assessment plan approval is to establish the appropriate expectations for the security control assessment. By not getting the security assessment plan approved by FEMA's OCIO before security assessment reviews were conducted, GMM risks inconsistencies with the plan and security objectives of the organization.

Finally, consistent with NIST guidance, GMM performed a security assessment in December 2017 of the engineering and test environment's controls, which identified 36 vulnerabilities (23 critical- and high-impact vulnerabilities and 13 medium- and low-impact vulnerabilities). The program also documented these vulnerabilities and associated findings and recommendations in a security assessment report. GMM conducted initial remediation actions (i.e., remediation of vulnerabilities that should be corrected immediately) for 12 of the critical- and high-impact vulnerabilities and a reassessment of those security controls confirmed that they were resolved by January 2018. Remediation of the remaining 11 critical- and high-impact vulnerabilities and 13 medium- and low- impact vulnerabilities were to be addressed by corrective action plans as part of the authorization to operate process, which is discussed in the next section.

## GMM Obtained Authorization to Operate, but Had Not Addressed Known Vulnerabilities or Tested All Controls

The authorization to operate GMM's engineering and test environment was granted on February 5, 2018. Among other things, this decision was based on the important stipulation that the remaining 11 critical- and high-impact vulnerabilities associated with multifactor authentication would be addressed within 45 days, or by March 22, 2018. However, the program did not meet this deadline and, instead, approximately 2 months after this deadline passed, obtained a waiver to remediate these vulnerabilities by May 9, 2019.

These vulnerabilities are related to a multifactor authentication capability.[60] Program officials stated that they worked with FEMA OCIO officials to attempt to address these vulnerabilities by the initial deadline, but they were unsuccessful in finding a viable solution. Therefore, GMM program officials developed a waiver at the recommendation of the OCIO to provide additional time to develop a viable solution. However, a multifactor authentication capability is essential to ensuring that users are who they say they are, prior to granting users access to the GMM engineering and test environment, in order to reduce the risk of harmful actors accessing the system.

In addition, as of September 2018, the program had not established corrective action plans for the 13 medium- and low-impact vulnerabilities. Program officials stated that they do not typically address low-impact vulnerabilities; however, this is in conflict with DHS guidance that specifies that corrective action plans must be developed for every weakness identified during a security control assessment and within a security assessment report. In response to our audit, in October 2018, GMM program officials developed these remaining corrective action plans. The plans indicated that these vulnerabilities were to be fully addressed by January 2019 and April 2019.

While the program eventually took corrective actions in response to our audit by developing the missing plans, the GMM program initially failed to follow DHS's guidance on preparing corrective actions plans for all security vulnerabilities. Until GMM consistently follows DHS's guidance, it will be difficult for FEMA to determine the extent to which GMM's security weaknesses identified during its security control assessments are remediated. Additionally, as we have reported at other

---

[60] The purpose of multifactor authentication is to make it more difficult for an unauthorized person to access a computer system by putting in place several factors of defense. The factors are defined as: (1) something you know (e.g., password), (2) something you have (e.g., token), or (3) something you are (e.g., biometric).

92        *United States Government Accountability Office*

agencies, vulnerabilities can be indicators of more significant underlying issues and, thus, without appropriate management attention or prompt remediation, GMM is at risk of unnecessarily exposing the program to potential exploits.[61]

Moreover, GMM was required to assess all untested controls by March 7, 2018, or no later than 30 days after the approval of the authorization to operate; however, it did not meet this deadline. Specifically, we found that, by October 2018, FEMA had not fully tested 190 security controls in the GMM engineering and test environment. These controls were related to areas such as security incident handling and allocation of resources required to protect an information system. In response to our findings, in October 2018, GMM program officials reported that they had since fully tested 27 controls and partially tested the remaining 163 controls.

Program officials stated that testing of the 163 controls is a shared responsibility between GMM and other parties (e.g., the cloud service provider). They added that GMM had completed its portion of the testing but was in the process of verifying the completion of testing by other parties. Program officials stated that the untested controls were not addressed sooner, in part, because of errors resulting from configuration changes in the program's compliance tool during a system upgrade, which have now been resolved. Until GMM ensures that all security controls have been tested, it remains at an increased risk of exposing programs to potential exploits.

## GMM Is Using Processes for Monitoring Controls

Consistent with the NIST framework, GMM established methods for assessing and monitoring security controls to be conducted after an authorization to operate has been approved. GMM has tailored its cybersecurity policies and practices for monitoring its controls to take into

---

[61] GAO, *Electronic Health Information: CMS Oversight of Medicare Beneficiary Data Security Needs Improvement*, GAO-18-210 (Washington, D.C.: Mar. 6, 2018).

account the frequent and iterative pace with which system functionality is continuously being introduced into the GMM environment.

Specifically, the GMM program established a process for assessing security impact changes to the system and conducting reauthorizations to operate within the rapid Agile delivery environment. As part of this process, GMM embedded cybersecurity experts on each Agile development team so that they are involved early and can impact security considerations from the beginning of requirements development through testing and deployment of system functionality.

In addition, the process involves important steps for ensuring that the system moves from development to completion, while producing a secure and reliable system. For example, it includes procedures for creating, reviewing, and testing new system functionality. As the new system functionality is integrated with existing system functionality, it is to undergo automated testing and security scans in order to ensure that the integrity of the security of the system has not been compromised. Further, an automated process is to deploy the code if it passes all security scans, code tests, and code quality checks.

GMM's process for conducting a reauthorization to operate within the rapid delivery Agile development environment is to follow FEMA guidance that states that all high-level changes made to a FEMA IT system must receive approval from both a change advisory board and the FEMA Chief Information Officer. The board and FEMA Chief Information Officer are to focus their review and approval on scheduled releases and epics (i.e., collections of user stories). Additionally, the Information System Security Officer is to review each planned user story and, if it is determined that the proposed changes may impact the integrity of the authorization, the Information System Security Officer is to work with the development team to begin the process of updating the system authorization.

Finally, GMM uses automated tools to track the frequency in which security controls are assessed and to ensure that required scanning data are received by FEMA for reporting purposes. Program officials stated that, in the absence of department-level and agency-level guidance, they have

# 94 *United States Government Accountability Office*

coordinated with DHS and FEMA OCIO officials to ensure that these officials are in agreement with GMM's approach to continuous monitoring. By having monitoring control policies and procedures in place, FEMA management is positioned to more effectively prioritize and plan its risk response to current threats and vulnerabilities for the GMM program.

## CONCLUSIONS

Given FEMA's highly complex grants management environment, with its many stakeholders, IT systems, and internal and external users, implementing leading practices for business process reengineering and IT requirements management is critical for success. FEMA has taken many positive steps, including ensuring executive leadership support for business process reengineering, documenting the agency's grants management processes and performance improvement goals, defining initial IT requirements for the program, incorporating input from end user stakeholders into the development and implementation process, and taking recent actions to improve its delivery of planned IT requirements. Nevertheless, until the GMM program finalizes plans and time frames for implementing its organizational change management actions, plans and communicates system transition activities, and maintains clear traceability of IT requirements, FEMA will be limited in its ability to provide streamlined grants management processes and effectively deliver a modernized IT system to meet the needs of its large range of users.

While GMM's initial cost estimate was reliable, key assumptions about the program since the initial estimate had changed and, therefore, it no longer reflected the current approach for the program. The forthcoming updated cost schedule is expected to better reflect the current approach. However, the program's unreliable schedule to fully deliver GMM by September 2020 is aggressive and unrealistic. The delays the program has experienced to date further compound GMM's schedule issues. Without a robust schedule that has been informed by a realistic assessment of GMM's development activities, leadership will be limited in its ability to

*FEMA Grants Modernization* 95

make informed decisions on what additional increases in cost or reductions in scope might be needed to achieve their goals.

Further, FEMA's implementation of cybersecurity practices for GMM in the areas of system categorization, selection and implementation, and monitoring will help the program. However, GMM lacked essential details for evaluating security controls, did not approve the security assessment plan before proceeding with the security assessment, did not follow DHS's guidance to develop corrective action plans for all security vulnerabilities, and did not fully test all security controls. As a result, the GMM engineering and test environment remains at an increased risk of exploitations.

## RECOMMENDATIONS FOR EXECUTIVE ACTION

We are making eight recommendations to FEMA:

The FEMA Administrator should ensure that the GMM program management office finalizes the organizational change management plan and time frames for implementing change management actions. (Recommendation 1)

The FEMA Administrator should ensure that the GMM program management office plans and communicates its detailed transition activities to its affected customers before they transition to GMM and undergo significant changes to their processes. (Recommendation 2)

The FEMA Administrator should ensure that the GMM program management office implements its planned changes to its processes for documenting requirements for future increments and ensures it maintains traceability among key IT requirements documents. (Recommendation 3)

The FEMA Administrator should ensure that the GMM program management office updates the program schedule to address the leading practices for a reliable schedule identified in this chapter. (Recommendation 4)

The FEMA Administrator should ensure that the FEMA OCIO defines sufficiently detailed planned evaluation methods and actual evaluation methods for assessing security controls. (Recommendation 5)

The FEMA Administrator should ensure that the FEMA OCIO approves a security assessment plan before security assessment reviews are conducted. (Recommendation 6)

The FEMA Administrator should ensure that the GMM program management office follows DHS guidance on preparing corrective action plans for all security vulnerabilities. (Recommendation 7)

The FEMA Administrator should ensure that the GMM program management office fully tests all of its security controls for the system. (Recommendation 8)

## AGENCY COMMENTS AND OUR EVALUATION

DHS provided written comments on a draft of this chapter, which are reprinted in appendix IV. In its comments, the department concurred with all eight of our recommendations and provided estimated completion dates for implementing each of them.

For example, with regard to recommendation 4, the department stated that FEMA plans to update the GMM program schedule to address the leading practices for a reliable schedule by April 30, 2019. In addition, for recommendation 7, the department stated that FEMA plans to ensure that corrective action plans are prepared by July 31, 2019, to address all identified security vulnerabilities for GMM. If implemented effectively, the actions that FEMA plans to take in response to the recommendations should address the weaknesses we identified.

We also received technical comments from DHS and FEMA officials, which we incorporated, as appropriate.

We are sending copies of this chapter to the Secretary of Homeland Security and interested congressional committees.

Sincerely yours,

Carol C. Harris
Director, Information Technology Management Issues

## APPENDIX I: OBJECTIVES, SCOPE, AND METHODOLOGY

Our objectives were to (1) determine the extent to which the Federal Emergency Management Agency (FEMA) is implementing leading practices for reengineering its grants management business processes and incorporating business needs into Grants Management Modernization (GMM) information technology (IT) requirements; (2) assess the reliability of the program's estimated costs and schedule; and (3) determine the extent to which FEMA is addressing key cybersecurity practices for GMM.

To address the first objective, we reviewed GAO's Business Process Reengineering Assessment Guide[62] and Software Engineering Institute's Capability Maturity Model for Integration for Development[63] to identify practices associated with business process reengineering and IT requirements management. We then selected six areas that, in our professional judgment, represented foundational practices that were of particular importance to the successful implementation of an IT modernization effort that is using Agile development processes. We also selected the practices that were most relevant based on where GMM was in the system development lifecycle and we discussed the practice areas with FEMA officials. The practices are:

- Ensuring executive leadership support for process reengineering
- Assessing the current and target business environment and business performance goals
- Establishing plans for implementing new business processes
- Establishing clear, prioritized, and traceable IT requirements

---

[62] GAO, *Business Process Reengineering Assessment Guide*—Version 3, GAO/AIMD-10.1.15 (Washington, D.C.: May 1997).
[63] Software Engineering Institute, *Capability Maturity Model® Integration for Development*, Version 1.3 (Pittsburgh, Pa.: November 2010).

## 98 *United States Government Accountability Office*

- Tracking progress in delivering IT requirements
- Incorporating input from end user stakeholders

We also reviewed selected chapters of GAO's draft Agile Assessment Guide (Version 6A), which is intended to establish a consistent framework based on best practices that can be used across the federal government for developing, implementing, managing, and evaluating agencies' IT investments that rely on Agile methods. To develop this guide, GAO worked closely with Agile experts in the public and private sector; some chapters of the guide are considered more mature because they have been reviewed by the expert panel. We reviewed these chapters to ensure that our expectations for how FEMA should apply the six practices for business process reengineering and IT requirements management are appropriate for an Agile program and are consistent with the draft guidance that is under development. Additionally, since Agile development programs may use different terminology to describe their software development processes, the Agile terms used in this chapter (e.g., increment, sprint, epic, etc.) are specific to the GMM program.

We obtained and analyzed FEMA grants management modernization documentation, such as current and target grants management business processes, acquisition program baseline, operational requirements document, concept of operations, requirements analyses workbooks, Grants Management Executive Steering Group artifacts, stakeholder outreach artifacts, Agile increment- and sprint-level planning and development artifacts, and the requirements backlog.[64]

We assessed the program documentation against the selected practices to determine the extent to which the agency had implemented them. We then assessed each practice area as:

---

[64] Since GMM uses Agile software development, which allows for specific plans and IT requirements to be defined on an incremental basis, we focused on GMM's plans and requirements for near-term efforts, which consisted of Increment 1 (i.e., the Assistance to Firefighters Grants Pilot).a

- fully implemented—FEMA provided complete evidence that showed it fully implemented the practice area;
- partially implemented—FEMA provided evidence that showed it partially implemented the practice area;
- not implemented—FEMA did not provide evidence that showed it implemented any of the practice area.

Additionally, we observed Agile increment and sprint development activities at GMM facilities in Washington, D.C. We also observed a demonstration of how the program manages its lower level requirements (i.e., user stories and epics) and maintains traceability of the requirements using an automated tool at GMM facilities in Washington, D.C.

We also interviewed FEMA officials, including the GMM Program Executive, GMM Program Manager, GMM Business Transformation Team Lead, and Product Owner regarding their efforts to streamline grants management business processes, collect and incorporate stakeholder input, and manage GMM's requirements. In addition, we interviewed FEMA officials from four out of 16 grant program offices and two out of 10 regional offices to obtain contextual information and illustrative examples of FEMA's efforts to reengineer grants management business processes and collect business requirements for GMM. Specifically,

- We selected the four grant program offices based on a range of grant programs managed, legacy systems used, and the amount of grant funding awarded. We also sought to select a cross section of different characteristics, such as selecting larger grant program offices, as well as smaller offices. In addition, we ensured that our selection included the Assistance to Firefighters Grants (AFG) program office because officials in this office represent the first GMM users and, therefore, are more actively involved with the program's Agile development practices. Based on these factors, we selected: Public Assistance Division, Individual Assistance Division, AFG, and National Fire Academy. Additionally, the four selected grant program offices are responsible for 16 of the total 45

# United States Government Accountability Office

grant programs and are users of five of the nine primary legacy IT systems. The four selected grant program offices also represent about 68 percent of the total grant funding awarded by FEMA from fiscal years 2005 through 2016.

- We selected two regional offices based on (1) the largest amount of total FEMA grant funding for fiscal years 2005 through 2016—Region 6 located in Denton, Texas; and (2) the highest percentage of AFG funding compared to the office's total grant funding awarded from fiscal years 2005 through 2016—Region 5 located in Chicago, Illinois.

To assess the reliability of data from the program's automated IT requirements management tool, we interviewed knowledgeable officials about the quality control procedures used by the program to assure accuracy and completeness of the data. We also compared the data to other relevant program documentation on GMM requirements. We determined that the data used were sufficiently reliable for the purpose of evaluating GMM's practices for managing IT requirements.

For our second objective, to assess the reliability of GMM's estimated costs and schedule, we reviewed documentation on GMM's May 2017 lifecycle cost estimate and on the program's schedule, dated May 2018.

- To assess the reliability of the May 2017 lifecycle cost estimate, we evaluated documentation supporting the estimate, such as the cost estimating model, the report on GMM's Cost Estimating Baseline Document and Life Cycle Cost Estimate, and briefings provided to the Department of Homeland Security (DHS) and FEMA management regarding the cost estimate. We assessed the cost estimating methodologies, assumptions, and results against leading practices for developing a comprehensive, accurate, well-documented, and credible cost estimate, identified in GAO's Cost Estimating and Assessment Guide.[65] We also interviewed program

---

[65] GAO, *Cost Estimating and Assessment Guide: Best Practices for Developing and Managing Capital Program Costs,* GAO-09-3SP (Washington, D.C.: March 2009). S

officials responsible for developing and reviewing the cost estimate to understand their methodology, data, and approach for developing the estimate. We found that the cost data were sufficiently reliable.

- To assess the reliability of the May 2018 GMM program schedule, we evaluated documentation supporting the schedule, such as the integrated master schedule, acquisition program baseline, and Agile artifacts.[66] We assessed the schedule documentation against leading practices for developing a comprehensive, well-constructed, credible, and controlled schedule, identified in GAO's Schedule Assessment Guide.[67] We also interviewed GMM program officials responsible for developing and managing the program schedule to understand their practices for creating and maintaining the schedule. We noted in our report the instances where the quality of the schedule data impacted the reliability of the program's schedule.

For both the cost estimate and program schedule, we assessed each leading practice as:

- fully addressed—FEMA provided complete evidence that showed it implemented the entire practice area;
- substantially addressed—FEMA provided evidence that showed it implemented more than half of the practice area;
- partially addressed—FEMA provided evidence that showed it implemented about half of the practice area;
- minimally addressed—FEMA provided evidence that showed it implemented less than half of the practice area;
- not addressed—FEMA did not provide evidence that showed it implemented any of the practice area.

---

[66] Since GMM uses Agile software development, which allows for high level plans to be defined in further detail on an incremental basis, we focused on GMM's near-term planning efforts which consisted of Increment 1 (i.e., the Assistance to Firefights Grants Pilot).

[67] GAO, *Schedule Assessment Guide: Best Practices for Project Schedules,* GAO-16-89G (Washington, D.C.: December 2015).

102       *United States Government Accountability Office*

Finally, we provided FEMA with draft versions of our detailed analyses of the GMM cost estimate and schedule. This was done to verify that the information on which we based our findings was complete, accurate, and up-to-date.

Regarding our third objective, to determine the extent to which FEMA is addressing key cybersecurity practices for GMM, we reviewed documentation regarding DHS and FEMA cybersecurity policies and guidance, and FEMA's authorization to operate for the program's engineering and test environment.[68] We evaluated the documentation against all six cybersecurity practices identified in the National Institute of Standards and Technology's (NIST) Risk Management Framework.[69] While NIST's Risk Management Framework identifies six total practices, for reporting purposes, we combined two interrelated practices—selection of security controls and implementation of security controls—into a single practice. The resulting five practices were: categorizing the system based on security risk, selecting and implementing security controls, assessing security controls, obtaining an authorization to operate the system, and monitoring security controls on an ongoing basis.

We obtained and analyzed key artifacts supporting the program's efforts to address these risk management practices, including the program's System Security Plan, the Security Assessment Plan and Report, Authorization to Operate documentation, and the program's continuous monitoring documentation. We also interviewed officials from the GMM program office and FEMA's Office of the Chief Information Officer, such as the GMM Security Engineering Lead, GMM Information System Security Officer, and FEMA's Acting Chief Information Security Officer, regarding their efforts to assess, document, and review security controls for GMM.

---

[68] The programs' engineering and test environment went live in February 2018 and was the most recent authorization to operate at the time that we began our review. This environment was intended to mirror the production environment's configuration and security controls. GMM subsequently conducted a separate authorization to operate process for the production environment, which went live in July 2018.

[69] NIST, *Guide for Applying the Risk Management Framework to Federal Information Systems: A Security Life Cycle Approach*, SP 800-37, Revision 1 (Gaithersburg, Md.: February 2010).

We assessed the evidence against the five practices to determine the extent to which the agency had addressed them. We then assessed each practice area as:

- fully addressed—FEMA provided complete evidence that showed it fully implemented the practice area;
- partially addressed—FEMA provided evidence that showed it partially implemented the practice area;
- not addressed—FEMA did not provide evidence that showed it implemented any of the practice area.

To assess the reliability of data from the program's automated security controls management tool, we interviewed knowledgeable officials about the quality control procedures used by the program to assure accuracy and completeness of the data. We also compared the data to other relevant program documentation on GMM security controls for the engineering and test environment. We found that some of the security controls data we examined were sufficiently reliable for the purpose of evaluating FEMA's cybersecurity practices for GMM, and we noted in our report the instances where the accuracy of the data impacted the program's ability to address key cybersecurity practices.

We conducted this performance audit from December 2017 to April 2019 in accordance with generally accepted government auditing standards. Those standards require that we plan and perform the audit to obtain sufficient, appropriate evidence to provide a reasonable basis for our findings and conclusions based on our audit objectives. We believe that the evidence obtained provides a reasonable basis for our findings and conclusions based on our audit objectives.

104     *United States Government Accountability Office*

# APPENDIX II: FEDERAL EMERGENCY MANAGEMENT AGENCY'S GRANT PROGRAMS

The Federal Emergency Management Agency (FEMA) awards many different types of grants to state, local, and tribal governments and nongovernmental entities. These grants are to help communities prevent, prepare for, protect against, mitigate the effects of, respond to, and recover from disasters and terrorist attacks.

The number of active grant programs varies based on programs being authorized or discontinued and how "grant programs" are defined. In 2018, FEMA Office of Chief Counsel officials identified 37 programs, whereas Grants Management Modernization (GMM) program officials identified 45 programs because they defined "grant programs" more broadly and further decomposed the programs to facilitate the development of the GMM solution. The following 45 active grant programs were identified by GMM, as of August 2018:

1. Assistance to Firefighters Grants
2. Chemical Stockpile Emergency Preparedness Program
3. Community Assistance Program - State Support Services Element
4. Complex Coordinated Terrorist Attacks Program
5. Cooperating Technical Partners
6. Cora Brown Fund
7. Countering Violent Extremism
8. Crisis Counseling Program
9. Disaster Case Management Grants
10. Disaster Housing Operations for Individuals and Households
11. Disaster Legal Services
12. Disaster Unemployment Assistance
13. Emergency Food and Shelter National Board Program
14. Emergency Management Baseline Assessments Grant
15. Emergency Management Institute Training Assistance
16. Emergency Management Performance Grants

17. Fire Management Assistance Grant
18. Fire Prevention and Safety Grants
19. Flood Mitigation Assistance
20. Hazard Mitigation Grant Program
21. Homeland Security Grant Program: Operation Stonegarden Grant Program
22. Homeland Security Grant Program: State Homeland Security Program
23. Homeland Security Grant Program: Urban Areas Security Initiative
24. Homeland Security National Training Program/National Domestic Preparedness Consortium
25. Homeland Security National Training Program/Continuing Training Grant
26. Homeland Security Preparedness Technical Assistance Program
27. Housing Assistance
28. Intercity Bus Security Grant Program
29. Intercity Passenger Rail Program
30. National Dam Safety Program
31. National Earthquake Hazard Reduction Program
32. National Fire Academy Training Assistance
33. National Incident Management System – Emergency Management Assistance Compact
34. Nonprofit Security Grant Program
35. Other Needs Assistance
36. Port Security Grant Program
37. Pre-Disaster Mitigation
38. Presidential Residence Protection Assistance
39. Public Assistance
40. Staffing for Adequate Fire and Emergency Response Grants
41. State Fire Training System Grant
42. Transit Security Grant Program
43. Tribal Homeland Security Grant Program

106 *United States Government Accountability Office*

44. Urban Search and Rescue Readiness Cooperative Agreements
45. Urban Search and Rescue Response Cooperative Agreements

## APPENDIX III: OVERVIEW OF AGILE SOFTWARE DEVELOPMENT

Agile software development is a type of incremental development that calls for the rapid delivery of software in small, short increments. The use of an incremental approach is consistent with the Office of Management and Budget's guidance as specified in its information technology (IT) Reform Plan,[70] as well as the legislation commonly referred to as the Federal Information Technology Acquisition Reform Act.[71]

Many organizations, especially in the federal government, are accustomed to using a waterfall software development model, which typically consists of long, sequential phases, and differs significantly from the Agile development approach. Agile practices integrate planning, design, development, and testing into an iterative lifecycle to deliver software early and often. Figure 7 provides a depiction of software development using the Agile approach, as compared to a waterfall approach.

---

[70] Office of Management and Budget, *25 Point Implementation Plan to Reform Federal Information Technology Management* (Washington, D.C.: Dec. 9, 2010). The implementation plan states that funding of major IT programs should only be approved when it uses a modular approach with usable functionality delivered every 6 months.

[71] 40 U.S.C. § 11319(b)(1)(B)(ii). The Federal Information Technology Acquisition Reform provisions of the Carl Levin and Howard P. "Buck" McKeon National Defense Authorization Act for Fiscal Year 2015, Pub. L. No. 113-291, div. A, title VIII, subtitle D, 128 Stat. 3292, 3438-3450 (Dec. 19, 2014) are commonly referred to as the Federal Information Technology Acquisition Reform Act. The act directs the Office of Management and Budget to require in its annual capital planning guidance that the chief information officers of covered agencies certify that IT investments are adequately implementing incremental development. The Office of Management and Budget defines adequate incremental development of software or services as the delivery of new or modified technical functionality to users at least every 6 months.

# FEMA Grants Modernization

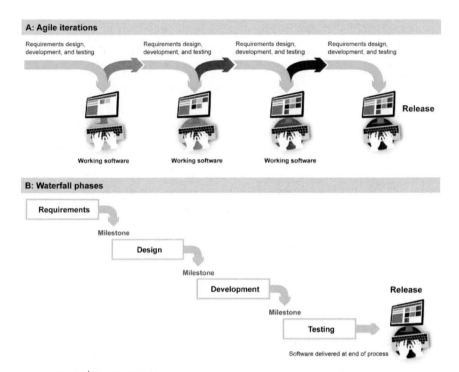

Source: GAO. | GAO-19-164

Figure 7. Comparison of Agile and Waterfall Software Development.

The frequent iterations of Agile development are intended to effectively measure progress, reduce technical and programmatic risk, and respond to feedback from stakeholders in changes to IT requirements more quickly than traditional methods. Despite these intended benefits, organizations adopting Agile must overcome challenges in making significant changes to how they are accustomed to developing software.[72]

The significant differences between Agile and waterfall development impact how IT programs are planned, implemented, and monitored in

---

[72] See prior reports highlighting challenges with adopting Agile practices, such as GAO, *Software Development: Effective Practices and Federal Challenges in Applying Agile Methods*, GAO-12-681 (Washington, D.C.: July 27, 2012); *Immigration Benefits System: U.S. Citizenship and Immigration Services Can Improve Program Management*, GAO-16-467 (Washington, D.C.: July 7, 2016); and *TSA Modernization: Use of Sound Program Management and Oversight Practices Is Needed to Avoid Repeating Past Problems*, GAO-18-46 (Washington, D.C.: Oct. 17, 2017).

terms of cost, schedule, and scope. For example, in waterfall development, significant effort is devoted upfront to document detailed plans and all IT requirements for the entire scope of work at the beginning of the program, and cost and schedule can be varied to complete that work.

However, for Agile programs the precise details are unknown upfront, so initial planning of cost, scope, and timing would be conducted at a high level, and then supplemented with more specific plans for each iteration. While cost and schedule are set for each iteration, requirements for each iteration (or increment) can be variable as they are learned over time and revised to reflect experiences from completed iterations and to accommodate changing priorities of the end users. The differences in these two software development approaches are shown in Figure 8.

Looking at Figure 8, the benefit provided from using traditional program management practices such as establishing a cost estimate or a robust schedule, is not obvious. However, unlike a theoretical environment, many government programs may not have the autonomy to manage completely flexible scope, as they must deliver certain minimal specifications with the cost and schedule provided.

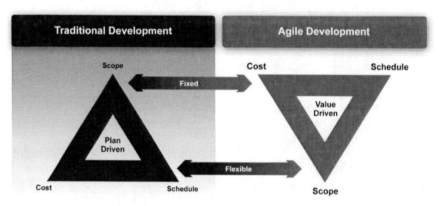

Source: GAO. | GAO-19-164

Figure 8. Comparison of Cost, Schedule, and Scope Management for Each Iteration among Software Development Approaches.

In those cases, it is vital for the team to understand and differentiate the IT requirements that are "must haves" from the "nice to haves" early in the planning effort. This would help facilitate delivery of the "must-haves" requirements first, thereby providing users with the greatest benefits as soon as possible.

# APPENDIX IV: COMMENTS FROM THE DEPARTMENT OF HOMELAND SECURITY

March 18, 2019

Carol C. Harris
Director, Information Technology Management Issues
U.S. Government Accountability Office
441 G Street, NW
Washington, DC 20548

Re: Management Response to Draft Report GAO-19-164, "FEMA GRANTS MODERNIZATION: Improvements Needed to Strengthen Program Management and Cybersecurity"

Dear Ms. Harris:

Thank you for the opportunity to review and comment on this draft report. The U.S. Department of Homeland Security (DHS) appreciates the U.S. Government Accountability Office's (GAO) work in planning and conducting its review and issuing this report.

The Department is pleased to note GAO's recognition of the many positive steps the Federal Emergency Management Agency (FEMA) has taken to implement leading practices for effective business process reengineering and information technology (IT) requirements. These include ensuring executive leadership support for business process reengineering and incorporating input from end user stakeholders. DHS and FEMA are committed to the successful implementation of the Grants Management Modernization (GMM) program, which aims to transform the way FEMA manages grants, strengthening FEMA's ability to execute its mission through a user-centered, business-driven approach.

The draft report contained eight recommendations with which the Department concurs. Attached find our detailed response to each recommendation. Technical comments were previously provided under separate cover.

# 110    *United States Government Accountability Office*

Again, thank you for the opportunity to review and comment on this draft report. Please feel free to contact me if you have any questions. We look forward to working with you again in the future.

Sincerely,

JIM H. CRUMPACKER, CIA, CFE
Director
Departmental GAO-OIG Liaison Office

### Attachment: Management Response to Recommendations Contained in GAO-19-164

GAO recommended that the FEMA Administrator:

**Recommendation 1:** Ensure that the GMM Program management office finalizes the organizational change management plan and time frames for implementing change management actions.

**Response:** Concur. The GMM Program Management Office (PMO) will ensure the change management efforts are further developed and implemented with the various grants programs in the Agency.

The GMM PMO has identified key resources to focus on maturing its change management efforts. These key resources include the GMM Business Manager, Regional Coordinator, Change Manager, Training Manager, and a Business Analyst who will partner with the various grant programs and champion GMM's change management across the agency. GMM will first update its Change Management Plan (CMP) to add additional details, where available, to include organizational change, workforce impacts, and readiness. GMM is currently reviewing its CMP and will develop a Plan of Action & Milestones (POAM) by July 31, 2019 to guide the program and establish timeframes for implementation. In the Change Management POAM, GMM will identify target dates to create an Organizational Change Management Strategy, Readiness Assessment, Training Plan, and Workforce Analysis. The development of these documents will support the overall implementation of change management efforts in GMM with users from all grant programs.

In addition to supporting organizational change management, GMM has helped stand up the Centralized Grants Policy & Doctrine Working Group (CWG) to identify opportunities for standardizing grant policies and/or processes in order to ensure alignment with the FEMA Manual 205-0-1, "Grants Management," as well as ensuring accurate and qualitative buildouts of the GMM system (aka FEMA GO). The CWG is a cross-Agency team of policy experts from the various grant programs. The initial phase of the team's efforts will be focused on resolving policy and process questions that arise during the development of the FEMA GO system that are beyond what is addressed in the Grants Management Manual. Decisions made by this team will be captured in updates to the Grants Management Manual, supporting standard operating procedures, and incorporated in the updated CMP.

Estimated Completion Date (ECD): July 31, 2020.

# FEMA Grants Modernization

**Recommendation 2:** Ensure that the GMM program management office plans and communicates its detailed transition activities to its affected customers before they transition to GMM and undergo significant changes to their processes.

**Response:** Concur. The GMM PMO will ensure a detailed transition of activities for users to optimally manage significant changes to their current business processes. The GMM PMO will conduct a readiness assessment to better understand our users and their ability to undergo significant changes to their grants business processes, per the timeline identified in the CMP POAM. The assessment will analyze how prepared and ready FEMA users are to use new functionality in FEMA GO, review how users are trained with current grants management and how much training is needed to support the transition to the FEMA GO system, identify areas needing more attention for users, and make recommendations that significantly increase the likelihood of GMM success and FEMA GO user adoption. The initial transition plan to support the Assistance to Firefighters Grants pilot will be completed by August 31, 2019.

ECD: December 31, 2019.

**Recommendation 3:** Ensure that the GMM program management office implements its planned changes to its processes for documenting requirements for future increments and ensures it maintains traceability among key IT requirements documents.

**Response:** Concur. GMM is leveraging industry best practices while implementing Agile and Kanban software development methodologies. The GMM team is documenting the Jira Software product backlog, which provides complete traceability through acceptance criteria and gets mapped to test plans and test cases. GMM will provide mapping of functions to the Jira backlog to ensure complete end-to-end traceability. Jira is the DHS software suite used by GMM to manage Agile software requirements and measure development progress.

ECD: July 31, 2019.

**Recommendation 4:** Ensure that the GMM program management office updates the program schedule to address the leading practices for a reliable schedule identified in this report.

**Response:** Concur. GMM Program leadership will ensure that the GMM PMO updates the program schedule to address the leading practices for a reliable schedule identified in this report.

In October 2018, the program added two master schedulers to the PMO team to work on the GMM Program Integrated Master Schedule (IMS). In addition, the program detailed a dedicated portfolio manager to begin building a program level Release Plan that incorporates product requirements across all FEMA lines of business and illustrates software development goals, objectives, and milestones for when features (new functionality) will be delivered to users.

The program level Release Plan will be further revised with input from the Systems and Platform using Agile Releases and Consolidation (SPARC) software development contractor. The initial planning task awarded to the SPARC contractor includes a requirement to develop a "comprehensive Integrated Master Schedule (IMS) that incorporates all projects, activities, and milestones necessary for the design, development, and implementation of the GMM target solution."

ECD: April 30, 2019.

**Recommendation 5:** Ensure that the FEMA OCIO defines sufficiently detailed planned evaluation methods and actual evaluation methods for assessing security controls.

**Response:** Concur. FEMA's Office of the Chief Information Officer (OCIO) Cyber Security Division (CSD) will plan and conduct security control evaluations as annotated in the Cybersecurity Security Assessment Plan Standard Operating Procedures. The CSD Security Control Assessor will work with the GMM program Information Systems Security Officer to ensure security controls are implemented and documented in the Security Assessment Report with sufficient detail to meet DHS Sensitive Policy Systems Directive 4300A and National Institute of Standards and Technology (NIST) 800-53 mandates.

ECD: July 31, 2019.

**Recommendation 6:** Ensure that the FEMA OCIO approves a security assessment plan before security assessment reviews are conducted.

**Response:** Concur. FEMA OCIO CSD will document and implement processes and procedures in accordance with NIST SP 800-37, "Guidelines for Applying the Risk Management Framework to Federal Information Systems," and "DHS Sensitive Policy Systems Directive 4300A," for the Security Control Assessor to review and validate in the Security Assessment Plan. The GMM system owner and independent verification and validation team lead will approve and sign the required Scanning Authorization Letter included in the Security Assessment Plan prior to conducting any system security assessments. This will grant Security Control Assessors the authority to scan and assess the system.

ECD: July 31, 2019.

# FEMA Grants Modernization

**Recommendation 7:** Ensure that the GMM Program management office follows DHS guidance on preparing corrective action plans for all security vulnerabilities.

**Response:** Concur. The GMM Program will expand its corrective action plans to comply with mandated guidance for corrective Plans of Action and Milestones to detail remediation of identified vulnerabilities. These guidelines will be compliant with DHS Instruction 4300A, Attachment-H (Plan of Action and Milestones).

On August 17, 2018, FEMA OCIO established a formal Agile Development, Security, and Operations (DevSecOps) process that allows the GMM program to securely deploy new software into a production environment in a true Agile process. This allows software deployments to occur in minutes/hours compared to days/weeks in a traditional waterfall-based software development process.

GMM is continuing to use automated DevSecOps pipelines and security tools to identify security vulnerabilities. This allows early identification and remediation as quickly as possible. The program has adopted security best practices as part of the overall delivery lifecycle. GMM is leveraging dynamic & static security scans which identifies code vulnerabilities as part of the DevSecOps deployment process. This step prevents any code vulnerabilities being introduced and provides a remediation path for course correction. The environment also undergoes periodic network scans to identify any security vulnerabilities which get patched on a regular basis. The platform is hosted on an accredited cloud infrastructure on a cloud architecture which is patched on a daily basis to address any zero-day vulnerability attack vector. GMM has also implemented additional defense-in-depth features to prevent against malicious attacks. During December 2018, GMM invited DHS cybersecurity professionals to conduct an exhaustive vulnerability assessment of the FEMA GO system, which were unable to identify any vulnerabilities. The scan results provided a good validation of the program's strong security posture.

ECD: July 31, 2019.

**Recommendation 8:** Ensure that the GMM Program management office fully tests all of its security controls for the system.

**Response:** Concur. The GMM Program Office will work with FEMA OCIO to ensure a detailed evaluation of all DHS and NIST security controls are annotated in the Security Assessment Plan. OCIO CSD Security Control Assessors will work with the GMM system owner and program ISSO to ensure security controls are implemented and documented with sufficient details to meet DHS Directive 4300A and NIST 800-53 mandates, allowing for comprehensive testing of the system.

# 114 United States Government Accountability Office

As of October 2018, GMM has worked with CSD to obtain and document all inherited controls and the systems that provide these controls. GMM is working to identify and compile the Points of Contact (POCs) for these systems, (for both DHS and FEMA). GMM will continue to work with these POCs to ensure that all inherited controls are tested by all parties who have a share in the provision of the control and that these are documented in FEMA's Information Assurance Compliance System (IACS). GMM has worked to improve the FEMA GO engineering/test environment documentation in IACS and will continuously do so.

DHS has a well-documented Security Management plan that provides guidance with respect to security management processes such as common controls and ongoing authorization. With the integration of new technology, and best practices such as Information Security Continuous Monitoring, cloud computing, and security control inheritance, the customary ways of addressing these areas of security are gradually transforming.

The GMM Program is planning to leverage a multi-pronged approach to test all of its security controls for the system. This includes the use of:
- automated tools,
- centralized logging tools such as Splunk, and
- periodic manual testing, to detect and alert on deviation from implemented security controls for the system.

ECD: July 31, 2019.

In: Key Government Reports. Volume 17     ISBN: 978-1-53616-003-1
Editor: Ernest Clark     © 2019 Nova Science Publishers, Inc.

*Chapter 3*

# DATA CENTER OPTIMIZATION: ADDITIONAL AGENCY ACTIONS NEEDED TO MEET OMB GOALS*

## *United States Government Accountability Office*

### ABBREVIATIONS

| | |
|---|---|
| Agriculture | Department of Agriculture |
| CIO | chief information officer |
| Commerce | Department of Commerce |
| DCOI | Data Center Optimization Initiative |
| Defense | Department of Defense |
| DHS | Department of Homeland Security |
| Education | Department of Education |
| Energy | Department of Energy |
| EPA | Environmental Protection Agency |
| FDCCI | Federal Data Center Consolidation Initiative |

---

* This is an edited, reformatted and augmented version of United States Government Accountability Office; Report to Congressional Committees, Accessible Version, Publication No. GAO-19-241, dated April 2019.

| | |
|---|---|
| FITARA | Federal Information Technology Acquisition Reform Act |
| GSA | General Services Administration |
| HHS | Department of Health and Human Services |
| HUD | Department of Housing and Urban Development |
| IT | information technology |
| Interior | Department of the Interior |
| Justice | Department of Justice |
| Labor | Department of Labor |
| NASA | National Aeronautics and Space Administration |
| NRC | Nuclear Regulatory Commission |
| NSF | National Science Foundation |
| OMB | Office of Management and Budget |
| OPM | Office of Personnel Management |
| SBA | Small Business Administration |
| SSA | Social Security Administration |
| State | Department of State |
| Transportation | Department of Transportation |
| Treasury | Department of the Treasury |
| USAID | U.S. Agency for International Development |
| VA | Department of Veterans Affairs |

# WHY GAO DID THIS STUDY

In December 2014, Congress enacted federal IT acquisition reform legislation that included provisions related to ongoing federal data center consolidation efforts. OMB's Federal Chief Information Officer launched DCOI to build on prior data center consolidation efforts; improve federal data centers' performance; and establish goals for inventory closures, cost savings and avoidances, and optimizing performance.

The 2014 legislation included a provision for GAO to annually review agencies' data center inventories and strategies. Accordingly, GAO's objectives were to (1) evaluate agencies' progress and plans for data center

*Data Center Optimization* 117

closures and cost savings; (2) assess agencies' progress against OMB's data center optimization targets; (3) and identify effective agency practices for achieving data center closures, cost savings, and optimization progress. To do so, GAO assessed the 24 DCOI agencies' data center inventories as of August 2018; reviewed their reported cost savings documentation; evaluated their data center optimization strategic plans; and assessed their progress against OMB's established optimization targets. GAO also solicited practices that selected agencies reported to be effective in meeting DCOI goals.

## WHAT GAO RECOMMENDS

GAO is making 36 recommendations to 22 agencies to improve performance against established DCOI goals. Eleven agencies agreed with the recommendations, three did not fully agree, one disagreed, and seven neither agreed nor disagreed, as discussed in the report.

## WHAT GAO FOUND

The 24 agencies participating in the Office of Management and Budget's (OMB) Data Center Optimization Initiative (DCOI) reported mixed progress toward achieving OMB's goals for closing data centers and realizing the associated savings by September 2018. As of August 2018, 13 agencies reported that they had met, or had plans to meet, all of their OMB-assigned closure goals by the deadline. However, 11 agencies reported that they did not have plans to meet their goals. Further, 16 agencies reported that, as of August 2018, they had met, or planned to meet, their cost savings targets, for a total of $2.36 billion in cost savings for fiscal years 2016 through 2018. This is about $0.38 billion less than OMB's DCOI savings goal of $2.7 billion. This shortfall is the result of 5 agencies reporting less in planned cost savings and avoidances in their

DCOI strategic plans, as compared to their savings targets established for them by OMB. Three agencies did not have a cost savings target and did not report any achieved savings.

In addition, the 24 agencies reported limited progress against OMB's five data center optimization targets for server utilization and automated monitoring, energy metering, power usage effectiveness, facility utilization, and virtualization. As of August 2018, the agencies reported that 3 had met three targets, 9 had met one target, and 10 met none of the targets. Two agencies did not have a basis to report on progress as they do not own any data centers. Further, as of August 2018, 20 agencies did not plan to meet all of OMB's fiscal year 2018 optimization goals. Specifically, only 2 agencies reported plans to meet all applicable targets; 6 reported that they did not plan to meet any of the targets (see figure).

We selected 6 agencies that had demonstrated success towards meeting their DCOI goals and those agencies reported a number of key practices that contributed to their efforts. The officials noted the importance of, among other things, obtaining executive leadership support for consolidation and optimization activities, employing an organization-wide communications plan, and focusing on data center closures. The officials also cited the use of past experience and lessons learned to inform improvements to future consolidation plans and processes.

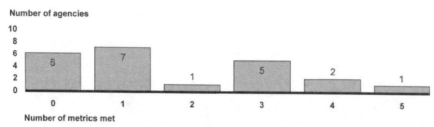

Source: GAO analysis of data from OMB's Information Technology Dashboard. | GAO-19-241.

Agencies' Planned Fiscal Year 2018 Progress against OMB's Five Data Center Optimization Metrics, as of August 2018.

April 11, 2019
Congressional Committees

# Data Center Optimization

The federal government's demand for information technology (IT) is ever increasing. In recent years, as federal agencies have modernized their operations, put more of their services online, and improved their information security profiles, their need for computing power and data storage resources has grown. Accordingly, this growing demand has led to a dramatic rise in the number of federal data centers and a corresponding increase in operational costs.

To reduce data center duplication and costs, the Office of Management and Budget's (OMB) Federal Chief Information Officer (CIO) launched two initiatives. The first, launched in 2010, was the Federal Data Center Consolidation Initiative (FDCCI), which aimed to reduce the number of data centers that were outdated or duplicative. The second initiative—the Data Center Optimization Initiative (DCOI)—was launched in August 2016 and superseded FDCCI. It shifted the focus to optimizing agencies' remaining data centers by requiring, among other things, that agencies consolidate inefficient infrastructure, optimize existing facilities, and transition to more efficient infrastructure, such as cloud services.[1]

Further, Congress recognized the importance of reforming the government-wide management of IT and, in December 2014, enacted *Federal Information Technology Acquisition Reform* provisions (commonly referred to as FITARA) as a part of the *Carl Levin and Howard P. 'Buck' McKeon National Defense Authorization Act for Fiscal Year 2015.*[2] Among the requirements related to federal data center consolidation, the law required:[3]

---

[1] According to the National Institute of Standards and Technology, cloud services provide one or more capabilities via the cloud computing model. The cloud computing model enables ubiquitous, convenient, on-demand network access to a shared pool of configurable computing resources (e.g., networks, servers, storage, applications, and services).

[2] Pub. L. No. 113-291, division A, title VIII, subtitle D, 128 Stat. 3292, 3438 (Dec. 19, 2014). In November 2017, the *FITARA Enhancement Act of 2017* was enacted to extend, among other things, the sunset date for the data center provisions of FITARA. The law set an expiration date of October 1, 2020 for provisions for data center consolidation and optimization. Pub. L. No. 115-88, 131 Stat. 1278 (Nov. 21, 2017).

[3] Pub. L. No. 113-291 § 834, 128 Stat. 3444 – 3448 (44 U.S.C. 3601 note). Unless otherwise noted, these requirements apply to the 24 agencies specified in section 834 (corresponding to those agencies covered by the *Chief Financial Officers Act of 1990.* 31 U.S.C. § 901(b)).

120 *United States Government Accountability Office*

- Covered departments and agencies (agencies)[4] to annually report to OMB about federal data center inventories and strategies to achieve consolidation, including yearly calculations of investment and cost savings.[5]
- OMB to develop goals for the amount of planned cost savings and optimization improvements that agencies are to achieve through FDCCI. OMB is to make the goals publicly available and compare progress against the goals.

In addition to these requirements, FITARA included a provision for GAO to annually review and verify the quality and completeness of federal data center inventories and strategies for consolidation submitted by the agencies covered by the law. Accordingly, our specific objectives were to (1) determine agencies' progress on data center closures and the related savings that have been achieved, and describe agencies' plans for future closures and savings; (2) assess agencies' progress against OMB's data center optimization targets; and (3) identify effective agency practices for achieving data center closures, cost savings, and optimization.

To review closures to date and plans for future closures, we obtained and analyzed August 2018 data center inventory documentation from the 24 DCOI agencies. We compared information on these agencies' completed and planned data center closures to OMB's fiscal year 2018 consolidation goals, as documented in its August 2016 memorandum (M-

---

[4] The 24 agencies that are required to participate in the Data Center Optimization Initiative are the Departments of Agriculture, Commerce, Defense, Education, Energy, Health and Human Services, Homeland Security, Housing and Urban Development, the Interior, Justice, Labor, State, Transportation, the Treasury, and Veterans Affairs; the Environmental Protection Agency, General Services Administration, National Aeronautics and Space Administration, National Science Foundation, Nuclear Regulatory Commission, Office of Personnel Management, Small Business Administration, Social Security Administration, and U.S. Agency for International Development. These are the same agencies covered by FITARA's data center consolidation provisions.

[5] In lieu of submitting a data center inventory and strategy, the Department of Defense may submit this information as part of a defense-wide plan and report on cost savings, as required under §§ 2867(b)(2) and 2867(d) of the *National Defense Authorization Act for Fiscal Year 2012* (10 U.S.C. § 2223a note).

## Data Center Optimization

16-19).[6] We determined the number of data centers that had been closed by adding the closures from fiscal year 2010 through August 2018, as reported by the agencies in their inventory submissions to OMB.[7] We identified future closures by counting data centers that agencies reported as planned closures, as of August 2018 through fiscal year 2023.

To verify the quality, completeness, and reliability of the agencies' data center inventories, we compared the information on completed and planned data center closures to similar information reported on OMB's IT Dashboard—a public website that provides information on federal agencies' major IT investments.[8] We determined that the data were sufficiently reliable to report on agencies' consolidation progress and planned closures.

To evaluate agencies' progress in, and plans for, achieving data center cost savings, we reviewed August 2018 cost savings and avoidance[9] documentation that the 24 DCOI agencies submitted in response to OMB's March 2013 PortfolioStat[10] and August 2016 data center initiative memorandums.[11] This documentation included the agencies' quarterly reports of cost savings and avoidances posted to their digital services websites and discussed in their DCOI strategic plans.

We determined cost savings achieved by adding agencies' reported savings and avoidances from the start of fiscal year 2012 through August 2018, as found in the August 2018 quarterly reports posted to the agencies' digital services websites. We identified planned savings by totaling the

---

[6] OMB, *Data Center Optimization Initiative (DCOI)*, Memorandum M-16-19 (Washington, D.C.: Aug. 1, 2016).

[7] Under FDCCI, which OMB launched in February 2010, agencies were required to begin closing data centers. However, current OMB guidance only requires agencies to report historical cost savings and avoidances realized since fiscal year 2012.

[8] We did not physically visit agencies' data center locations to verify their inventory totals.

[9] Beginning in March 2013, OMB required agencies to report on both cost savings and cost avoidances. OMB defines cost savings as a reduction in actual expenditures below the projected level of costs to achieve a specific objective and defines a cost avoidance as the result of an action taken in the immediate time frame that will decrease costs in the future.

[10] Launched by OMB in 2012, PortfolioStat requires agencies to conduct an annual, agency-wide IT portfolio review to, among other things, reduce commodity IT spending and demonstrate how their IT investments align with the agency's mission and business functions.

[11] OMB, *Fiscal Year 2013 PortfolioStat Guidance: Strengthening Federal IT Portfolio Management*, Memorandum M-13-09 (Washington, D.C.: Mar. 27, 2013) and Memorandum M-16-19.

# 122 *United States Government Accountability Office*

agencies' projected savings and avoidances from fiscal years 2016 through 2018, as reported in their DCOI strategic plans.

To assess the quality, completeness, and reliability of each agency's data center consolidation cost savings information, we used the latest version of each agency's update of the August 2018 quarterly cost savings report and DCOI strategic plan. We also reviewed the quarterly reports and DCOI strategic plans for missing data and other errors, such as missing cost savings information.

In addition, we compared agencies' reported cost savings and avoidances with data from our most recently issued report on data center consolidation.[12] Further, we obtained written responses from agency officials regarding the steps they took to ensure the accuracy and reliability of their cost savings data. As a result, we determined that the data were sufficiently reliable to report on agencies' data center consolidation cost-savings information.

To assess agencies' progress against OMB's data center optimization targets, we obtained the August 2018 data center optimization progress information of 22 DCOI agencies, as reported on the IT Dashboard.[13] To assess the agencies' planned optimization progress, we obtained the planned optimization performance from the 22 agencies' DCOI strategic plans. We then compared the agencies' current and planned optimization progress information to OMB's fiscal year 2018 optimization targets, as documented in its August 2016 memorandum.[14]

To assess the reliability of agencies' optimization progress information on OMB's IT Dashboard, we reviewed the information for errors or missing data, compared agencies' optimization progress information across multiple reporting quarters to identify any inconsistencies in their reported progress, and discussed with agency officials the steps they took to ensure the accuracy and reliability of the reported optimization progress. We

---

[12] *Data Center Optimization: Continued Agency Actions Needed to Meet Goals and Address Prior Recommendations,* GAO-18-264 (Washington, D.C.: May 23, 2018).

[13] Two agencies—the Departments of Education and Housing and Urban Development— reported that they do not own any data centers and, therefore, do not have a basis to measure and report on optimization progress.

[14] OMB, Memorandum M-16-19.

# Data Center Optimization

123

determined that the data were sufficiently reliable to report on agencies' optimization progress.

In addition, to assess the reliability of the planned optimization milestones in the DCOI strategic plans, we reviewed agencies' documentation to identify any missing or erroneous data. We also compared the planned data center optimization milestones contained in agencies' documentation against current optimization progress information obtained from the IT Dashboard; we then discussed any discrepancies or potential errors that we identified with agency officials to determine the causes or request additional information. As a result of these efforts, we were able to determine whether each agency's strategic plan information was sufficiently reliable for reporting on plans to meet or not meet OMB's fiscal year 2018 optimization targets.

To identify effective agency practices for achieving data center closures, cost savings, and optimization progress, we selected two of the highest-performing agencies for each of these three data center optimization areas (closures, cost savings, and optimization performance) that we reported on in our May 2018 report.[15] For closures, we selected the Departments of Agriculture (Agriculture) and Justice (Justice) as two agencies that had, as of August 2017, reached or exceeded their DCOI tiered and non-tiered data center closure targets.[16]

For cost savings, we selected the Department of Commerce (Commerce) and the General Services Administration (GSA) as two agencies reporting some of the highest DCOI cost savings as of August 2017. For optimization performance, we selected the Social Security Administration (SSA) and the Environmental Protection Agency (EPA), the only two agencies reporting, as of August 2017, that they had met more than half of OMB's optimization targets.

We sent each of these 6 agencies a list of open-ended questions designed to solicit information on practices that the agencies found to be

---

[15] GAO-18-264.

[16] The term "tiered" and its definition are derived by OMB from the Uptime Institute's Tier Classification System. However, OMB notes that no specific certification is required in order for a data center to be considered tiered by OMB. According to OMB M-16-19, all data centers not marked as tiered were to be considered non-tiered.

124  *United States Government Accountability Office*

effective in closing and optimizing data centers and identifying the resulting cost savings. In doing so, our intent was to compile anecdotal information that could assist other agencies struggling with DCOI implementation. We do not consider the examples they provided to be findings; nor should they be taken to be representative of all the agencies participating in DCOI. Appendix I provides greater details regarding our objectives, scope, and methodology.

We conducted this performance audit from April 2018 to April 2019 in accordance with generally accepted government auditing standards. Those standards require that we plan and perform the audit to obtain sufficient, appropriate evidence to provide a reasonable basis for our findings and conclusions based on our audit objectives. We believe that the evidence obtained provides a reasonable basis for our findings and conclusions based on our audit objectives.

## BACKGROUND

According to OMB, federal agencies reported that they operated 432 data centers in 1998, 2,094 in July 2010, and 9,995 in August 2016.[17] Operating such a large number of centers has been, and continues to be, a significant cost to the agencies.[18] For example, in 2007, EPA estimated that the annual cost for electricity to operate federal servers and data centers across the government was about $450 million.

Further, according to the Department of Energy (Energy), a typical government data center has 100 to 200 times the energy use intensity of a commercial building.[19] However, in 2009, OMB reported server utilization rates as low as 5 percent across the federal government's estimated

---

[17] Between 1998 and 2016, OMB used several different definitions for a data center, which contributed to the increase in the number of reported centers. This issue is discussed in more detail later in this chapter.

[18] Costs include hardware, software, real estate, electricity, and heating and cooling.

[19] GAO, *Data Center Consolidation: Agencies Need to Complete Inventories and Plans to Achieve Expected Savings,* GAO-11-565 (Washington, D.C.: July 19, 2011).

*Data Center Optimization* 125

150,000 servers.[20] All of these factors contributed to OMB recognizing the need to establish a coordinated, government-wide effort to improve the efficiency, performance, and environmental footprint of federal data center activities.

## OMB and the Federal CIO Established FDCCI

Concerned about the size of the federal data center inventory and the potential to improve the efficiency, performance, and environmental footprint of federal data center activities, OMB's Federal CIO established FDCCI in February 2010. This initiative's four high-level goals were to reduce the overall energy and real estate footprint of government data centers; reduce the cost of data center hardware, software, and operations; increase the overall IT security posture of the government; and shift IT investments to more efficient computing platforms and technologies.

In February 2010, OMB required all of the agencies participating in the FDCCI to submit a data center inventory and a consolidation plan.[21] In October 2010, OMB also clarified the definition of a data center and noted that, for the purposes of FDCCI, a data center was to be defined as any room used for the purpose of processing or storing data that is larger than 500 square feet and meets stringent availability requirements. Under this definition, OMB reported that agencies had identified 2,094 data centers as of July 2010.

However, in 2011, the Federal CIO expanded the definition to include a facility of any size and OMB published its revised definition in March 2012.[22] Based on the revised definition, OMB estimated that there were a total of 3,133 federal data centers in December 2011. In addition, its goal was to consolidate approximately 40 percent, or 1,253 of these data centers, for a savings of approximately $3 billion by the end of 2015.

---

[20] OMB, *Inventory of Federal Data Center Activity*, Budget Data Request No. 09-41 (Washington, D.C.: Aug. 10, 2009).
[21] The same 24 agencies participated in the FDCCI and DCOI.
[22] OMB, *Implementation Guidance for the Federal Data Center Consolidation Initiative* (Washington, D.C.: Mar. 19, 2012).

Figure 1 shows data center server racks at SSA's National Support Center in 2017.

Source: Social Security Administration. | GAO-19-241.

Figure 1. Example of Data Center Server Racks at the Social Security Administration's National Support Center in 2017.

The number of federal data centers reported by agencies has continued to grow since 2011. In May 2018, we reported that agencies had collectively identified a total of 12,062 data centers in their inventories as of August 2017—an increase of about 9,000 data centers compared to OMB's October 2011 estimate.[23] According to the Federal CIO, the increase in the number of data centers was primarily due to the expanded definition of a data center (discussed later in this chapter) and improved inventory reporting by the agencies. See figure 2 for a depiction of the increase in the number of data centers from 1998 through August 2018.

Further, OMB placed greater emphasis on data center optimization to improve the efficiency of federal data centers when it issued memorandum

---

[23] GAO-18-264.

M-13-09 in March 2013.[24] Specifically, OMB stated that, to more effectively measure the efficiency of an agency's data center assets, agencies would also be measured by the extent to which their primary data centers are optimized for total cost of ownership by incorporating metrics for data center energy, facility, labor, and storage, among other things.

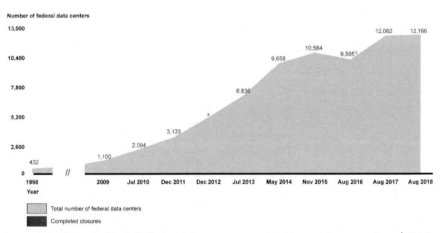

Source: GAO analysis of Office of Management and Budget and agency data. | GAO-19-241.

[a]OMB did not publicly report the total number of data centers in 2012 and expanded its definition of a data center in March 2012, which partially accounts for the sharp increase in the number of data centers.

[b]OMB again revised the definition of a data center in August 2016.

Figure 2. The Number of Reported Federal Data Centers from 1998 through August 2018.

Subsequently, in May 2014, OMB issued memorandum M-14-08, which established a set of data center optimization metrics to measure agency progress, along with target values for each metric.[25] All agencies were expected to achieve the target values by the end of fiscal year 2015.

---

[24] OMB, Memorandum M-13-09.
[25] OMB, *Fiscal Year 2014 PortfolioStat*, Memorandum M-14-08 (Washington- D.C.: May 7- 2014).

# 128      *United States Government Accountability Office*

## IT Acquisition Reform Law Enhanced Data Center Consolidation and Optimization Efforts

Recognizing the importance of reforming the government-wide management of IT, Congress enacted FITARA in December 2014. Among other things, the law required agencies to:[26]

- Submit to OMB a comprehensive inventory of the data centers owned, operated, or maintained by or on behalf of the agency.
- Submit, by the end of fiscal year 2016, a multi-year strategy to achieve the consolidation and optimization of the agency's data centers.[27] The strategy was to include performance metrics that were consistent with the government-wide data center consolidation and optimization metrics.
- Report progress toward meeting government-wide data center consolidation and optimization metrics on a quarterly basis to OMB's Administrator of the Office of Electronic Government.

In addition, according to FITARA, the Office of Electronic Government at OMB was to:

- Establish metrics applicable to the consolidation and optimization of data centers (including server efficiency), ensure that agencies' progress toward meeting government-wide data center consolidation and optimization metrics is made publicly available, review agencies' inventories and strategies to determine whether they are comprehensive and complete, and monitor the implementation of each agency's strategy.

---

[26] Pub. L. No. 113-291 § 834, 128 Stat. 3444 – 3448 (44 U.S.C. 3601 note). Unless otherwise noted, these requirements apply to the 24 agencies specified in section 834 (corresponding to those agencies covered by the *Chief Financial Officers Act of 1990*. 31 U.S.C. § 901(b)).

[27] In lieu of submitting a data center inventory and strategy, the Department of Defense may submit this information as part of a defense-wide plan and report on cost savings, as required under §§ 2867(b)(2) and 2867(d) of the *National Defense Authorization Act for Fiscal Year 2012* (10 U.S.C. § 2223a note).

*Data Center Optimization* 129

- Develop and make publicly available not later than December 19, 2015, a goal broken down by year for the amount of planned cost savings and optimization improvements to be achieved through FDCCI and, for each year thereafter until October 1, 2020, compare reported cost savings and optimization improvements against those goals.[28]

## OMB Established DCOI to Address FITARA Data Center Provisions

OMB issued memorandum M-16-19 in August 2016 to establish DCOI and included guidance on how to implement the data center consolidation and optimization provisions of FITARA.[29] Among other things, the guidance required agencies to consolidate inefficient infrastructure, optimize existing facilities, improve their security posture, and achieve cost savings. For example, each agency was required to maintain a complete inventory of all data center facilities owned, operated, or maintained by or on its behalf, and measure progress toward defined optimization performance metrics on a quarterly basis as part of its data center inventory submission.

OMB's memorandum also directed each agency to develop a DCOI strategic plan that defined its data center strategy for fiscal years 2016 through 2018. Among other things, this strategy was to include a timeline for agency consolidation and optimization activities, with an emphasis on cost savings and optimization performance benchmarks that the agency could achieve between fiscal years 2016 and 2018. For example, each agency was required to develop cost savings targets due to consolidation and optimization actions and report any realized cost savings. OMB required each agency to publicly post its DCOI strategic plan to its agency-

---

[28] As mentioned previously, the *FITARA Enhancement Act of 2017* extended FITARA's data center consolidation and optimization provisions until October 1, 2020. Pub. L. No. 115-88, 131 Stat. 1278 (Nov. 21, 2017).

[29] OMB, Memorandum M-16-19.

130     *United States Government Accountability Office*

owned digital strategy website by September 30, 2016, and to post subsequent strategic plan updates by April 14, 2017 and April 13, 2018.

Further, the memorandum stated that OMB was to maintain a public dashboard (referred to as the IT Dashboard) to display government-wide and agency-specific progress in areas such as planned and achieved data center closures, consolidation-related cost savings, and data center optimization performance information. In this regard, OMB began including data center consolidation and optimization progress information on the IT Dashboard in August 2016.

OMB's memorandum also provided new guidance for the classification of a physical data center and expanded the definition of a data center. According to the revised definition, a room with at least one server that provides services (whether in a production, test, staging, development, or any other environment) should be considered a data center, while a room containing only print servers, routing equipment, switches, security devices (such as firewalls), or other telecommunication components, was not to be considered a data center.[30]

In light of this new definition, OMB directed each agency to perform a comprehensive review of its data centers and maintain a complete and updated data center inventory. Further, OMB directed each agency to categorize each of its data centers as either a tiered data center or a non-tiered data center. OMB's memorandum defined a tiered data center as one that uses each of the following:

- a separate physical space for IT infrastructure;
- an uninterruptible power supply;
- a dedicated cooling system or zone; and
- a backup power generator for a prolonged power outage.

---

[30] OMB, Memorandum M-16-19.

## Data Center Optimization 131

According to the memorandum, all other data centers were to be considered non-tiered.[31]

Moreover, OMB guidance included a series of performance metrics in the areas of data center closures, cost savings, and optimization progress.

- *Data center closures:* According to the guidance, agencies were to close at least 25 percent of tiered data centers government-wide, excluding those approved as inter-agency shared services providers, by the end of fiscal year 2018.[32] Further, agencies were to close at least 60 percent of non-tiered data centers government-wide by the end of fiscal year 2018. OMB's guidance further notes that, in the long term, all agencies should continually strive to close all non-tiered data centers, noting that server rooms and closets pose security risks and management challenges and are an inefficient use of resources.

- *Cost savings:* According to the guidance, agencies were to reduce government-wide annual costs attributable to physical data centers by at least 25 percent, resulting in savings of at least $2.7 billion for fiscal years 2016 through 2018.[33]

- *Data center optimization:* According to the guidance, agencies were to measure progress against a series of new data center performance metrics[34] in the areas of server utilization, energy metering, power usage, facility utilization, and virtualization.[35] Further, OMB's guidance established target values for each metric that agencies were to achieve by the end of fiscal year 2018.

---

[31] The term "tiered" and its definition are derived by OMB from the Uptime Institute's Tier Classification System. However, OMB notes that no specific certification is required in order for a data center to be considered tiered by OMB.

[32] For more information about shared services, see OMB, *Federal Information Technology Shared Services Strategy* (Washington, D.C.: May 2, 2012).

[33] OMB established a goal of $2.7 billion in Memorandum M-16-19. Subsequently, OMB increased the goal to $2.74 billion when it published agency-specific targets on the IT Dashboard.

[34] These metrics supersede OMB's previous set of optimization metrics established in 2014.

[35] Virtualization is a technology that allows multiple software-based machines with different operating systems to run in isolation, side-by-side, on the same physical machine.

132     *United States Government Accountability Office*

OMB's guidance further noted that agency progress against these performance metrics was to be measured by OMB on a quarterly basis, using agencies' data center inventory submissions and OMB-defined closures, cost savings, and optimization targets.

## OMB Published Proposed Changes to DCOI in November 2018

In November 2018, OMB published proposed changes to DCOI for public comment.[36] The changes focus federal consolidation and optimization efforts on agencies' larger, tiered data centers and also de-emphasize the consolidation of non-tiered facilities and other smaller spaces. The draft guidance also revises the classification of data centers and data center optimization metrics.

The draft guidance redefines a data center as a purpose-built, physically separate, dedicated space that meets certain criteria. Similarly, OMB does not plan to continue to report on spaces not designed to be data centers. According to the draft, OMB also plans to work with agencies to set agency-specific goals for data center closures and cost savings and to update these targets from those set in OMB's August 2016 memorandum to match agencies' current status and progress.[37]

Additionally, the proposed changes to DCOI make several changes to the metrics currently used by agencies to monitor the performance of their data centers. Specifically, of the five metrics currently in use (described in detail later in this chapter), OMB proposes updating three, removing two, and adding one new metric.

The draft guidance states that public comments will be collected through the end of December 2018, but does not provide a date for when the proposed changes will be finalized and implemented. However, the draft does state that the new guidance will sunset on September 30, 2020, a date that coincides with the extension of FITARA's data center provisions.

---

[36] OMB, *Data Center Optimization Initiative*, accessed November 26, 2018, https://datacenters. cio.gov/policy/.
[37] OMB, Memorandum M-16-19.

## Agencies Have Taken Limited Action to Address Prior GAO Recommendations

Since the enactment of FITARA in December 2014, we have reviewed and verified annually for the quality and completeness of each agency's (covered by the law) inventory and DCOI strategy. We have also published reports documenting the findings from each of our reviews.[38] In addition, we have examined and reported on agencies' efforts to optimize their data centers, as well as the challenges encountered and successes achieved.[39]

In a report that we issued in March 2016, we noted that agencies had reported significant data center closures—totaling more than 3,100 through fiscal year 2015—with the Departments of Agriculture, Defense (Defense), the Interior (Interior), and the Treasury (Treasury) accounting for 84 percent of the total.[40] Although the agencies fell short of OMB's fiscal year 2015 consolidation goal, their plans identified about 2,100 additional centers planned for closure through fiscal year 2019.

Agencies also reported significant consolidation cost savings and avoidances—totaling about $2.8 billion through fiscal year 2015 and expected to increase to over $8.0 billion in future years. The Departments of Commerce, Defense, Homeland Security (DHS), Transportation (Transportation), and the Treasury accounted for 96 percent of the total planned savings.

However, we pointed out that many agencies lacked complete cost savings goals for the next several years despite having closures planned. In addition, we reported that 22 agencies had made limited progress against OMB's fiscal year 2015 data center optimization performance metrics, such as the utilization of data center facilities. Accordingly, we recommended that the agencies take actions to complete their cost savings

---

[38] GAO, *Data Center Consolidation: Agencies Making Progress, but Planned Savings Goals Need to Be Established [Reissued on March 4, 2016*, GAO-16-323 (Washington, D.C.: Mar. 3, 2016) and *Data Center Optimization: Agencies Need to Complete Plans to Address Inconsistencies in Reported Savings*, GAO-17-388 (Washington, D.C.: May 18, 2017).

[39] GAO, *Data Center Optimization: Agencies Need to Address Challenges and Improve Progress to Achieve Cost Savings Goal*, GAO-17-448 (Washington, D.C.: Aug. 15, 2017).

[40] GAO-16-323.

134 *United States Government Accountability Office*

targets and improve optimization progress. As of December 2018, 18 of the 32 recommendations from this chapter had yet to be fully addressed.

In May 2017, we reported that the agencies were reporting significant data center closures—totaling more than 4,300 through August 2016—with Agriculture, Defense, Interior, and the Treasury accounting for 84 percent of the total.[41] The agencies' plans for 2016 had identified more than 1,200 additional centers for closure through fiscal year 2019.

Agencies also reported significant consolidation and optimization cost savings and avoidances, which totaled about $2.3 billion through August 2016. However, reductions in the amount of achieved savings reported to OMB, particularly by the Treasury, resulted in a net decrease of more than $400 million in these savings, compared to amounts we previously reported as planned in 2015.

Further, our report noted that, as of December 2016, agencies' total planned cost savings of about $656 million were more than $3.3 billion less compared to the amounts that we reported in 2015, and more than $2 billion less than OMB's fiscal year 2018 cost savings goal of $2.7 billion. This reduction in planned savings was the result of eight agencies reporting less in planned cost savings and avoidances in their DCOI strategic plans compared to the savings amounts previously reported to us in November 2015. The reduction also reflected the absence of cost savings information for one agency (Defense) that did not submit its strategic plan in time for our review.

In addition, our May 2017 report identified weaknesses in agencies' DCOI strategic plans.[42] Of the 23 agencies that had submitted their strategic plans at the time of our review, 7 agencies—Agriculture, the Department of Education (Education), DHS, and the Department of Housing and Urban Development (HUD); GSA; the National Science Foundation (NSF); and the Office of Personnel Management (OPM)—had addressed all five required elements of a strategic plan, as identified by OMB (such as providing information related to data center closures and cost savings metrics). The remaining 16 agencies that submitted their plans

---

[41] GAO-17-388.
[42] GAO-17-388.

## Data Center Optimization

135

either partially met or did not meet the requirements. We also pointed out that there were inconsistencies in the reporting of cost savings in the strategic plans of 11 agencies.

Given these findings, we recommended that OMB improve its oversight of agencies' DCOI strategic plans and their reporting of cost savings and avoidances. We also recommended that 16 agencies and Defense (which did not submit a plan in time for our review) complete the missing elements in their strategic plans, and that 11 agencies ensure the reporting of consistent cost savings and avoidance information to OMB. As of December 2018, 10 of the 30 recommendations had not been fully addressed.

In a subsequent report that we issued in August 2017, we noted that 22 of the 24 agencies required to participate in the OMB DCOI had reported (collectively) limited progress against OMB's fiscal year 2018 performance targets for the five optimization metrics. The 2 remaining agencies, Education and HUD, did not own any data centers and, therefore, did not have a basis to report on progress.[43] Specifically, for each of the five targets, no more than 5 agencies reported that they had met or exceeded that specific target. We reported that this limited progress against OMB's optimization targets was due, in part, to agencies not fully addressing our prior recommendations in this area.

In addition, we noted in the report that most agencies had not yet implemented automated monitoring tools to measure server utilization, as required by the end of fiscal year 2018. Specifically, 4 agencies reported that they had fully implemented such tools, 18 reported that they had not yet done so, and 2 did not have a basis to report on progress because they did not own any data centers. Accordingly, we recommended that OMB require that agencies include plans, as part of existing OMB reporting mechanisms, to implement automated monitoring tools at their agency-owned data centers. We also recommended that the 18 agencies that did not have fully documented plans take action, within existing OMB reporting mechanisms, to complete plans describing how they intended to

---

[43] GAO-17-448.

136      *United States Government Accountability Office*

achieve OMB's requirement to implement automated monitoring tools at all agency-owned data centers by the end of fiscal year 2018. As of December 2018, none of our 19 recommendations had been fully addressed.

Most recently, in May 2018, we noted that the 24 agencies participating in DCOI had reported mixed progress toward achieving OMB's goals for closing their data centers by September 2018. Thirteen agencies reported that they had either already met, or planned to meet, all of their OMB-assigned goals by the deadline. However, 4 agencies reported that they did not have plans to meet all of their assigned goals and 2 agencies were working with OMB to establish revised targets.

With regard to agencies' progress in achieving cost savings, 20 agencies reported, as of August 2017, that they had achieved $1.04 billion in cost savings for fiscal years 2016 and 2017. In addition, the agencies' DCOI strategic plans identified an additional $0.58 billion in planned savings— for a total of $1.62 billion for fiscal years 2016 through 2018. This total was approximately $1.12 billion less than OMB's DCOI savings goal of $2.7 billion. This shortfall was the result of 12 agencies reporting less in planned cost savings and avoidances in their DCOI strategic plans, as compared to the savings targets established for them by OMB.

In addition, the 24 agencies reported limited progress against OMB's five data center optimization targets for server utilization and automated monitoring, energy metering, power usage effectiveness, facility utilization, and virtualization. As of August 2017, 1 agency had met four targets, 1 agency had met three targets, 6 agencies had met either one or two targets, and 14 agencies reported meeting none of the targets. Further, as of August 2017, most agencies were not planning to meet OMB's fiscal year 2018 optimization targets. Specifically, 4 agencies reported plans to meet all of their applicable targets by the end of fiscal year 2018; 14 reported plans to meet some of the targets; and 4 reported that they did not plan to meet any targets.

Because GAO had made a number of recommendations to OMB and the 24 DCOI agencies to help improve the reporting of data center-related cost savings and to achieve optimization targets, we did not make new

Data Center Optimization 137

recommendations and noted that, as of March 2018, 74 of the 81 prior recommendations had not been fully addressed. While agencies have made considerable progress, as of December 2018, 47 of the 81 recommendations had not been fully addressed.

## AGENCIES REPORTED MIXED RESULTS IN EFFORTS AND PLANS TO MEET OMB'S TARGETS FOR DATA CENTER CLOSURES AND COST SAVINGS

According to OMB guidance, agencies were expected to close at least 25 percent of tiered data centers government-wide,[44] by the end of fiscal year 2018.[45] In addition, agencies were to close at least 60 percent of non-tiered data centers government-wide by this same deadline. Further, agencies were expected to reduce government-wide annual costs attributable to physical data centers by a least 25 percent by the end of fiscal year 2018, resulting in savings of at least $2.7 billion.

### About Half of the Agencies Planned to Meet OMB's Targets for Data Center Closures

The 24 agencies reported mixed results regarding their data center closure progress and plans, when compared with OMB's goal for each agency to close at least 25 percent of their tiered data centers and at least 60 percent of their non-tiered centers. Specifically, as of August 2018, 13 agencies reported that they had already met the goal of closing 25 percent of their tiered data centers, another 3 agencies reported that they planned to

---

[44] Data centers approved as inter-agency shared service providers were excluded from the need to consolidate. For more information about shared services, see OMB, *Federal Information Technology Shared Services Strategy* (Washington, D.C.: May 2, 2012).

[45] OMB, Memorandum M-16-19.

meet the goal by the end of fiscal year 2018, and 6 agencies reported that they did not plan to meet the goal.[46]

Further, as of August 2018, 11 agencies reported that they had already met the goal for closing 60 percent of their non-tiered centers, 3 agencies reported that they planned to meet the goal by the end of fiscal year 2018, and 9 agencies reported that they did not plan to meet the goal by the end of fiscal year 2018.[47] Table 1 displays a breakdown of the number of reported tiered and non-tiered data centers and completed and planned closures by agency, as of August 2018.

As shown in the figure below, the 24 agencies reported a total of 6,250 data center closures as of August 2018, which represented about half of the total reported number of federal data centers. In addition, the agencies planned 1,009 closures by the end of fiscal year 2018, with an additional 191 closures planned through fiscal year 2023 for a total of 1,200 more closures.

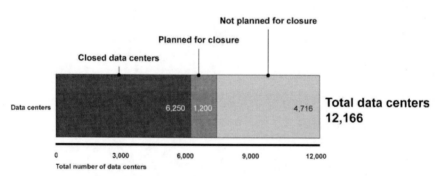

Source: GAO analysis of agency data. | GAO-19-241.

Figure 3. As Reported by the Agencies, Total Number of Federal Agency Data Centers Closed, Planned for Closure, or Not Planned for Closure since 2010, as of August 2018.

---

[46] The Department of Education did not report any tiered data centers in its inventory and the National Science Foundation only reported 1 tiered data center. As a result, neither agency had a target for closing tiered data centers.

[47] The Social Security Administration did not report any non-tiered data centers and therefore did not have a target for non-tiered closures.

# Table 1. Number of Reported Tiered and Non-tiered Federal Agency Data Centers with Completed and Planned Closures through Fiscal Year 2018, as of August 2018

| Agency | Tiered | | | | Non-tiered | | | |
|---|---|---|---|---|---|---|---|---|
| | Total data centers | Closed through August 2018 | Additional planned closures through fiscal year 2018 | Percent of closed and planned closures/total | Total data centers | Closed through August 2018 | Additional planned closures through fiscal year 2018 | Percent of closed and planned closures/ total |
| Department of Agriculture | 35 | 23 | 6 | 83 | 2,237 | 2,230 | 3 | 100[a] |
| Department of Commerce | 256 | 32 | 1 | 13 | 122 | 74 | 1 | 61 |
| Department of Defense | 934 | 202 | 74 | 30 | 2,680 | 826 | 742 | 59 |
| Department of Education | 0 | 0 | 0 | 0 | 2 | 2 | 0 | 100 |
| Department of Energy | 110 | 23 | 0 | 21 | 204 | 71 | 9 | 39 |
| Department of Health and Human Services | 93 | 28 | 4 | 34 | 299 | 80 | 2 | 27 |
| Department of Homeland Security | 38 | 15 | 0 | 39 | 237 | 35 | 0 | 15 |
| Department of Housing and Urban Development | 4 | 2 | 0 | 50 | 63 | 19 | 44 | 100 |
| Department of the Interior | 93 | 28 | 0 | 30 | 328 | 162 | 0 | 49 |
| Department of Justice | 41 | 24 | 4 | 68 | 69 | 60 | 3 | 91 |
| Department of Labor | 10 | 2 | 3 | 50 | 76 | 46 | 4 | 66 |
| Department of State | 53 | 10 | 1 | 21 | 395 | 37 | 4 | 10 |
| Department of Transportation | 223 | 12 | 0 | 5 | 233 | 162 | 1 | 70 |
| Department of the Treasury | 61 | 26 | 2 | 46 | 2,404 | 1,693 | 35 | 72 |
| Department of Veterans Affairs[b] | 288 | 41 | 11 | 18 | 128 | 54 | 18 | 56 |
| Environmental Protection Agency | 5 | 1 | 0 | 20 | 78 | 42 | 4 | 59 |
| General Services Administration | 42 | 36 | 0 | 86 | 93 | 82 | 0 | 88 |

# Table 1. (Continued)

| Agency | Tiered | | | | Non-tiered | | | |
|---|---|---|---|---|---|---|---|---|
| | Total data centers | Closed through August 2018 | Additional planned closures through fiscal year 2018 | Percent of closed and planned closures/total | Total data centers | Closed through August 2018 | Additional planned closures through fiscal year 2018 | Percent of closed and planned closures/ total |
| National Aeronautics and Space Administration | 55 | 33 | 2 | 64 | 4 | 4 | 0 | 100 |
| National Science Foundation | 1 | 0 | 0 | 0[c] | 1 | 1 | 0 | 100 |
| Nuclear Regulatory Commission | 5 | 3 | 0 | 60 | 14 | 9 | 0 | 64 |
| Office of Personnel Management | 7 | 3 | 1 | 57 | 2 | 1 | 1 | 100 |
| Small Business Administration | 9 | 0 | 3 | 33 | 43 | 10 | 26 | 84 |
| Social Security Administration | 3 | 1 | 0 | 33 | 0 | 0 | 0 | 0 |
| U.S. Agency for International Development | 2 | 2 | 0 | 100 | 86 | 3 | 0 | 3 |
| Total | 2,368 | 547 | 112 | 28 | 9,798 | 5,703 | 897 | 67% |

Source: GAO analysis of agency data. | GAO-19-241.

[a]The Department of Agriculture plans to close 99.8 percent of its non-tiered data centers.

[b]Department of Veterans Affairs, Office of Inspector General, *Lost Opportunities for Efficiencies and Savings During Data Center Consolidation*, 16- 04396-44 (Washington, D.C.: Jan. 30, 2019). In January 2019, after VA provided comments on a draft of this chapter, the VA Office of the Inspector General released a report that concluded VA had not reported a projected 860 facilities as data centers, due to incorrect internal agency guidance on what should be classified as a data center. The department agreed with the report's associated recommendations to develop additional guidance on determining what facilities are subject to DCOI and to establish a process for conducting a VA-wide inventory of data centers. The VA Office of the Inspector General reports the status of these recommendations as closed, based on actions taken by the department.

[c]The National Science Foundation did not have a target for tiered data center closures.

*Data Center Optimization* 141

This would further reduce the number of open data centers to about 39 percent of the number reported in the agencies' inventories. Figure 3 provides a summary breakdown of agencies' data center inventories that were closed, planned for closure, or not planned for closure, as of August 2018.

As noted, while about half of the agencies had met, or had planned to meet, their OMB targets as of August 2018, the other half planned to miss one or both of them. Officials from the 11 agencies that did not plan to meet one or both of their closure goals provided various reasons for why they had not planned to do so. For example, several agencies indicated that they were seeking revised closure goals because they viewed their goals as unattainable. Specifically, officials from Interior's Office of the CIO stated that a number of the department's non-tiered data centers were either mission-critical or not cost effective to close. Thus, the officials said Interior was working with OMB to establish a revised closure goal.

Similarly, Transportation's Director for IT Compliance stated that the department was working with OMB to establish a revised closure goal. The department reported having 186 tiered data centers in Federal Aviation Administration control towers that it believes should be excluded from its count of data centers when OMB sets the department's goal for closures. In addition, officials in Defense's Office of the CIO stated that the OMB closure targets for the department were based on including special purpose processing nodes that are mission critical and, therefore, are not subject to being closed. The officials noted that the department intends to continue operating its enterprise data centers, close its smaller data centers, and work with OMB to remove the special purpose processing nodes from DCOI consideration.

When OMB launched DCOI in 2016, agencies originally had until the end of fiscal year 2018 to meet OMB's stated time frame for closing their data centers. However, the extension of FITARA's data center consolidation and optimization provisions through fiscal year 2020, and OMB's planned revisions to DCOI goals, provide the 11 agencies that had not planned to meet one or both of OMB's closure targets with additional time to meet their goals. Until these agencies take action to close enough

142  *United States Government Accountability Office*

data centers to meet OMB's targets, they may not realize the efficiencies and cost savings that were expected from DCOI.

## Almost Two-Thirds of Agencies Planned to Meet OMB-Assigned Savings Targets

Since 2013, federal agencies have been required to report on data center cost savings, with guidance from OMB regarding how agencies were to report cost savings and avoidances.[48] Specifically, the guidance required agencies to report both data center consolidation cost savings and avoidances, among other areas, as part of a quarterly reporting process. FITARA also called for each agency to submit a multi-year strategy for achieving the consolidation and optimization of data centers that included year-by-year quarterly calculations of investment and cost savings through fiscal year 2018, which has now been extended to 2020.

In addition, in August 2016, OMB M-16-19 provided guidance on how agencies should implement the requirements of FITARA. Specifically, agencies were to develop a strategic plan that included information on historical cost savings and avoidances due to data center consolidation and optimization through fiscal year 2015. This guidance stated that agency strategic plans were also to include year-by-year calculations of target and actual agency-wide spending and cost savings on data centers from fiscal years 2016 through 2018. Further, the guidance established a DCOI combined cost savings goal of $2.7 billion for all federal agencies to achieve from fiscal years 2016 through 2018. This overall goal was then broken down into agency-specific targets on the IT Dashboard.

In August 2018, 22 agencies reported through the quarterly reporting process that they had achieved $1.94 billion in cost savings for fiscal years 2016 through 2018, while 2 agencies reported that they had not achieved

---

[48] OMB Memorandum M-13-09 defines cost savings as a reduction in actual expenditures below the projected level of costs to achieve a specific objective and defines cost avoidances as results from an action taken in the immediate time frame that will decrease costs in the future.

## Data Center Optimization

any savings. Further, 21 agencies identified an additional $0.42 billion planned through fiscal year 2018, for a total of $2.36 billion in planned savings from fiscal years 2016 through 2018. Nevertheless, this total is about $0.37 billion less than OMB's goal of $2.7 billion for overall DCOI savings. Figure 4 compares the total achieved savings as reported by the 24 agencies for fiscal years 2016 through 2018 and the agencies' additional planned savings through 2018 to OMB's DCOI savings goal for fiscal years 2016 through 2018.

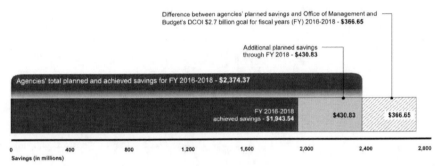

Source: GAO analysis of agency data. | GAO-19-241.

Figure 4. Agencies' Reported Achieved and Planned Data Center Optimization Initiative Cost Savings Compared to OMB's Goal, Fiscal Years 2016-2018, as of August 2018.

The 24 participating DCOI agencies had achieved $1.94 billion in savings as of August 2018. In addition, agencies identified an additional $0.43 billion, for a difference of $0.37 billion between planned and achieved savings from fiscal years 2016 through 2018. Table 2 provides specific data related to each agency's total planned savings, total achieved savings, and additional planned savings through 2018.

As shown in table 2, 13 agencies reported that they had met or planned to meet or exceed their OMB targets, and 3 agencies that did not have an OMB target also identified achieved savings. In contrast, 5 agencies reported that they did not plan to meet their targets. Three agencies did not have a savings target and did not report any achieved savings.

# 144     *United States Government Accountability Office*

## Table 2. Agencies' Reported Planned and Achieved Data Center Optimization Initiative Savings, Fiscal Years 2016-2018, Compared with Office of Management and Budget (OMB) Targets, as of August 2018 (dollars in millions)

| Agency | Total achieved for 2016 through 2018 | OMB savings targets | Additional planned through 2018 | Difference between OMB target and agencies' planned and achieved savings |
|---|---|---|---|---|
| Department of Agriculture | $25.82 | $23.62 | - | $2.20 |
| Department of Commerce | 1,115.45 | 94.97 | - | 1,020.48 |
| Department of Defense[a] | 205.46 | 1,800 | - | (1,594.54) |
| Department of Education | 0.84 | - | 0.24 | 1.07 |
| Department of Energy | 25.33 | - | - | 25.33 |
| Department of Health and Human Services | 107.70 | 77.84 | 48.38 | 78.24 |
| Department of Homeland Security | 112.22 | 154.94 | 254.70 | 211.98 |
| Department of Housing and Urban Development | - | - | - | - |
| Department of the Interior | 10.15 | 88.19 | 5.80 | (72.24) |
| Department of Justice | 68.92 | 65.86 | 5.43 | 8.49 |
| Department of Labor | 22.79 | 23.94 | 17.76 | 16.61 |
| Department of State | 109.90 | 17.07 | - | 92.83 |
| Department of Transportation | 36.93 | 30.26 | 3.08 | 9.75 |
| Department of the Treasury | 51.75 | 86.16 | 65.04 | 30.63 |
| Department of Veterans Affairs | 3.80 | 66.04 | - | (62.24) |
| Environmental Protection Agency | - | - | - | - |
| General Services Administration | 7.37 | 8.35 | 8.04 | 7.06 |
| National Aeronautics and Space Administration | 28.67 | 15.10 | 4.47 | 18.04 |
| National Science Foundation | - | - | - | - |
| Nuclear Regulatory Commission | 2.24 | 1.21 | 2.00 | 3.03 |
| Office of Personnel Management | 4.65 | 21.92 | 14.40 | (2.87) |

## Data Center Optimization 145

| Agency | Total achieved for 2016 through 2018 | OMB savings targets | Additional planned through 2018 | Difference between OMB target and agencies' planned and achieved savings |
|---|---|---|---|---|
| Small Business Administration | 1.04 | 0.86 | 0.92 | 1.11 |
| Social Security Administration | - | 164.69 | 0.58 | (164.12) |
| U.S. Agency for International Development | 2.51 | - | - | 2.51 |
| Total | 1,943.54 | 2,741.02 | 430.83 | (366.65) |

Source: GAO analysis of agency and OMB data I GAO-19-241.

[a]In a November 2014 response to our report, GAO-14-713, the Department of Defense noted that, in addition to the $2.6 billion in cost savings planned by fiscal year 2017, the department expected that figure to increase to $4.7 billion in future years as efficiencies were gained. Subsequently, the department changed its methodology for calculating cost savings and lowered its planned cost savings estimates accordingly.

Agencies provided various reasons for why they did not plan to meet their savings targets. For example, the Department of Veterans Affairs (VA) reported that the implementation of its DCOI-related projects in fiscal years 2016 through 2018 was dependent on funding approval and might not result in cost savings and avoidances until later in the projects' life cycles (i.e., fiscal year 2019 or later). In another example, GSA stated that the OMB target may be difficult for the agency to reach due, in part, to the methods OMB used to set the target for fiscal years 2016 through 2018. According to GSA, OMB used the data that GSA had reported on the IT Dashboard regarding the agency's expenditure for data center infrastructure and reduced that amount by 25 percent.

Agencies have now been working toward OMB's DCOI savings goals since fiscal year 2016; however, almost half of the agencies are still not planning to meet OMB's targets. Until agencies plan to meet and achieve OMB's data center-related savings targets, they will likely not realize the expected financial benefits from DCOI.

146    *United States Government Accountability Office*

## MOST AGENCIES CONTINUED TO REPORT LIMITED PROGRESS TOWARD MEETING OPTIMIZATION METRICS TARGETS

FITARA required OMB to establish metrics to measure the optimization of data centers, including server efficiency, and to ensure that agencies' progress toward meeting the metrics is made public. Pursuant to FITARA, OMB established a set of five data center optimization metrics intended to measure agencies' progress in the areas of server utilization and automated monitoring, energy metering, power usage effectiveness, facility utilization, and virtualization. According to OMB, while the server utilization and automated monitoring metric applied to agency-owned tiered and non-tiered data centers, the four remaining metrics applied only to agency-owned tiered centers.[49]

OMB's memorandum also established a target value for each of the five metrics, which agencies were expected to achieve by the end of fiscal year 2018. OMB measures agencies' progress against the optimization targets using the agencies' quarterly data center inventory submission and publicly reports this information on its IT Dashboard. Table 3 provides a description of the five data center optimization metrics and target values.

As of August 2018, most (22 of the 24) DCOI agencies continued to report limited progress in meeting OMB's fiscal year 2018 data center optimization targets identified on the IT Dashboard. The remaining 2 agencies—Education and HUD—reported that they did not have any agency-owned data centers in their inventory and, therefore, did not have a basis to measure and report optimization progress.

With regard to the data center optimization targets, agencies reported the greatest progress against two metrics: power usage effectiveness and virtualization metrics. Specifically, 8 agencies reported that they had met OMB's target for power usage effectiveness and 6 agencies reported that

---

[49] While agencies can also report data centers as outsourced, co-located, or cloud provided in their inventory, OMB's optimization metrics only apply to data centers identified as agency-owned.

*Data Center Optimization* 147

they had met the target for virtualization. However, for the energy metering, facility utilization, and server utilization and automated monitoring metrics, no more than 3 agencies reported meeting each. Figure 5 summarizes the 24 agencies' progress in meeting each optimization target, as of August 2018.

As of August 2018, NSF, SSA, and EPA reported the most progress against OMB's metrics among the 22 agencies with a basis to report—each met 3 targets. Nine agencies reported that they had met only one target, and 10 agencies reported they had not met any of the targets.

**Table 3. Office of Management and Budget (OMB) Data Center Optimization Metrics and Targets**

| Metrics | Description | Applicable agency-owned data centers | Target value (to be achieved by the end of fiscal year 2018) |
|---|---|---|---|
| Server utilization and automated monitoring | Percent of time busy, measured directly by continuous, automated monitoring software, discounted by the fraction of data centers fully equipped with automated monitoring. | Tiered and non-tiered data centers | At least 65 percent |
| Energy metering | Percent of total gross floor area in an agency's tiered data center inventory located in tiered data centers that have power metering. | Tiered data centers | 100 percent |
| Power usage effectiveness | Proportion of total data center energy used by IT equipment. | Tiered data centers | 1.5 or lower (1.4 or lower for new data centers) |
| Facility utilization | Portion of total gross floor area in tiered data centers that is actively utilized for racks that contain IT equipment. | Tiered data centers | At least 80 percent |
| Virtualization | Ratio of operating systems to physical servers. | Tiered data centers | 4 or higher |

Source: OMB | GAO-19-241.

Further, OMB began requiring the implementation of automated monitoring tools in August 2016; however, as of August 2018, of the 22

148 *United States Government Accountability Office*

agencies with a basis to report, 5 reported that they had either not implemented the tools at any data centers, or had experienced shortcomings in their implementation.

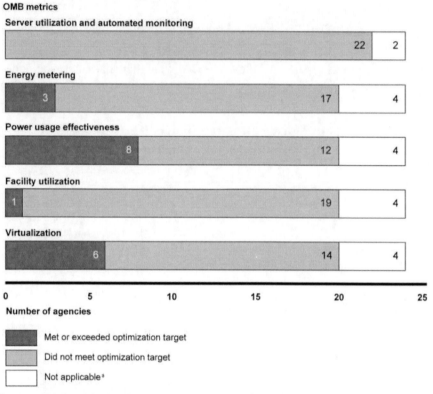

Source: GAO analysis of data from OMB's Information Technology Dashboard. | GAO-19-241.

[a]Two agencies did not have any reported agency-owned data centers in their inventory and, therefore, did not have a basis to measure and report on their progress towards optimization. In addition, two other agencies did not own any tiered data centers and, therefore, did not have a basis to measure and report on four of the five metrics.

Figure 5. Progress towards Meeting Office of Management and Budget (OMB) Data Center Optimization Targets, as Reported by the Agencies, as of August 2018.

## Table 4. Data Center Optimization Performance towards Meeting Office of Management and Budget (OMB) Optimization Targets, as Reported by the Agencies, as of August 2018

| Agency | Server utilization & automated monitoring[a] | Energy metering | Power usage effectiveness | Facility utilization | Virtualization |
|---|---|---|---|---|---|
| Department of Agriculture | Not Met | Not Met | Not Met | Not Met | Fully Met |
| Department of Commerce | Not Met | Not Met | Not Met | Not Met | Not Met |
| Department of Defense | Not Met b | Not Met | Not Met | Not Met | Not Met |
| Department of Education[c] | n/a | n/a | n/a | n/a | n/a |
| Department of Energy | Not Met | Not Met | Fully Met | Not Met | Not Met |
| Department of Health and Human Services | Not Met | Not Met | Not Met | Not Met | Not Met |
| Department of Homeland Security | Not Met | Not Met | Not Met b | Not Met | Not Met |
| Department of Housing and Urban Development[c] | n/a | n/a | n/a | n/a | n/a |
| Department of the Interior | Not Met | Not Met | Not Met | Not Met | Not Met |
| Department of Justice | Not Met | Not Met | Not Met | Not Met | Not Met |
| Department of Labor | Not Met b | Not Met | Not Met | Not Met | Fully Met |
| Department of State | Not Met b | Not Met | Fully Met | Not Met | Not Met |
| Department of Transportation | Not Met b | Not Met | Not Met | Not Met | Not Met |
| Department of the Treasury | Not Met b | Not Met | Fully Met | Not Met | Not Met |
| Department of Veterans Affairs | Not Met | Not Met | Not Met | Not Met | Not Met |
| Environmental Protection Agency | Not Met | Fully Met | Fully Met | Not Met | Fully Met |
| General Services Administration[d] | Not Met | n/a | n/a | n/a | n/a |
| National Aeronautics and Space Administration | Not Met | Not Met | Fully Met | Not Met | Not Met |
| National Science Foundation | Not Met | Fully Met | Fully Met | Not Met | Fully Met |

# Table 4. (Continued)

| Agency | Server utilization & automated monitoring[a] | Energy metering | Power usage effectiveness | Facility utilization | Virtualization |
|---|---|---|---|---|---|
| Nuclear Regulatory Commission | Not Met b | Not Met | Not Met b | Not Met | Fully Met |
| Office of Personnel Management | Not Met | Not Met | Not Met | Not Met | Fully Met |
| Small Business Administration | Not Met | Not Met | Fully Met | Not Met | Not Met |
| Social Security Administration | Not Met | Fully Met | Fully Met | Fully Met | Not Met |
| U.S. Agency for International Development[d] | Not Met | n/a | n/a | n/a | n/a |

Source: GAO analysis of data from OMB's IT Dashboard. | GAO-19-241.

[a]For this metric only, OMB's IT Dashboard displays agency progress for tiered and non-tiered data centers separately. However, for the purpose of this table, and to be consistent with how this metric was established in OMB's August 2016 memorandum (M-16-19), we combined the progress information for tiered and non-tiered data centers into a single assessment.

[b]According to OMB's IT Dashboard, the agency did not report any progress made on this metric. This is due to the agency lacking the monitoring tools required to measure progress and report it.

[c]Agency did not have any reported agency-owned data centers in its inventory and, therefore, does not have a basis to measure and report on optimization progress.

[d]Agency did not have any reported agency-owned tiered data centers in its inventory and, therefore, does not have a basis to measure and report on four of the five metrics.

*Data Center Optimization* 151

For example, the Department of State (State) reported that it had limited centralized monitoring capability and is installing automated monitoring tools in several phases.

Thus, these 5 agencies were not able to report any progress against either or both of the server utilization or power usage effectiveness metrics because their data centers lacked the required monitoring tools to measure progress in these areas. The remaining 17 agencies reported that they had implemented the tools in at least one data center. Table 4 depicts the performance of the agencies in meeting OMB targets for data center optimization, as of August 2018.

As of August 2018, multiple agencies had made changes to their data center inventory and operational environment, such as closing all agency-owned tiered data centers or implementing automated monitoring tools.[50] These changes impacted which metrics were applicable or an agency's ability to report on the status of its optimization metrics. For example, GSA reported that it no longer had any agency-owned tiered data centers, and, therefore, did not have a basis to report on four of the five optimization metrics. Additionally, NSF, which previously had only owned one non-tiered data center, migrated from the non-tiered center to a tiered data center as part of its headquarters relocation. Accordingly, NSF began reporting on the metrics applicable to its tiered facility.

Further, the Nuclear Regulatory Commission (NRC) did not report on power usage effectiveness due to delays in awarding a new contract that was to include monitoring tools that would impact the ability to report on this metric. Agency officials stated that NRC plans to have the monitoring tools in place during fiscal year 2019. Overall, these changes since last year's report have resulted in no significant changes to the progression of these agencies on their optimization metrics.

In addition, agencies' limited progress against OMB's optimization targets was due, in part, to not fully addressing our prior recommendations in this area. As previously mentioned, in March 2016, we reported[51] on weaknesses in agencies' data center optimization efforts, including that 22

---

[50] These changes were made after issuance of our May 2018 report, GAO-18-264.
[51] GAO-16-323.

152      *United States Government Accountability Office*

agencies[52] did not meet OMB's fiscal year 2015 optimization targets.[53] We noted that this was partially due to the agencies having challenges in optimizing their data centers, including in their decentralized organizational structures that made consolidation and optimization difficult, and in competing priorities for resources. In addition, consolidating certain data centers was problematic because the volume or type of information involved required the data center to be close in proximity to the users. Accordingly, we recommended that the agencies take action to improve optimization progress, to include addressing any of the identified challenges. Most agencies agreed with our recommendations or had no comments. However, as of December 2018, only 4 of the 22 agencies had fully addressed them.

The continuing shortcomings in data center optimization can also be attributed, in part, to agencies viewing OMB's optimization metric targets as unrealistic. For example, Transportation stated in its DCOI strategic plan that it could not meet multiple optimization metrics due to funds not being available and competing priorities. In addition, Treasury indicated in its DCOI strategic plan that it struggles to report on automated monitoring because many of its data centers do not have the ability to centrally aggregate and report on central processing unit data. Further, DHS officials noted that it has 7 smaller tiered data centers where it has determined that it is not cost effective to equip those centers with the tools needed to report on metrics such as power usage effectiveness. Given these types of challenges, the targets for each optimization metric may not be realistic for every agency. Unless agencies take action to meet the applicable OMB optimization metrics, their data centers may not operate efficiently enough to provide expected cost savings.

---

[52] These 22 agencies are the Departments of Agriculture, Commerce, Defense, Education, Energy, Health and Human Services, Homeland Security, Housing and Urban Development, the Interior, Justice, Labor, State, Transportation, the Treasury, and Veterans Affairs; the Environmental Protection Agency, General Services Administration, National Aeronautics and Space Administration, Nuclear Regulatory Commission, Office of Personnel Management, Social Security Administration, and U.S. Agency for International Development.

[53] In May 2014, OMB established fiscal year 2015 targets for the first set of 11 optimization metrics. In August 2016, OMB revised the optimization metrics, kept 2 of the original 11, dropped the other 9, and issued 3 new metrics.

## Only Two Agencies Planned to Meet OMB's Fiscal Year 2018 Optimization Targets

In addition to reporting current optimization progress on the IT Dashboard, OMB required agencies to include in their DCOI strategic plans planned performance levels for fiscal year 2018 for each optimization metric.

However, according to the 24 agencies' DCOI strategic plan information as of August 2018, only 2—Commerce and the U. S. Agency for International Development (USAID)—reported plans to fully meet their applicable targets by the end of fiscal year 2018. Of the remaining agencies, 14 reported plans to meet some, but not all, of the targets; 6 reported that they did not plan to meet any targets, and—as already discussed—Education and HUD did not have a basis to report planned optimization milestones because they did not report having any agency-owned data centers.[54] Figure 6 summarizes agencies' progress, as of August 2018, in meeting OMB's optimization targets and planned progress to be achieved by September 2018.

At the time of our review, only two agencies planned to meet all of their applicable targets, and it was doubtful that the agencies would be able to achieve OMB's collective optimization target of at least $2.7 billion in cost savings by the end of fiscal year 2018.[55] Until the remaining agencies take the steps necessary to meet their optimization targets, it is unlikely that these agencies will achieve the expected benefits of optimization and the resulting cost savings.

---

[54] USAID did not have any tiered data centers in its data center inventory. Therefore, the agency only has a basis to report on its plans to meet the one OMB optimization metric applicable to its non-tiered data centers (i.e., server utilization and automated monitoring).

[55] Agencies' data center cost savings and optimization progress information displayed on OMB's IT Dashboard is updated by OMB on a quarterly basis, based on data center cost savings and inventory data collected from agencies at the end of February, May, August, and November of each year. The November 2018 update was expected to include data for the full fiscal year and was available too late to be included in our review.

# 154     *United States Government Accountability Office*

**Planned and achieved performance (as of August 2018)**

| Department of Agriculture | |
|---|---|
| Department of Commerce | |
| Department of Defense | |
| Department of Education [a] | N/A     N/A |
| Department of Energy | |
| Department of Health & Human Services | |
| Department of Homeland Security | |
| Department of Housing and Urban Development [a] | N/A     N/A |
| Department of the Interior | |
| Department of Justice | |
| Department of Labor | |
| Department of State | |
| Department of Transportation | |
| Department of the Treasury | |
| Department of Veterans Affairs | |
| Environmental Protection Agency | |
| General Services Administration [b] | N/A |
| National Aeronautics and Space Administration | |
| National Science Foundation | |
| Nuclear Regulatory Commission | |
| Office of Personnel Management | |
| Small Business Administration | |
| Social Security Administration | |
| United States Agency for International Development [b] | |

Legend:
- ■ **Achieved** (current) metric performance
- ▨ Additional **planned** metric performance, by the end of fiscal year 2018
- ☐ Metrics that are currently not planned to be met

Source: GAO analysis of OMB's Information Technology Dashboard. | GAO-19-241.

[a] Agency did not report any agency-owned data centers in its inventory and, therefore, did not have a basis to measure and report on optimization progress.

[b] Agency did not report any agency-owned tiered data centers in its inventory and, therefore, did not have a basis to measure and report on four of the five metrics.

Figure 6. Agency-Reported Plans to Meet or Exceed the Office of Management and Budget's (OMB) Data Center Optimization Targets.

## SELECTED AGENCIES HIGHLIGHTED SUCCESSFUL DCOI PRACTICES

As we noted previously in this chapter, many agencies have reported challenges that have hindered their efforts to meet OMB's DCOI targets. However, a number of agencies have also reported success in meeting OMB's targets ahead of DCOI's end of fiscal year 2018 deadline. As noted in our methodology section, six agencies that were among the best performers in achieving data center closures, cost savings, and optimization performance reported a number of key practices that had contributed to their success. These practices were:

- obtaining executive leadership support for consolidation and optimization activities;
- using experiences and lessons learned to refine consolidation planning;
- increasing the use of cloud and shared services to consolidate or optimize data center operations;
- emphasizing closing data centers to meet OMB targets and achieve cost savings;
- increasing the use of virtualization to optimize data centers; and
- employing an organization-wide communications plan to facilitate adoption of consolidation and optimization activities.

### Obtaining Executive Leadership Support for Consolidation and Optimization Activities

Five of the six agencies (Agriculture, Commerce, Justice, EPA, and GSA) reported that their success in consolidation and optimization activities was due to obtaining support from executive leadership for the agency's consolidation efforts. Each agency obtained sponsorship and support from its executive leadership (e.g., Deputy Secretary or agency

156      *United States Government Accountability Office*

CIO), such as through a memorandum or policy that directed all agency offices to participate in, or comply with, the consolidation effort. For example,

- The Deputy Secretary for Agriculture issued a memorandum in 2017 that, among other things, declared the department's intent to consolidate from 39 data centers down to 2 by the end of 2019. According to officials in the Office of the CIO, this memorandum from the Secretary's office focused all data center owners on the same project task of reducing the data center inventory.
- The Commerce CIO and the department's CIO Council provided overall governance through organizational policies, processes, and procedures for the department's data center consolidation effort. Leveraging this departmental guidance, each component of Commerce developed its own consolidation plan that identified specific approaches and activities. Using these plans, the department and its components focused on reducing spending on redundant software, infrastructure, and data center operations.
- The Deputy Attorney General issued a memorandum in 2014 to the heads and CIOs of all components. This memorandum formally established Justice's Data Center Transformation Initiative, established the Department Program Review Board to provide oversight for the initiative, and also directed the consolidation of all data centers into 3 enterprise facilities. In addition, Justice's CIO issued a memorandum to component CIOs that provided additional details on how to execute planned activities and established further governance associated with the initiative. These memoranda provided clear leadership buy-in and support for the department's data center consolidation and optimization activities that could be used to resolve any challenges or issues at the departmental level.
- EPA attributed much of its DCOI success to a top-down approach from its CIO office, saying that such support was critical to achieve data center closures. For example, EPA leadership decided

*Data Center Optimization* 157

to adopt and enforce geographical consolidation of data centers within major areas to minimize costs of consolidation while still meeting closure objectives. In doing so, the agency leadership provided clear direction and support for the agency's consolidation effort by adopting the strategy to consolidate data centers within specific geographic regions.

- GSA reported that it obtained leadership commitment that made its data center consolidation and optimization activities a priority. The agency noted that having strong CIO and executive leadership was important for sponsoring technology modernization. As a result of the buy-in, the agency reported that it had minimized resistance to change and improved acceptance of its consolidation and optimization activities.

## Using Experiences and Lessons Learned to Refine Consolidation Planning

Four agencies (Agriculture, Commerce, Justice, and SSA) reported that their success with consolidation and optimization activities was due to the use of a refined consolidation plan or process. Each of these agencies developed an initial consolidation plan or process for closing data centers, and then refined their procedures based on their experiences and lessons learned as data centers were closed. For example,

- Agriculture developed a set of streamlined processes to facilitate DCOI closures that were based on the experiences gained from successful data center closures under FDCCI. The set of processes consisted of 5 steps:
  o The planning step included the discovery and documentation of all data center assets, including applications and IT hardware, in a given data center. In addition, this step involved identifying the necessary resources to move the applications and associated data to a target data center.

158 *United States Government Accountability Office*

- o The preparation step included identification of the target data center and development of a project schedule.
- o The data migration step included moving both applications and data to the target data center or cloud-services, as planned.[56]
- o The testing step included ensuring the applications and data that were moved were integrated into the target data center, and functional testing to ensure that the applications worked and data was accessible.
- o The application cutover step included putting the migrated applications and data into operation and closing the original data center.

Using and refining this set of processes allowed the department to become more efficient in closing its data centers. After closing 46 data centers in fiscal years 2011 through 2014, the department closed 2,185 data centers over the next 2 years. In total, Agriculture reported that it had closed 2,253 data centers as of August 2018.

- • Commerce established departmental guidance and then each departmental component leveraged that guidance to develop its own consolidation plan. The plans identified specific approaches and activities intended to achieve the stated goals and milestones. According to Commerce, the department and its components leveraged their IT planning processes and established IT governance to, among other things, reduce spending on redundant commodity software, infrastructure, and operations.
- • Justice's Office of the CIO developed a master plan for the department's data center consolidation effort in June 2015. The plan included a planning framework, transformation approach, and a master schedule for data center moves and closures. It also

---

[56] According to the National Institute of Standards and Technology (NIST), cloud services provide one or more capabilities via the cloud computing model. The cloud computing model enables ubiquitous, convenient, on-demand network access to a shared pool of configurable computing resources (e.g., networks, servers, storage, applications, and services).

included process steps similar to those used by Agriculture. Further, Justice's plan noted that the department would use its initial closure efforts to gain experience and to refine its plans. Justice reported that it used the plan's schedule and semi-monthly progress reports to ensure that consolidation activities stayed on schedule, or the department could make adjustments as needed. As a result, the department closed 84 of its 110 data centers and achieved more than $128 million in cost savings and avoidances as of August 2018.

- SSA used a project management framework process and controls that it believed efficiently addressed requirements, critical path, and risk management. In addition, SSA reported that it used an incremental development approach to its data center optimization plans, with each project expected to accomplish specific tasks that would lead to another project.[57] Accordingly, SSA noted that the agency used a multi-year plan with many initiatives focused on specific goals. Using this approach, the agency successfully moved SSA's operations and infrastructure from an older facility to the newly-built National Support Center. The agency reports that this facility is state-of-the-art and provides similar capabilities and efficiencies to major cloud service providers.

## Increasing the Use of Cloud and Shared Services to Consolidate or Optimize Data Center Operations

Three agencies (Commerce, GSA, and SSA) also attributed their success in consolidation and optimization activities to increasing their agency's use of cloud and shared services. In doing so, each agency

---

[57] Incremental, or modular, development is where an investment may be broken down into discrete projects, increments, or useful segments, each of which are undertaken to develop and implement the products and capabilities that the larger investment must deliver. Dividing investments into smaller parts helps to reduce investment risk, deliver capabilities more rapidly, and permit easier adoption of newer and emerging technologies.

## 160 *United States Government Accountability Office*

emphasized the move of data center assets and systems to cloud services to optimize their data centers and reduce costs. For example,

- Commerce identified moving to cloud services and utilizing shared services[58] as being most effective in closing data centers. As an example, the department cited the National Oceanic and Atmospheric Administration's (NOAA) "cloud-first" policy that emphasized using cloud services rather than an agency-owned physical data center whenever feasible. The agency attributed its ability to handle increased traffic as an operational benefit of its increased use of cloud services. For example, NOAA did not have the capacity in its agency-owned facilities to meet the computing demands and requirements of a sudden increase in web traffic on the websites for NOAA and the National Hurricane Center, such as during Hurricanes Irma and Harvey in 2017. Commerce stated that using cloud services allowed NOAA to handle 4.7 billion page hits during Hurricane Harvey over a 6-day span, ensuring the websites were not adversely impacted by the increase in traffic.

- GSA reported that it focused on moving services from agency-owned tiered and non-tiered data centers to cloud services or to shared centers. As a result, GSA had closed 118 data centers as of August 2018, including all of the agency's tiered centers.

- SSA developed an agency cloud initiative that encourages the adoption of cloud technologies as part of the agency's infrastructure modernization. The agency reported that it is employing a hybrid cloud strategy that is comprised of both private cloud and public cloud services for the agency's back office applications.[59] By doing so, the agency will consolidate and

---

[58] OMB, *Federal IT Shared Services Strategy*, (Washington, D.C.: May 2, 2012). A shared service is a function that is provided for consumption by multiple organizations within or between federal agencies.

[59] According to NIST, a hybrid cloud is a composition of two or more clouds (on-site or off-site, private or public) that remain as distinct entities but are bound to share data and applications. A private cloud gives a single organization the exclusive access to and usage of the cloud service and related infrastructure and computational resources. A public cloud is one in which the cloud infrastructure and computing resources are made available to the

# Data Center Optimization 161

standardize SSA's IT infrastructure systems and software to simplify management of those resources and reduce costs.

## Emphasizing the Closure of Data Centers to Meet OMB Targets and Achieve Cost Savings

Three agencies (Agriculture, Justice, and EPA) reported that their success in consolidation and optimization activities was due to focusing on the closure of data centers. In doing so, they emphasized the importance of closing data centers to reduce costs and achieve cost savings and avoidances. For example,

- Agriculture determined that the costs to improve DCOI performance metrics in its agency-owned data centers were prohibitive. Accordingly, the department decided that the only viable alternative was to close data centers to remove underperforming centers and improve optimization metrics performance and reduce costs. As a result, Agriculture reported that it had closed 2,253 data centers through August 2018. In addition, the department reported that it had improved its security posture, reduced its real estate footprint, and achieved realized cost savings and avoidance of $51.8 million from fiscal year 2012 through 2018.
- Justice reported that it took a practical approach to selecting the data centers that would remain as its enterprise facilities, considering factors such as the number of physical servers that could be eliminated, the efficiency of the remaining hardware, and potential labor savings. The department reported that it focused on retaining more efficient data centers (e.g., those with more efficient use of electricity or virtualization), rather than simply keeping its biggest existing data centers. As a result, Justice has

---

general public over a public network. A public cloud is owned by an organization providing cloud services, and serves a diverse pool of clients.

162         *United States Government Accountability Office*

closed 84 of its 110 data centers and achieved more than $128 million in cost savings and avoidances as of August 2018.

- EPA identified geographical consolidation as its best approach to meeting DCOI goals. Specifically, in its data center consolidation plan, the agency stated that, for geographic areas where it had multiple data centers, a single facility was identified into which data center IT assets would be consolidated. Using this approach, EPA had closed 43 of its 83 data centers as of August 2018.

## Increasing the Use of Virtualization to Optimize Data Centers

Three agencies (Commerce, EPA, and SSA) reported that their success in consolidation and optimization activities also was due to focusing on the increased use of virtualization[60] to run more software on the same or a reduced amount of servers. In doing so, the agencies expected to reduce costs by avoiding the purchase of additional servers to meet computing demands or eliminating unnecessary hardware and floor space in their data centers. For example,

- Commerce focused on moving systems from physical hardware to virtual servers, as part of its component offices' plans to update technology and in cases where the systems did not require a specific type of server. Using this approach, the department reported that it had reduced the number of physical servers in its data centers, and was working to improve server utilization. The department also cited the ability to automatically increase or decrease computing capability through virtualization, such as when NOAA handled the increased traffic to its hurricane-related web pages during Hurricanes Irma and Harvey in 2017.
- EPA used the agency's data center consolidation plan to implement an agency-wide "physical-to-virtual" policy that

---

[60] Virtualization is a technology that allows multiple software-based machines with different operating systems to run in isolation, side-by-side, on the same physical machine.

# Data Center Optimization

163

required offices to convert existing physical servers to virtual servers wherever possible. The agency also defined server and software standards for virtualized platforms.

- SSA reported that the agency's goal, using its "Virtual 1st" policy, was to have failover capability within the data center, disaster recovery capability for both data centers, and balanced load capacity between data centers.[61] The agency reported that it has continued to virtualize not only servers but storage and network applications, as well. For example, SSA stated that it has taken steps to virtualize as much storage as possible and used similar techniques to reduce the physical hardware footprint on the data center floor, as well as power, cooling, and network bandwidth requirements.

## Employing an Organization-Wide Communications Plan to Facilitate Adoption of Consolidation and Optimization Activities

Two agencies (Justice and GSA) reported that their success in consolidation and optimization activities was due to employing an organization-wide communications plan. In doing so, the agencies adopted a structured method for communicating with agency offices to improve acceptance and adoption of consolidation and optimization activities. This also facilitated conflict resolution. For example,

- Justice reported that it prioritized communications related to its Data Center Transformation Initiative and established an all-encompassing approach to initiative-related communications. To help communicate all related directives, strategies, plans, statuses, and accomplishments, the department used a variety of methods that included:

---

[61] Failover capability is the ability to automatically switch over (typically without human intervention or warning) to a redundant or standby information system upon the failure or abnormal termination of the previously active system.

164 *United States Government Accountability Office*

- o regular meetings to share information,
- o a dedicated email box to provide easy communication for answers or information, without the need to know specific individuals,
- o an intranet web page that provided general information, instructions, templates, decisions, status information, and accomplishments related to the initiative; and
- o email broadcasts on an as-needed basis.

- GSA reported that it communicated and collaborated frequently with business stakeholders to identify the best time frames to move systems, stagger transfers to minimize impact, and determine which systems could be virtualized. The agency indicated that these important factors required continuous communication between system owners, system administrators, and business leadership. As a result, the agency experienced minimal staff resistance to change and a commitment to reach a consensus on moving forward with the agency's consolidation efforts.

The aforementioned practices included elements of sound management techniques, such as gathering leadership support for a project and developing a communications plan to foster adoption of organizational changes. The practices also included activities that aligned with the core tenets of DCOI to consolidate inefficient infrastructure, optimize existing facilities, and achieve cost savings. Further, these practices each proved effective for multiple agencies and, while they were not the only practices that could be effective, they represent concepts that could provide the foundation for an effective data center consolidation and optimization program.

## CONCLUSION

Federal data center consolidation efforts have been underway since 2010 and OMB's fiscal year 2018 targets provided clear and transparent

*Data Center Optimization* 165

goals that helped define the tangible benefits that DCOI was expected to provide. However, most agencies continue to report mixed progress against those targets. Although agencies have taken action to close about half of the data centers in their combined inventories, 11 agencies did not plan to meet all of their closure targets. Further, the data center closures were expected to drive cost savings and avoidances and, to the agencies' credit, the closures have led to more than $2.37 billion in planned and achieved cost savings and avoidances from fiscal years 2016 through 2018. However, five agencies did not plan to meet their cost savings targets. Until agencies consolidate the data centers required to meet their targets, as well as identify and report the associated cost savings, they will be challenged to realize expected efficiencies and the full benefits of DCOI will not be fully realized. Similarly, although OMB first established optimization metrics in May 2014, agencies continue to report only limited progress against the current performance targets. While two agencies do not have a basis to report any progress as they do not own any data centers, only two agencies reported that they planned to achieve all of DCOI's fiscal year 2018 optimization targets. Ensuring the optimized performance of data centers is a key component to meeting OMB's DCOI-wide savings goal and the 20 agencies that did not have plans to meet their targets call into question whether DCOI will realize its full potential savings.

Although many agencies have struggled to meet their individual DCOI targets, other agencies have successfully met OMB's goals for data center closures, savings, and optimization. Six such agencies that we identified reported on the importance of gathering leadership support, effective communication, and alignment with the core tenets of DCOI. Key practices such as these can play an important role in helping agencies better meet the overall goals and mission of DCOI.

## RECOMMENDATIONS

We are making a total of 36 recommendations to 22 of the 24 agencies in our review. Specifically:

166 *United States Government Accountability Office*

The Secretary of Agriculture should take action to meet the data center optimization metric targets established by OMB under DCOI. (Recommendation 1)

The Secretary of Commerce should take action to meet the data center closure targets established under DCOI by OMB. (Recommendation 2)

The Secretary of Defense should take action to meet the data center closure targets established under DCOI by OMB. (Recommendation 3)

The Secretary of Defense should identify additional savings opportunities to achieve the targets for data center-related cost savings established under DCOI by OMB. (Recommendation 4)

The Secretary of Defense should take action to meet the data center optimization metric targets established under DCOI by OMB. (Recommendation 5)

The Secretary of Energy should take action to meet the data center closure targets established under DCOI by OMB. (Recommendation 6)

The Secretary of Energy should take action to meet the data center optimization metric targets established under DCOI by OMB. (Recommendation 7)

The Secretary of the Department of Health and Human Services (HHS) should take action to meet the data center closure targets established under DCOI by OMB. (Recommendation 8)

The Secretary of HHS should take action to meet the data center optimization metric targets established under DCOI by OMB. (Recommendation 9)

The Secretary of DHS should take action to meet the data center closure targets established under DCOI by OMB. (Recommendation 10)

The Secretary of DHS should take action to meet the data center optimization metric targets established under DCOI by OMB. (Recommendation 11)

The Secretary of Interior should take action to meet the data center closure targets established under DCOI by OMB. (Recommendation 12)

The Secretary of Interior should take action to meet the data center-related cost savings established under DCOI by OMB. (Recommendation 13)

The Secretary of Interior should take action to meet the data center optimization metric targets established under DCOI by OMB. (Recommendation 14)

The Attorney General should take action to meet the data center optimization metric targets established for Justice under DCOI by OMB. (Recommendation 15)

The Secretary of the Department of Labor (Labor) should take action to meet the data center optimization metric targets established under DCOI by OMB. (Recommendation 16)

The Secretary of State should take action to meet the data center closure targets established under DCOI by OMB. (Recommendation 17)

The Secretary of State should take action to meet the data center optimization metric targets established under DCOI by OMB. (Recommendation 18)

The Secretary of Transportation should take action to meet the data center closure targets established under DCOI by OMB. (Recommendation 19)

The Secretary of Transportation should take action to meet the data center optimization metric targets established under DCOI by OMB. (Recommendation 20)

The Secretary of Treasury should take action to meet the data center optimization metric targets established under DCOI by OMB. (Recommendation 21)

The Secretary of VA should take action to meet the data center closure targets established under DCOI by OMB. (Recommendation 22)

The Secretary of VA should take action to meet the data center-related cost savings established under DCOI by OMB. (Recommendation 23)

The Secretary of VA should take action to meet the data center optimization metric targets established under DCOI by OMB. (Recommendation 24)

The Administrator of EPA should take action to meet the data center closure targets established under DCOI by OMB. (Recommendation 25)

168        *United States Government Accountability Office*

The Administrator of EPA should take action to meet the data center optimization metric targets established under DCOI by OMB. (Recommendation 26)

The Administrator of GSA should take action to meet the data center optimization metric targets established under DCOI by OMB. (Recommendation 27)

The Administrator of the National Aeronautics and Space Administration (NASA) should take action to meet the data center optimization metric targets established under DCOI by OMB. (Recommendation 28)

The Director of NSF should take action to meet the data center optimization metric targets established under DCOI by OMB. (Recommendation 29)

The Chairman of NRC should take action to meet the data center optimization metric targets established under DCOI by OMB. (Recommendation 30)

The Director of OPM should take action to meet the data center-related cost savings established under DCOI by OMB. (Recommendation 31)

The Director of OPM should take action to meet the data center optimization metric targets established under DCOI by OMB. (Recommendation 32)

The Administrator of the Small Business Administration (SBA) should take action to meet the data center optimization metric targets established under DCOI by OMB. (Recommendation 33)

The Commissioner of SSA should take action to meet the data center-related cost savings established under DCOI by OMB. (Recommendation 34)

The Commissioner of SSA should take action to meet the data center optimization metric targets established under DCOI by OMB. (Recommendation 35)

The Administrator of USAID should take action to meet the data center closure targets established under DCOI by OMB. (Recommendation 36)

*Data Center Optimization*  169

## AGENCY COMMENTS AND OUR EVALUATION

We requested comments on a draft of this chapter from OMB and the 24 agencies that we reviewed. Of the 22 agencies to which we made recommendations, 11 agencies agreed with our recommendations; three agencies agreed with some portion, but not all of the recommendations; one agency disagreed with our recommendations; and seven agencies did not state whether they agreed or disagreed with the recommendations. In addition, OMB and two agencies to which we did not make recommendations stated that they had no comments. Further, multiple agencies provided technical comments, which we have incorporated, as appropriate.

The following 11 agencies agreed with our recommendations:

- In written comments from Commerce, State, NASA, SBA, and SSA, the agencies stated that they agreed with the recommendations and indicated their intent to address them. State also provided technical comments, which we have incorporated, as appropriate. The agencies' comments are reprinted in appendices II through VI.

- In written comments, Energy agreed with our recommendations to meet its data center closure and optimization metric targets, and described actions that the department planned to take in order to address the recommendations. Energy initially estimated that it would complete these actions by March 1, 2019; however, the department subsequently revised its estimated completion date to April 15, 2019. Energy also provided technical comments, which we have incorporated, as appropriate. Energy's comments are reprinted in appendix VII.

- In written comments, VA agreed with our recommendations to meet its data center closure, cost savings, and optimization metric targets. In addition, the department requested that we close our recommendation related to data center closures on the basis of its planned actions to implement a new inventory data collection tool

170 *United States Government Accountability Office*

and methodology to improve how the department collects data center inventory information, and a positive trend in its data center closures. The department estimated that its planned actions would be completed in March 2019 and reported that, as of November 2018, it had closed 78 data centers in fiscal year 2018, as compared with 24 in fiscal year 2017.

However, as noted earlier in this chapter, we found that VA did not plan to meet the closure goal for either tiered or non-tiered data centers, which was the basis for our recommendation. While we acknowledge and encourage VA's reported closure progress, the department still has not met its DCOI closure goals, as we recommended. Further, VA did not provide an update on the status of its planned actions in time for us to address them in this chapter. As such, we maintain that this recommendation is still appropriate.

In addition, VA referred to OMB's proposed changes to DCOI guidance when describing actions that it planned to take to meet the department's cost savings and optimization metrics targets. However, OMB staff told us that the August 2016 DCOI guidance will remain in effect until the revised DCOI guidance is formally issued. Once OMB's new DCOI guidance is finalized, we plan to assess agency progress against any revised targets, and we will continue to monitor the department's efforts to address our recommendation. VA's comments are reprinted in appendix VIII.

We received emails from officials of Agriculture, Justice, Transportation, and OPM which stated that these agencies agreed with the recommendations we directed to them.[62] In addition, three agencies agreed with some portion, but not all of our recommendations directed to them:

---

[62] We received these emails from Agriculture's Director for Strategic Planning, Policy, Egovernment and Audits on March 1, 2019; Justice's Audit Liaison Specialist in the Justice Management Division on December 20, 2018; Transportation's Director for Audit Relations and Program Improvement on December 21, 2018; and OPM's Director for Internal Oversight and Compliance on February 21, 2019.

## Data Center Optimization 171

- In written comments, Defense stated that it agreed with our recommendation to meet its data center closure targets. However, the department partially agreed with our two other recommendations: to identify additional data center-related savings opportunities and to meet OMB's data center optimization metric targets.

In partially agreeing with our recommendation on data center savings, Defense asserted that it had already identified significant cost savings through activities such as the identification of system migration candidates and the use of cloud services, among others. The department further stated that, while it would continue to optimize its data centers, the need for IT would continue to grow, and this growth might ultimately lead to an increase in total data center costs, despite overall per unit cost reductions.

However, the department's planned savings of $205.46 million represented only 11 percent of its $1.8 billion savings goal by the end of fiscal year 2018 and, as such, this limited progress by the department formed the basis for our recommendation. As discussed in our report, OMB plans to revise DCOI guidance and work with agencies to set agency-specific targets. According to OMB staff, until the guidance is revised, the current guidance and its targets are still applicable. For these reasons, we maintain that our recommendation is still appropriate.

Further, in partially agreeing with our recommendation to meet optimization metric targets, Defense stated that the department will continue to drive towards the achievement of data center optimization targets. It added, however, that it would not invest resources to improve the efficiency of data centers planned for closure and that, as a result, the composite view of Defense's data center efficiency would fall short of meeting OMB's targets.

Our review found that Defense did not plan on meeting any of OMB's five data center optimization metric targets by the end of fiscal year 2018. This finding was the basis for our recommendation. We acknowledge Defense's position that

172          *United States Government Accountability Office*

investing resources into optimizing data centers that are already planned for closure would not be the best use of taxpayer dollars. We also noted in our report that OMB had proposed revising its optimization metrics, and that any such changes had not yet been finalized. Our recommendation is not intended to imply that an agency should meet a particular version of OMB targets but, rather, that the agency should meet any targets that are established by OMB. This would include any future changes to DCOI targets. Accordingly, we maintain that our recommendation is still appropriate and will continue to monitor the department's efforts to address our recommendation. Defense's comments are reprinted in appendix IX.

- In written comments, DHS stated that it agreed with our recommendation to meet its data center closure targets and disagreed with our recommendation to meet its data center optimization metric targets. Specifically, the department noted that it had met its tiered data center closure targets, and was reviewing the status of its remaining open non-tiered data centers. The department added that it expected to complete this activity by March 31, 2019. However, the department did not provide an update on its efforts in time to be included in this chapter.

While we encourage DHS's continued efforts to close its remaining non-tiered data centers, we note that the department's letter cites an inventory of 18 open non-tiered facilities, which differs significantly from the 202 non-tiered centers counted in our draft report, and which DHS officials confirmed in November 2018. According to the department, this discrepancy is because OMB issued revised inventory reporting requirements in November 2018, and these revised requirements exempted certain types of facilities from DCOI reporting and resulted in the lower number.

These changes in reporting requirements are similar to the proposed, but not yet finalized, revisions to the DCOI policy that are discussed earlier in this chapter. However, OMB staff told us

## Data Center Optimization 173

that the August 2016 DCOI guidance will remain in effect until the revised DCOI guidance is formally issued. Once OMB's new DCOI guidance is finalized, we plan to assess agency progress against any revised targets, and we will continue to monitor the department's efforts to address our recommendation.

Further, in disagreeing with our recommendation on meeting optimization metrics, the department stated that, while the recommendation was applicable under the original DCOI guidance that OMB issued in August 2016, OMB's proposed changes to DCOI guidance would exempt most, if not all, DHS agency-owned data centers from the optimization metrics. Consequently, the department requested that our recommendation be closed.

In our review, we found that the department did not plan on meeting any of OMB's five data center optimization metric targets established under DCOI. This finding was the basis for our recommendation on meeting optimization metrics. Also, while OMB has proposed changes to its metrics, as we noted previously, it has not provided a date for when any such proposed changes will be finalized and implemented; and, according to OMB staff, until the changes to DCOI guidance are finalized, the current guidance is still applicable. Further, our recommendations do not specify that an agency should meet any particular version of OMB targets, but rather, that an agency should meet the targets established by OMB. This would include any future changes to DCOI targets. Accordingly, we maintain that our recommendation is still appropriate. DHS also provided technical comments, which we have incorporated, as appropriate. DHS's comments are reprinted in appendix X.

- In written comments, Interior stated that it partially agreed with our recommendation to meet its data center closure targets and disagreed with our two recommendations to meet its data center-related cost savings target and its data center optimization metric targets. For all three recommendations, the department stated that OMB had proposed changes to DCOI guidance that would result in

174      *United States Government Accountability Office*

new targets for closures, cost savings, and optimization metrics and that Interior planned to adopt the new policy and work through OMB to establish its new targets.

As noted in our report, Interior met its target for tiered data center closures, but did not plan to meet the closure goal for non-tiered data centers. Further, the department planned on achieving only $15.95 million of its $88.19 million savings target (18 percent) by the end of fiscal year 2018, and did not plan on meeting any of OMB's five data center optimization metric targets. These three findings were the basis for our recommendations to the department.

We also noted that, as part of OMB's proposed changes to DCOI guidance, it planned to work with agencies to set agency-specific targets for data center closures and planned to modify the metrics currently used by agencies to monitor the performance of their data centers. However, as previously mentioned, OMB has not provided a date for when these proposed changes will be finalized and implemented and, according to OMB staff, until the changes to DCOI guidance are finalized, the 2016 guidance is still applicable. Furthermore, our recommendations do not specify that an agency should meet any particular version of OMB targets, but should meet any targets that are established by OMB. This would include any future changes to DCOI targets. As such, we maintain that our recommendations are appropriate. Interior's comments are reprinted in appendix XI.

One agency disagreed with all of our recommendations:

- In written comments, HHS disagreed with our two recommendations to meet its data center closure targets and data center optimization metric targets. In regard to both recommendations, the department disagreed with being held to what it termed "expired requirements" from DCOI guidance, pending the assignment of new targets being established by OMB.

As noted in our report, HHS met its target for tiered data center closures, but did not plan to meet the closure target for non-tiered data centers. We also found that HHS did not meet any of OMB's five optimization metric targets and had planned to meet only one of the five by end of fiscal year 2018. These findings were the basis for the two recommendations that we made to the department.

We also noted that, as part of OMB's proposed changes to DCOI guidance, OMB planned to work with agencies to set agency-specific targets for data center closures and planned to modify the metrics currently used by agencies to monitor the performance of their data centers. However, as previously mentioned, OMB did not provide a date for when these proposed changes will be finalized and implemented and, according to its staff, until the changes to DCOI guidance are finalized, the current guidance is still applicable. Further, our recommendations do not specify that an agency should meet any particular version of OMB targets, but rather, that the agency should meet the targets established by OMB. This would include any future changes to DCOI targets. Accordingly, we maintain that our recommendations are still appropriate. HHS's comments are reprinted in appendix XII.

Further, seven agencies did not agree or disagree with the recommendations:

- In written comments, EPA did not state whether it agreed or disagreed with our recommendations to meet its data center closure and data center optimization metrics targets. However, the agency requested that we close our recommendations, citing its reported progress in closing 21 of 34 targeted data centers and OMB's proposed changes in its draft DCOI guidance that could result in revised closure targets and optimization metrics.
  As stated in our report, we found that EPA did not plan to meet its closure target for tiered or non-tiered data centers, nor did it plan to

176     *United States Government Accountability Office*

meet its data center optimization targets; these findings were the basis for our recommendations. We also noted that, as part of OMB's proposed changes to DCOI, OMB planned to work with agencies to set agency-specific targets for data center closures and planned to modify the metrics currently used by agencies to monitor the performance of their data centers. However, OMB has not provided a date for when these proposed changes will be finalized and implemented and, according to OMB staff, until the changes to DCOI guidance are finalized, the current guidance is still applicable. Further, our recommendations do not specify that an agency should meet any particular version of OMB targets, but that it should meet the targets established by OMB. This would include any future changes to DCOI targets. Accordingly, we maintain that our recommendations are appropriate and should remain open. EPA also provided technical comments, which we have incorporated, as appropriate. The agency's comments are reprinted in appendix XIII.

- In written comments, GSA did not state whether it agreed or disagreed with our recommendation to meet the agency's data center optimization metrics targets. Specifically, the agency stated that it had complied with revised inventory reporting requirements, which OMB provided to agencies in November 2018 and which eliminated non-tiered data centers from the requirement to meet optimization targets. As a result, the agency noted that it no longer had a basis to measure and report on the one metric our report cited as applicable to GSA (i.e., server utilization and automated monitoring) and asked that we withdraw the recommendation.

These changes in reporting requirements are similar to the proposed, but not yet finalized, revisions to the DCOI policy that are discussed earlier in the report. However, OMB staff told us that the August 2016 DCOI guidance is still in effect until the revised DCOI guidance is formally issued. Until OMB's new DCOI guidance is finalized and agency progress against any revised targets can be evaluated, we maintain that our recommendation to

## Data Center Optimization 177

meet the agency's optimization metrics targets is appropriate, and we will continue to monitor the agency's efforts to address it. GSA's comments are reprinted in appendix XIV.

- In written comments, NSF did not state whether it agreed or disagreed with our recommendation. The agency's comments are reprinted in appendix XV.
- In written comments, NRC agreed with the draft report, but did not state whether it agreed or disagreed with our recommendation. The agency's comments are reprinted in appendix XVI.
- In written comments USAID did not state whether it agreed or disagreed with the draft report's recommendation but agreed with our finding that the agency no longer had any tiered data centers. However, USAID stated that it had met DCOI's closure targets for the agency by closing its 4 non-tiered data centers, and requested that we close our recommendation to meet those targets.

While we encourage USAID's continued efforts to close its remaining non-tiered data centers, we note that the agency's letter cites an inventory of 4 non-tiered facilities, which differs significantly from the 83 non-tiered centers counted in our draft report, and which USAID officials confirmed in October 2018. As USAID communicated in subsequent emails, this discrepancy is because OMB issued revised inventory reporting requirements in November 2018 and these revised requirements exempted certain types of facilities from DCOI reporting, which resulted in the lower number.

These changes in reporting requirements are similar to the proposed, but not yet finalized, revisions to the DCOI policy that are discussed earlier in the report. However, OMB staff told us that the August 2016 DCOI guidance is still in effect until the revised DCOI guidance is formally issued. Until OMB's new DCOI guidance is finalized and agency progress against any revised targets can be evaluated, we maintain that our data center closure recommendation is appropriate, and we will continue to monitor

# 178 *United States Government Accountability Office*

the agency's efforts to address it. The agency's comments are reprinted in appendix XVII.

- In emails received from Labor's GAO liaison in the department's Office of the Assistant Secretary for Policy on January 8, 2019, and from an audit liaison in Treasury's Office of the CIO on February 1, 2019, both departments did not state whether they agreed or disagreed with our respective recommendations.

Finally, in emails received from a Management and Program Analyst in Education's Office of the Secretary/Executive Secretariat on January 8, 2019; an audit liaison in HUD's Office of the CIO, Audit Compliance Branch on February 15, 2019; and a GAO liaison in OMB's Office of General Counsel on February 25, 2019, these agencies stated that they had no comments on the draft report.

We are sending copies of this chapter to interested congressional committees, the Director of OMB, the secretaries and heads of the departments and agencies addressed in this chapter, and other interested parties.

Carol C. Harris
Director, Information Technology
Acquisition Management Issues

## List of Committees

The Honorable James M. Inhofe
Chairman

The Honorable Jack Reed
Ranking Member
Committee on Armed Services
United States Senate

The Honorable Ron Johnson
Chairman

The Honorable Gary C. Peters
Ranking Member
Committee on Homeland Security and Governmental Affairs
United States Senate

The Honorable Adam Smith
Chairman

The Honorable Mac Thornberry
Ranking Member
Committee on Armed Services
House of Representatives

The Honorable Elijah Cummings
Chairman

The Honorable Jim Jordan
Ranking Member
Committee on Oversight and Reform
House of Representatives

# APPENDIX I: OBJECTIVES, SCOPE, AND METHODOLOGY

Our objectives for this engagement were to (1) determine agencies' progress in data center closures and achievement in related savings to date and describe plans for future savings, (2) evaluate the agencies' progress against OMB's data center optimization targets, and (3) identify effective agency practices for achieving data center closures, cost savings, and optimization.

180      *United States Government Accountability Office*

To address the first objective, for data center closures, we obtained and analyzed August 2018 data center inventory documentation from the 24 departments and agencies (agencies)[63] that participate in OMB's Data Center Optimization Initiative (DCOI).[64] To determine data center closures to date, we totaled their reported closures from fiscal year 2010 through August 2018 and to identify future closures, we totaled their reported planned closures through fiscal year 2018. We also compared agencies' completed and planned closures to OMB's fiscal year 2018 consolidation goals, as documented in its August 2016 memorandum (M-16-19).[65]

To verify the quality, completeness, and reliability of each agency's data center inventory, we compared information on completed and planned data center closures to similar information reported on OMB's IT Dashboard—a public website that provides information on federal agencies' major IT investments.[66] We also checked for missing data and other errors, such as missing closure status information. In some cases identified, we followed-up with agency officials to obtain further information. We determined that the data were sufficiently complete and reliable to report on agencies' consolidation progress and planned closures.

For cost savings and avoidance[67] we obtained and analyzed documentation from the 24 DCOI agencies. This documentation is required by OMB's March 2013 and August 2016 memorandums and included the agencies' quarterly reports of cost savings and avoidances posted to their

---

[63] The 24 agencies that are required to participate in the Data Center Optimization Initiative are the Departments of Agriculture, Commerce, Defense, Education, Energy, Health and Human Services, Homeland Security, Housing and Urban Development, the Interior, Justice, Labor, State, Transportation, the Treasury, and Veterans Affairs; the Environmental Protection Agency, General Services Administration, National Aeronautics and Space Administration, National Science Foundation, Nuclear Regulatory Commission, Office of Personnel Management, Small Business Administration, Social Security Administration, and U.S. Agency for International Development.

[64] Agencies' data center optimization progress information displayed on OMB's IT Dashboard is updated by OMB on a quarterly basis based on data center inventory data collected from agencies at the end of February, May, August, and November of each year.

[65] OMB, *Data Center Optimization Initiative (DCOI)*, Memorandum M-16-19 (Washington, D.C.: Aug. 1, 2016).

[66] We did not physically visit agencies' data center locations to verify their inventory totals.

[67] Beginning in March 2013, OMB required agencies to report on both cost savings and cost avoidances. OMB defines cost savings as a reduction in actual expenditures below the projected level of costs to achieve a specific objective and defines a cost avoidance as the result of an action taken in the immediate time frame that will decrease costs in the future.

Data Center Optimization 181

digital services websites and their DCOI strategic plans.[68] To determine cost savings achieved, we totaled agencies' reported savings and avoidances from the start of fiscal years 2012 through August 2018, as found in the August 2018 quarterly reports posted to the agencies' digital services websites.[69] To identify future planned savings, we totaled the agencies' projected savings and avoidances from fiscal years 2016 through 2018, as reported in their DCOI strategic plans.

To assess the quality, completeness, and reliability of each agency's data center consolidation cost savings information, we used the latest version of each agency's quarterly cost savings report and DCOI strategic plan, as of August 2018. We also reviewed the quarterly reports and DCOI strategic plans for missing data and other errors, such as missing cost-savings information. In addition, we compared agencies cost savings and avoidances with data from our most recent data center consolidation report.[70] As a result, we determined that the data were sufficiently complete and reliable to report on agencies data center consolidation cost-savings information.

For our second objective, we analyzed the August 2018 data center optimization progress information of the 24 DCOI agencies. This progress information was obtained from the IT Dashboard—an OMB public website that provides information on federal agencies' major IT investments. To assess agencies' planned optimization progress, we obtained the planned optimization performance from the 22 agencies' DCOI strategic plans. We then compared the agencies' current and planned optimization progress information to OMB's fiscal year 2018 optimization targets, as documented in its August 2016 memorandum.[71]

---

[68] OMB, Memorandum M-16-19 and *Fiscal Year 2013 PortfolioStat Guidance: Strengthening Federal IT Portfolio Management*, Memorandum M-13-09 (Washington, D.C.: Mar. 27, 2013).

[69] Under FDCCI, which OMB launched in February 2010, agencies were required to begin closing data centers. However, current OMB guidance only requires agencies to report historical cost savings and avoidances realized since fiscal year 2012.

[70] GAO, *Data Center Optimization: Continued Agency Actions Needed to Meet Goals and Address Prior Recommendations*, GAO-18-264 (Washington, D.C.: May 23, 2018).

[71] OMB, Memorandum M-16-19.

182     *United States Government Accountability Office*

Although OMB's memorandum establishes a single optimization target value for the server utilization and automated monitoring metric, the IT Dashboard displays agencies' progress for tiered and non-tiered data centers separately. To report consistently with OMB's implementation memorandum, we combined the progress information for tiered and non-tiered data centers into a single assessment in this chapter.

In addition, to assess the reliability of the planned optimization milestones in the DCOI strategic plans, we reviewed agencies' documentation to identify any missing or erroneous data. We also compared the planned data center optimization milestones contained in agencies' documentation against current optimization progress information obtained from the IT Dashboard; we then discussed any discrepancies or potential errors that we identified with agency officials to determine the causes or request additional information. As a result of these efforts, we were able to determine whether each agency's strategic plan information was sufficiently reliable for reporting on plans to meet or not meet OMB's fiscal year 2018 optimization targets.

To assess the reliability of agencies' optimization progress information on OMB's IT Dashboard, we reviewed the information for errors or missing data, such as progress information that was not available for certain metrics. We also compared agencies' optimization progress information across multiple reporting quarters to identify any inconsistencies in agencies' reported progress. We discussed with staff from OMB's Office of the Federal Chief Information Officer any discrepancies or potential errors identified to determine the causes.

To identify effective agency practices for achieving data center closures, cost savings, and optimization progress, we selected two of the highest performing departments or agencies for each of those three data center areas that we reported on in our May 2018 report.[72]

---

[72] GAO-18-264.

## Data Center Optimization

183

For the data center inventory closures area, we selected the Departments of Agriculture (Agriculture) and Justice (Justice) from among the five agencies that had, as of August 2017, reached or exceeded both their tiered and non-tiered data center closure targets for the end of fiscal year 2018. For the cost savings area, we identified two departments and two small agencies reporting the highest cost savings DCOI to date, as of August 2017. From those, we selected one department (Commerce) and one small agency (the General Services Administration) to provide balance relative to agency size. For effective practices related to optimization performance, we reviewed agencies' reported optimization performance as of August 2017 and selected the two highest-performing agencies in this area (the Social Security Administration and the Environmental Protection Agency), since they were the only two agencies reporting that they met more than half of OMB's optimization targets. Selecting these agencies was designed to provide anecdotal information that could assist agencies struggling with DCOI implementation. The examples they provided are not findings nor should they be taken to be representative of all the agencies participating in DCOI.

We asked each selected agency to identify practices that they found effective in implementing DCOI at their agency and in meeting OMB's established targets in each of the areas, not just the area for which they were selected. We also solicited examples that demonstrated how those practices helped agency implementation or the benefits from implementing DCOI. Additionally, we considered information and examples that these agencies provided as part of our work to identify FITARA best practices. We analyzed the responses to determine the practices and reported those that were identified by at least two agencies.

We conducted this performance audit from April 2018 to April 2019 in accordance with generally accepted government auditing standards. Those standards require that we plan and perform the audit to obtain sufficient, appropriate evidence to provide a reasonable basis for our findings and conclusions based on our audit objectives. We believe that the evidence obtained provides a reasonable basis for our findings and conclusions based on our audit objectives.

# Appendix II: Comments from the Department of Commerce

February 27, 2019

Ms. Carol C. Harris
Director, Information Technology
Acquisition Management Issues
U.S. Government Accountability Office
441 G Street, NW
Washington, DC 20548

Dear Ms. Harris:

Thank you for the opportunity to review and comment on the Government Accountability Office's (GAO) draft report titled *DATA CENTER OPTIMIZATION: Additional Agency Actions Needed to Meet OMB Goals* (GAO-19-241, March 2019).

On behalf of the Department of Commerce, I have enclosed our comments on the draft report. The GAO-19-241 report on Data Center Optimization Initiative is a fair and thorough assessment of ongoing activities and progress. The Department agrees with the recommendation and is planning to close an additional 22 data centers by the end of Fiscal Year 2022.

Sincerely,

Wilbur Ross

**Department of Commerce's Comments on
GAO Draft Report titled
*DATA CENTER OPTIMIZATION: Additional Agency Actions Needed to Meet OMB Goals*
(GAO-19-241, March 2019)**

The Department of Commerce has reviewed the draft report, and we concur with the recommendation.

### General Comments

We do not have any comments.

### Comments on Recommendations

The Government Accountability Office (GAO) made one (1) recommendation(s) to the Department of Commerce in the report.

**Recommendation 1:** The Secretary of Commerce should take action to meet the data center closure targets established under DCOI by OMB (page 45).

**Commerce Response:** The Department agrees with the recommendation and is targeting Q3 FY22 to complete this important work.

# Appendix III: Comments from the Department of State

United States Department of State
*Comptroller*
Washington, DC 20520

FEB 2 7 2019

Thomas Melito
Managing Director
International Affairs and Trade
Government Accountability Office
441 G Street, N.W.
Washington, D.C. 20548-0001

Dear Mr. Melito:

We appreciate the opportunity to review your draft report, "DATA CENTER OPTIMIZATION: Additional Agency Actions Needed to Meet OMB Goals" GAO Job Code 102743.

The enclosed Department of State comments are provided for incorporation with this letter as an appendix to the final report.

United States Government Accountability Office

United States Department of State
*Comptroller*
Washington, DC 20520

FEB 2 7 2019

Thomas Melito
Managing Director
International Affairs and Trade
Government Accountability Office
441 G Street, N.W.
Washington, D.C. 20548-0001

Dear Mr. Melito:

We appreciate the opportunity to review your draft report, "DATA CENTER OPTIMIZATION: Additional Agency Actions Needed to Meet OMB Goals" GAO Job Code 102743.

The enclosed Department of State comments are provided for incorporation with this letter as an appendix to the final report.

Sincerely,

Jeffrey C. Mounts (Acting)

**Department of State Response to the Draft Report**

**DATA CENTER OPTIMIZATION: Additional Agency Actions Needed to Meet OMB Goals**
**(GAO-19-241; GAO Code 102743)**

Thank you for the opportunity to comment on the GAO draft report *"Data Center Optimization: Additional Agency Actions Needed to Meet OMB Goals."*

**Recommendations:**

The Secretary of State should take action to meet the data center closure targets established under DCOI by OMB [Recommendation 17]

The Secretary of State should take action to meet the data center optimization metric targets established under DCOI by OMB [Recommendation 18]

**Response:**

The Department of State Bureau of Information Resource Management (IRM) concurs with recommendation 17 and looks forward to working toward the applicable targets in the forthcoming guidance from OMB.

The Department of State concurs with recommendation 18. IRM continues to increase the August 2018 total by following the multi-year strategy designed to the FITARA requirement for achieving the consolidation and optimization of data centers by the end of fiscal year 2020

# APPENDIX IV: COMMENTS FROM THE NATIONAL AERONAUTICS AND SPACE ADMINISTRATION

National Aeronautics and Space Administration
**Headquarters**
Washington, DC 20546-0001

FEB 1 9 2019

Reply to Attn of:   Office of the Chief Information Officer

Ms. Carol C. Harris
Director
Acquisition Management Issues
United States Government Accountability Office
Washington, DC 20548

Dear Ms. Harris:

The National Aeronautics and Space Administration (NASA) appreciates the opportunity to review and comment on the Government Accountability Office (GAO) draft report entitled, "Data Center Optimization: Additional Agency Actions Need to Meet OMB Goals" (GAO-19-241) dated December 12, 2018.

In the draft report, GAO makes one recommendation to NASA intended to drive cost savings and avoidances relating to the Data Center Optimization Initiative (DCOI). Specifically, GAO recommends the following:

**Recommendation 1:** The Administrator of NASA should take action to meet the data center optimization metric targets established under DCOI by OMB.

**Management's Response:** NASA concurs with the recommendation. NASA will take action to meet the data center optimization metric targets established under DCOI by OMB. The DCOI metric targets that were the subject of this report expired at the end of FY18. OMB is working with Federal agencies to revise these metrics. When the new metrics are available, NASA will take action to meet the revised metrics to the extent possible.

**Estimated Completion Date:** February 28, 2020.

Sincerely,

Renee P. Wynn
Chief Information Officer

# Appendix V: Comments from the Small Business Administration

February 15, 2019

Ms. Carol C. Harris
Director, Information Technology Acquisition Management Issues
U. S. Government Accountability Office
441 G Street, N.W.
Washington, DC 20548

Dear Ms. Harris:

Thank you for providing the U. S. Small Business Administration (SBA) with a copy of the Government Accountability Office (GAO) draft report titled "Data Center Optimization: Additional Agency Actions Needed to Meet OMB Goals" GAO-19-241 (102743). The draft report analyzes agencies' progress and plans for data center closures and cost savings, assessment against OMB's data center optimization targets, and identify effective agency practices for achieving those objectives. SBA reviewed the draft report and agrees with the one recommendation GAO issued to SBA.

**Recommendation 33:** The Administrator of the Small Business Administration should take action to meet the data center optimization metric targets established under DCOI by OMB.

**SBA Response:** Concur. SBA Office of the Chief Information Officer (OCIO) and the appropriate program offices will develop further plans to meet the data center optimization metric targets established under DCOI by OMB. As referenced in this report, OMB recently changed the data center optimization metrics. As such, SBA is revising SBA's DCOI plan and anticipates completion of its revised DCOI plan in March 2019. Due to the changes in DCOI metrics, SBA's action plan and date to meet these revised DCOI metrics is to be determined.

Thank you for the opportunity to comment on this draft report.

Sincerely,

MARIA ROAT
Digitally signed by MARIA ROAT
Date: 2019.02.15 12:53:58 -05'00'

Maria Roat
Chief Information Officer

# APPENDIX VI: COMMENTS FROM THE SOCIAL SECURITY ADMINISTRATION

SOCIAL SECURITY
Office of the Commissioner

January 10, 2019

Ms. Carol C. Harris
Director, Information Technology
 Acquisition Management Issues
United States Government Accountability Office
441 G Street, NW
Washington, DC 20548

Dear Ms. Harris:

Thank you for the opportunity to review the draft report, "DATA CENTER OPTIMIZATION: Additional Agency Actions Needed to Meet OMB Goals" (GAO-19-241). Please see our enclosed comments.

Sincerely,

Stephanie Hall
Acting Deputy Chief of Staff

**SSA COMMENTS ON THE GOVERNMENT ACCOUNTABILITY OFFICE DRAFT REPORT, "DATA CENTER OPTIMIZATION: ADDITIONAL AGENCY ACTIONS NEEDED TO MEET OMB GOALS" (GAO-19-241)**

**GENERAL COMMENTS**

In accordance with the Office of Management and Budget's (OMB) Data Center Optimization Initiative (DCOI) mandate M-16-19, we will work to ensure we properly measure items that yield optimal information technology operations and efficiencies. We continue to engineer and implement data center optimization management to improve energy and cooling efficiency at both our data centers. We will also continue to automate asset inventory into the Data Center Infrastructure Management tool to include application mapping.

Our responses to the recommendations are below.

**SSA's Recommendation 1 – GAO's Recommendation 34**

Take action to meet the data center-related cost savings established under DCOI by OMB.

**Response**

We agree.

**SSA's Recommendation 2 – GAO's Recommendation 35**

Take action to meet the data center optimization metric targets established under DCOI by OMB.

**Response**

We agree.

# APPENDIX VII: COMMENTS FROM THE DEPARTMENT OF ENERGY

**Department of Energy**
Washington, DC 20585

January 10, 2019

Ms. Carol C. Harris
Director, Information Technology and Management Issues
U.S. Government Accountability Office
441 G Street, N.W.
Washington, D.C. 20548

Dear Ms. Harris:

Thank you for the opportunity to provide the Department of Energy's (DOE or Department) management response to the Government Accountability Office's (GAO) draft report *Data Center Optimization: Additional Agency Actions Needed to Meet OMB Goals (GAO-19-241)*. We understand that GAO conducted this audit to (1) determine agencies' progress in data center closures and achievement in related savings to date and describe plans for future closures and savings; (2) assess agencies' progress against Office of Management and Budget's (OMB's) data center optimization targets and (3) identify effective agency practices for achieving data center closures, cost savings, and optimization progress.

DOE concurs with the recommendations, and continues to work toward meeting or exceeding its targeted metrics and closure goals established under OMB's Data Center Optimization Initiative (DCOI). Details are in the attached Enclosure.

Sincerely,

Stephen (Max) Everett
Chief Information Officer

**Recommendation 6:** The Secretary of Energy should take action to meet the data center closure targets established under DCOI by OMB.

**Management Decision:** Concur

DOE continues to make progress toward meeting its target goals for data center closure. To date, we have closed 98 data centers (23 tiered and 75 non-tiered).

On November 26, 2018, OMB published a new draft Data Center Optimization Initiative (DCOI) Memorandum changing the focus from closure to optimizing data centers. This memorandum revises the definition of Data Center, which may require reclassifying a number of our non-tiered data centers to 'invalid', thus potentially removing a significant number of entries from our reported inventory.

The OMB's draft memorandum requires agencies to identify "Key Mission Facility" data centers. Data centers identified as "Key Mission Facility" may be exempt from closure and performance reporting. This will reduce the number of data center closures needed to meet our goals.

DOE has initiated an update of our automated reporting platform with the appropriate definitions and metric fields in order to capture the new reporting requirements. We will update our DCOI Implementation Plan and schedule to reflect the new changes.

**Estimated Completion Date:** March 1, 2019

**Recommendation 7:** The Secretary of Energy should take action to meet the data center optimization metric targets established under DCOI by OMB.

**Management Decision:** Concur

DOE will continue to work to meet or exceed its targeted metrics.

On November 26, 2018, OMB published a new draft DCOI Memorandum changing the key metric requirements for each Agency. The changes in performance metrics have a significant impact to the overall reporting. For example, Power Usage Effectiveness (PUE), and Facilities Utilization are no longer required reporting metrics. The draft memorandum modified other metrics such as Virtualization, Energy Metering, and Server Utilization and added new metrics w, such as, Data Center Availability and Underutilized Servers.

DOE has initiated updates to our automated reporting platform with the appropriate metric fields in order to capture the new reporting requirements. The Department put into place Data Center Information Management (DCIM) software that will enable each data center to measure its operations at an enterprise level. We will update our DCOI Implementation Plan and schedule to reflect the new changes.

**Estimated Completion Date:** March 1, 2019

# APPENDIX VIII: COMMENTS FROM THE DEPARTMENT OF VETERANS AFFAIRS

THE SECRETARY OF VETERANS AFFAIRS
WASHINGTON

January 22, 2019

# 192 *United States Government Accountability Office*

Ms. Carol C. Harris
Director
Information Technology
 Acquisition Management Issues
U.S. Government Accountability Office
441 G Street, NW
Washington, DC 20548

Dear Ms. Harris:

The Department of Veterans Affairs (VA) has reviewed the Government Accountability Office (GAO) draft report: *"DATA CENTER OPTIMIZATION: Additional Agency Actions Needed to Meet OMB Goals"* (GAO-19-241).

The enclosure sets forth the actions to be taken to address the draft report recommendations.

VA appreciates the opportunity to comment on your draft report.

Sincerely,

*Robert L. Wilkie*

Robert L. Wilkie

Department of Veterans Affairs (VA) Comments to
Government Accountability Office (GAO) Draft Report
*"DATA CENTER OPTIMIZATION: Additional Agency
Actions Needed to Meet OMB Goals"*
(GAO-19-241)

**Recommendation 1: The Secretary of VA should take action to meet the data center closure targets established under DCOI by OMB. (Recommendation 22)**

**VA Comment**: Concur. The Department of Veterans Affairs (VA) is committed to working with the Office of Management and Budget (OMB) to meet all Data Center Optimization Initiative (DCOI) requirements. Over the past year, VA Office of Information and Technology (OIT) has closely collaborated with OMB to identify synergies and weaknesses to improve the way in which OMB evaluates VA (and other agencies) progress towards meeting OMB requirements (VA is submitting a briefing to OMB, Attachment A, as an example of VA's ongoing collaboration with OMB on data center optimization). Currently, OMB is drafting new guidance on data center consolidation and optimization efforts for Federal agencies (Attachment B). The draft is available for public comment, and the final version is expected to be released early in 2019.

## Data Center Optimization

## 193

OIT, in concert with OMB, evolved its data center program to better meet the data center closure targets established under DCOI and prepare for the new guidance. The new program leveraged feedback from Area Managers to build a user-friendly tool to collect input for the data center inventory, making it easier for staff to report. A memorandum introducing the new program, as well as OIT-developed user guides are attached, illustrating VA's effort to collaborate with IT and non-IT staff to collect information outside of the required OMB fields to populate a comprehensive inventory (Attachments C, D, and E). VA has continued to evolve its tool and user guides to conform with the new OMB policy on data centers.

The new program also focused on educating Area Managers and non-OIT stakeholders on Federal data center inventory requirements to further improve accuracy and efficiency of reported data center information. This upgraded methodology was designed to meet the OMB reporting requirements by collecting relevant information and inventory that can be used to better identify data centers to consolidate or close. OIT's new program has already produced results which will help inform implementation of OMB's anticipated new guidance. For example, VA closed 78 data centers in Fiscal Year (FY) 2018, a significant increase from the 24 data centers closed in FY 2017 (as reported in VA's November 2018 DCIO Inventory Submission to OMB, Attachment F). Because of the collaborative work between OIT and OMB, OIT is prepared to continue this positive trend of data center closures and meet OMB's requirements. Based on the above described actions, OIT requests closure of the recommendation.

**Recommendation 2:** The Secretary of VA should take action to meet the data center-related cost savings established under DCOI by OMB. (Recommendation 23)

**VA Comment:** Concur. During monthly program update meetings held between OIT and OMB, OIT discussed the feasibility and financial impact associated with meeting data center-related cost savings established under DCOI (M-16-19). Given the VA environment, most of VA's data center closures are due to consolidation efforts (i.e., moving servers from one room to another) rather than the elimination of physical space. OMB agreed that the $85.35 million target set by DCOI would not be feasible for VA to achieve.

OMB's new guidance will shift its focus away from cost savings realized from closures and will instead center on savings from optimization efforts. To prepare for OMB's new requirements, OIT is working with non-OIT staff to use tools that provide visibility into VA's assets and leverage virtualizing capabilities. Consistent with OMB's new guidance, VA will focus on cost savings realized through optimization efforts, such as virtualizing services whenever feasible. OMB's draft guidance is enclosed (Attachment C). The target completion date is March 2019.

**Recommendation 3:** The Secretary of VA should take action to meet the data center optimization metric targets established under DCOI by OMB. (Recommendation 24)

**VA Comment:** Concur. VA has taken action to meet the data center optimization metrics targets established by OMB. As part of VA's effort, OIT has established a Tiger Team to deploy discovery tools to locate assets and leverage virtualization services, as well as monitoring tools. This will help ascertain the following:

- Number of hours of unplanned outages in data centers;
- Number of planned hours of data center availability; and
- Impacts to major systems in data centers.

Additionally, these tools will help VA improve its optimization efforts, including power consumption, underutilized servers, and efficient use of physical and virtual resources. This will allow VA to meet optimization metrics set forth by OMB guidance. The target completion date is March 2019.

# APPENDIX IX: COMMENTS FROM THE DEPARTMENT OF DEFENSE

**DEPARTMENT OF DEFENSE**
6000 DEFENSE PENTAGON
WASHINGTON, D.C. 20301-6000

CHIEF INFORMATION OFFICER

JAN 3 1 2019

Ms. Carol C. Harris
Director, Information Technology
U.S. Government Accountability Office
441 G Street, NW, Washington, DC 20548

Dear Ms. Harris:

    This is the Department of Defense (DoD) response to the GAO Draft Final Report, GAO-19-241, "DATA CENTER OPTIMIZATION: Additional Agency Actions Needed to Meet OMB Goals," dated December 12, 2018 (GAO Code 102743). The Department is in general agreement with the overall content of the draft final audit report. Enclosed are detailed comments on the report recommendations.

Sincerely,

Dana Deasy

# Data Center Optimization

**195**

## ENCLOSURE

### GAO FINAL REPORT DATED DECEMBER 12, 2018
### GAO-19-241 (GAO CODE 102743)

### "DATA CENTER OPTIMIZATION: ADDITIONAL AGENCY ACTIONS NEEDED TO MEET OMB GOALS"

### DEPARTMENT OF DEFENSE COMMENTS
### TO THE GAO RECOMMENDATION

**RECOMMENDATION 3:** The Secretary of Defense should take action to meet the data center closure targets established under DCOI by OMB.

**DoD RESPONSE:** Concur. DoD will continue to take action to meet the data center closure targets established under OMB's DCOI guidance. Beyond the measures DoD has already taken to expedite data center closures (e.g., numerous Joint Base and Agency site assessments and closure directives), DoD CIO is revising its Data Center Reference Architecture to eliminate the Installation Processing Node (IPN) data center and directing DoD Components to migrate associated workloads to enterprise level data centers and approved DoD cloud environments. Finally, OMB's anticipated changes to DCOI will include an exclusion of non-severable data center-like facilities, which will reduce the affected data center population. These actions will enable DoD to achieve OMB prescribed closure targets.

**RECOMMENDATION 4:** The Secretary of Defense should identify additional savings opportunities to achieve the targets for data center-related cost savings established under DCOI by OMB.

**DoD RESPONSE:** Partially concur. DoD has already identified significant cost savings through the identification of system migration candidates, the optimization of its enterprise computing environment, and past data center closure activity, and the use of cloud services. While DoD continues to optimize its data centers, the need for IT will continue to grow. This growth in IT demand may ultimately lead to an increase in total data center costs despite the overall per unit cost reductions.

**RECOMMENDATION 5:** The Secretary of Defense should take action to meet the data center optimization metric targets established under DCOI by OMB.

**DoD RESPONSE:** Partially concur. As discussed, DoD will continue to drive towards the achievement of data center optimization targets, to include the identification of additional data centers for closure. However, DoD will not invest resources into improving the efficiency of these closing data centers. Therefore, while DoD continues to optimize, composite views of DoD's data center efficiency will fall short of meeting OMB's efficiency targets. DoD will focus its energy and resources on ensuring that the enterprise-level data centers, which comprise the target end-state, meet or exceed OMB prescribed efficiencies.

# APPENDIX X: COMMENTS FROM THE DEPARTMENT OF HOMELAND SECURITY

March 1, 2019

Carol C. Harris
Director, Information Technology
  Acquisition Management Issues
U.S. Government Accountability Office
441 G Street, NW
Washington, DC 20548

Re:   Management Response to Draft Report GAO-19-241, "DATA CENTER OPTIMIZATION: Additional Agency Actions Needed to Meet OMB Goals"

Dear Ms. Harris:

Thank you for the opportunity to review and comment on this draft report. The U.S. Department of Homeland Security (DHS) appreciates the U.S. Government Accountability Office's (GAO) work in planning and conducting its review and issuing this report.

The Department is pleased to note GAO's positive recognition of DHS' progress on achieving Office of Management and Budget (OMB) Federal data center optimization objectives. DHS continues to optimize its physical data center footprint and has closed a total of 55 data centers as part of consolidation efforts. DHS remains committed to optimizing data center service delivery by leveraging Cloud hosting options[1].

The draft report contained two recommendations, one with which the Department concurs and one with which it non-concurs. While the draft report provides valuable insights, recent updates by OMB to data center optimization initiative (DCOI) guidance essentially negate GAO's recommendations. This is because data centers affected either have already been exempted from DCOI closure and other optimization requirements or are currently being reviewed for exemption which we anticipate will occur. Attached find our detailed response to the recommendations. Technical comments were previously provided under separate cover.

---

[1] DHS adopted the National Institute of Standards and Technology (NIST) definitions of the Cloud, including Public, Community, Hybrid, and Private clouds. DHS's use of Cloud technology will reduce the need for legacy data centers. As part of ongoing efforts to optimize our remaining data centers, DHS is committed to adopting Hybrid and Private cloud computing as the primary modernization and optimization pathway.

# Data Center Optimization

197

Again, thank you for the opportunity to review and comment on this draft report. Please feel free to contact me if you have any questions. We look forward to working with you again in the future.

Sincerely,

JIM H. CRUMPACKER, CIA, CFE
Director
Departmental GAO-OIG Liaison Office

### Attachment: Management Response to Recommendations Contained in GAO 19-241 Draft Report

GAO recommended that the Secretary of Homeland Security:

**Recommendation 10**: Take action to meet the data center closure targets established under DCOI by OMB.

**Response**: Concur. DHS has already met OMB's tiered data center closure target and an FY 2018 update to the DCOI guidance exempts DHS' 18 non-tiered data centers. More specifically:

Tiered Summary: DHS met OMB's closure metric for Tiered data centers as of August 2018, and has closed 2 additional Tiered sites, as of the November 2018 Integrated Data Call (IDC) update. In addition, DHS has met GAO's version of the Tiered closure metric (which incorporates data back to 2010), and the Department previously met the overall Federal Data Center Consolidation Initiative 40 percent closure metric for all sites (Tiered and non-Tiered).

| OMB-IT Dashboard version: Tiered Closure Metric Target for DHS | DHS Progress Toward Metric (As of November 2018) | Status |
|---|---|---|
| 6 Tiered sites Closed based on the DCOI re-baseline | 8 | Met |

| GAO version: Tiered Closure Metric Target for DHS | DHS Progress Toward Metric (As of November 2018 data call) | Status |
|---|---|---|
| 25 percent of Tiered (Valid) inventory | 46 percent | Met |

Non-Tiered Summary: During FY 2018, OMB engaged in extensive working group discussions with Federal agencies, including DHS, to weigh the benefits against the burden of the original optimization requirements placed on agency owned data centers.

As a result, OMB issued a change in DCOI guidance in the November 2018 OMB IDC. This change provides that tiered and non-tiered data centers that house non-severable systems and services are not suitable for improvements targeted by the original DCOI performance measures. Therefore, per OMB November 2018 updates to DCOI guidance, such data centers are exempt from both DCOI closure and optimization requirements.

# 198 United States Government Accountability Office

- DHS closed 6 non-tiered data centers prior to the updated November 2018 DCOI guidance

- DHS is currently reviewing the status of 18 open non-tiered collocated, outsourced, or consolidated data centers including laboratories, training facilities, and other key mission facilities. We believe that most, if not all, will be found to meet the requirements of non-severable systems and services that are not suitable for the original DCOI performance requirements. Final decisions and updates will be included at the IT Dashboard for the February 2019 OMB IDC.

Estimated Completion Date: March 31, 2019.

**Recommendation 11:** Take action to meet the data center optimization metric targets established under DCOI by OMB.

**Response:** Non-concur. This recommendation was applicable to DHS agency owned data centers under original OMB DCOI guidance published in 2016. At that time, automation requirements in agency owned tiered and non-tiered data centers were at the heart of the DCOI performance requirements on which this recommendation is based.

However, the DCOI changes OMB promulgated for the November 2018 IDC, which apply to agency owned tiered and non-tiered data centers that house non-severable systems and services, state these concerns are not suitable for improvements targeted by the original DCOI performance measures. After review of each of 7 tiered and 2 non-tiered agency-owned data centers, DHS determined that these 9 agency-owned data centers are exempt from both DCOI closure and optimization requirements.

DHS tiered and non-tiered agency owned data centers are in the category of facilities that house non-severable systems and services and DHS is in process of updating all reports to OMB to identify these data centers as exempt from DCOI closure and optimization requirements.

- Seven DHS tiered agency owned data centers, representing less than 8 percent of DHS data center gross floor area (GFA), corrected their status to non-severable in the November 2018 IDC exempting them from closure and optimization requirements.

- Five DHS non-tiered agency owned data centers, representing less than 5 percent of DHS data center GFA will update their status to non-severable in the February 2018 IDC exempting them from closure and optimization requirements.

These corrections exempt all DHS agency owned data centers from DCOI closure and compliance requirements that are encompassed in this recommendation and OMB guidance, which apply only to agency owned data centers. Consequently, DHS is no longer required to close or optimize this very narrow and small percent of our overall data center GFA.

We request that GAO consider this recommendation resolved and closed as implemented.

# Appendix XI: Comments from the Department of the Interior

United States Department of the Interior
OFFICE OF THE SECRETARY
Washington, DC 20240

FEB 1 9 2019

Ms. Carol C. Harris
Director, Information Technology Acquisition
  Management Issues
U.S. Government Accountability Office
441 G Street, NW
Washington, DC 20548

Dear Ms. Harris:

Thank you for giving the Department of the Interior (Department) the opportunity to review and comment on the draft Government Accountability Office (GAO) report entitled, *Data Center Optimization: Additional Agency Actions Needed to Meet OMB Goals* (GAO-19-241). We appreciate GAO's review of data center optimization.

GAO issued several recommendations including three to the Department. Below is a summary of actions planned to implement the recommendations:

**Recommendation 12: The Secretary of the Interior should take action to meet the data center closure targets established under the Data Center Optimization Initiative (DCOI) by the Office of Management and Budget (OMB).**

Response: The Department partially concurs with recommendation 12. The Department exceeded OMB targets for "Tiered" data centers and applied cost-benefit and mission-need criteria to decide which non-tiered data centers to close. In November 2018, OMB published proposed changes to DCOI[1] policy that will result in new targets replacing the old targets. Therefore, the Department will adopt the new DCOI[2] policy and work through OMB to establish the new targets.

**Recommendation 13: The Secretary of the Interior should take action to meet the data center-related cost savings established under DCOI by OMB.**

Response: The Department does not concur with recommendation 13, because we recognize the existing guidance will soon be revised. In November 2018, OMB published proposed changes to DCOI policy that will result in new cost-savings goals replacing the old goals. Therefore, the

---

[1] OMB Published Proposed Changes to DCOI in November 2018, page 16 of GAO-19-241 Draft Report
[2] OMB, Data Center Optimization Initiative, accessed November 26, 2018, https://datacenters.cio.gov/policy/

Department will adopt the new DCOI policy and work through OMB to establish the new cost-savings goals once the new guidance becomes final.

**Recommendation 14: The Secretary of the Interior should take action to meet the data center optimization metric targets established under DCOI by OMB.**

Response: The Department does not concur with recommendation 14, because we recognize the existing guidance will soon be revised. In November 2018, OMB published proposed changes to DCOI policy that will result in revised metrics. Therefore, the Department will adopt the new DCOI policy and work through OMB to establish the metric targets once the new guidance becomes final.

Sincerely,

Scott J. Cameron
Principal Deputy Assistant Secretary
for Policy, Management and Budget

# APPENDIX XII: COMMENTS FROM THE DEPARTMENT OF HEALTH AND HUMAN SERVICES

DEPARTMENT OF HEALTH & HUMAN SERVICES

OFFICE OF THE SECRETARY

Assistant Secretary for Legislation
Washington, DC 20201

JAN 1 1 2019

Carol C. Harris
Director, Information Technology
  Acquisition Management Issues
U.S. Government Accountability Office
441 G Street NW
Washington, DC 20548

Dear Ms. Harris:

Attached are comments on the U.S. Government Accountability Office's (GAO) report entitled, *"Data Center Optimization: Additional Agency Actions Needed to Meet OMB Goals"* (GAO-19-241).

# Data Center Optimization

201

The Department appreciates the opportunity to review this report prior to publication.

Sincerely,

Matthew D. Bassett
Assistant Secretary for Legislation

## GENERAL COMMENTS FROM THE DEPARTMENT OF HEALTH & HUMAN SERVICES ON THE GOVERNMENT ACCOUNTABILITY OFFICE'S DRAFT REPORT ENTITLED – DATA CENTER OPTIMIZATION: ADDITIONAL AGENCY ACTIONS NEEDED TO MEET OMB GOALS (GAO-19-241)

The U.S. Department of Health & Human Services (HHS) appreciates the opportunity from the Government Accountability Office (GAO) to review and comment on this draft report.

### Recommendation 8
The Secretary of HHS should take action to meet the data center closure targets established under Data Center Optimization Initiative (DCOI) by the Office of Management and Budget (OMB).

### HHS Response
HHS non-concurs with GAO's recommendation.

While HHS did meet the tiered data center closure target under the previous DCOI closure targets, HHS does not concur with continuing to meet the expired requirements and looks forward to achieving the new targets proposed by OMB. As the old targets may no longer apply as intended, HHS would not be as prudent as possible with public funds expending resources to meet a prior measures that are no longer valid.

### Recommendation 9
The Secretary of HHS should take action to meet the data center optimization metric targets established under DCOI by OMB.

### HHS Response
HHS non-concurs with GAO's recommendation.

HHS does not concur with continuing to meet the expired requirements and looks forward to achieving the new targets proposed by OMB. As the old targets may no longer apply as intended, HHS would not be as prudent as possible with public funds expending resources to meet a prior measures that are no longer valid.

## APPENDIX XIII: COMMENTS FROM THE ENVIRONMENTAL PROTECTION AGENCY

UNITED STATES ENVIRONMENTAL PROTECTION AGENCY
WASHINGTON, D.C. 20460

MAR 0 5 2019

OFFICE OF
MISSION SUPPORT

Carol C. Harris
Director, Information Technology Acquisition Management Issues
U.S. Government Accountability Office
441 G St. NW
Washington, DC 20548

Dear Ms. Harris:

The Office of Mission Support (formerly the Office of Environmental Information (OEI)) reviewed the Final Report, GAO-19-241, *Data Center Optimization: Additional Agency Actions Needed to Meet OMB Goals* (102743). The purpose of this memorandum is to provide the Environmental Protection Agency's (EPA's) response to the report. In the Draft Report, GAO had two recommendations for the EPA.

**Recommendation 1**
GAO recommends that, "The Administrator of the Environmental Protection Agency should take action to meet the data center closure targets established under DCOI by OMB."

**Response:**
EPA has taken the steps necessary to meet data center closure targets as established in accordance with OMB Memorandum, M-16-19, *Data Center Optimization Initiative (DCOI)*. To date, EPA has successfully closed 21 out of the targeted 34 data centers. In November 2018, OMB released a draft memorandum establishing a new DCOI which will effectively rescind OMB M-16-19 and provide new guidelines to achieve targeted improvements in key optimization areas. EPA has reviewed and provided comments on the draft memorandum. In anticipation of the final release of the updated DCOI policy, EPA has started preparatory activities to achieve the updated DCOI requirements and work with OMB to formalize new targets for data center closures and other performance metrics. Given the anticipated release of OMB's new DCOI policy and EPA's current data center closure rate, EPA recommends this recommendation be closed.

## Recommendation 2

GAO recommends that, "The Administrator of EPA should take action to meet the data center optimization metric targets established under DCOI by OMB."

## Response:

EPA worked to achieve the data center optimization metrics in accordance with M-16-19 and successfully met or exceeded 3 of the 5 metrics (energy metering, PUE, and virtualization ratio). As referenced above, OMB is in the process of establishing a new DCOI. On review of this document, the data center optimization metrics will be defined by an agency which may result in metrics different from those outlined in M-16-19. EPA has already started preparatory activities to define data center optimization metrics and will work with OMB to formalize these metrics. Given the anticipated release of OMB's new DCOI policy and the change in the data center optimization metrics, EPA recommends this recommendation be closed.

Sincerely,

Vaughn Noga
Chief Information Officer
and Deputy Assistant Administrator for
Environmental Information

# APPENDIX XIV: COMMENTS FROM THE GENERAL SERVICES ADMINISTRATION

The Administrator

January 31, 2019

The Honorable Gene L. Dodaro
Comptroller General of the United States
U.S. Government Accountability Office
Washington, DC 20548

Dear Mr. Dodaro:

The U.S. General Services Administration (GSA) appreciates the opportunity to review and comment on the Government Accountability Office (GAO) draft report titled *Data Center Optimization: Additional Agency Actions Needed to Meet OMB Goals* (GAO-19-241).

There is one recommendation addressed to the Administrator of General Services:

- The Administrator of General Services should take action to meet the data center optimization metric targets established under the Data Center Optimization Initiative by the Office of Management and Budget (OMB) (Recommendation 27).

In November 2018, after data was provided for the draft report, OMB eliminated non-tiered data centers from the reporting requirements for the "Server Utilization and Automated Monitoring" metric, which was the only metric applicable to GSA. As a result, GSA no longer has a basis to measure and report on this metric. In light of this development, GSA respectfully requests that GAO consider withdrawing its recommendation.

Additionally, GSA respectfully requests correction to a typographical error in the draft report that overstates GSA's savings:

> On Page 27, Table 2, Column 3 ("Additional planned [savings] through 2018"), the report reflects that GSA's additional planned savings was $8.04 million. However, in August 2018, GSA reported its achieved savings as $7.37 million and its additional planned savings as $0.67 million. It appears that GAO may have mistakenly added these two figures and used the sum ($8.04 million) as GSA's additional planned savings. Column 3 of this table should be revised to reflect that GSA's additional planned savings is $0.67 million. This also necessitates a change to Column 4 ("Difference between OMB target and agencies' planned and achieved savings"), from $7.06 million to $0.31 million.
>
> Based on the figures reported in August, GSA's total achieved and planned savings would have been $8.04 million, which is below the $8.35 million goal assigned by OMB. However, by the end of FY 2018, GSA exceeded its
>
>> additional planned savings amount, and actually saved $1.44 million. This brings GSA's actual total savings to $8.81 million, which exceeds the assigned goal.

Sincerely,

Emily W. Murphy
Administrator

# APPENDIX XV: COMMENTS FROM THE NATIONAL SCIENCE FOUNDATION

National Science Foundation
Office of the Chief Information Officer

February 15, 2019

Ms. Carol Harris
Director, Information Technology Management Issues
U.S. Government Accountability Office
441 G St., NW
Washington DC 20226

Ms. Carol Harris
Director, Information Technology Management Issues
U.S. Government Accountability Office
441 G St., NW
Washington DC 20226

Dear Ms. Harris:

Thank you for the opportunity to review and comment on the Government Accountability Office (GAO) draft report entitled *Data Center Optimization: Additional Agency Actions Needed to Meet OMB Goals (GAO-19-241)*. Our response to your recommendation is provided below.

**Recommendation 29:** "The Director of NSF should take action to meet the data center optimization metric targets established under DCOI by OMB."

**NSF RESPONSE:** As identified in GAO's report, NSF has addressed all five required elements of a strategic plan for data center optimization as identified by the Office of Management and Budget (OMB), and has met three of five metric targets established under the Data Center Optimization Initiative (DCOI) by OMB. Understanding that OMB is planning to develop new guidance and metrics for data center optimization metrics, NSF will continue to work with OMB to update savings and closure targets appropriate to mission and budget with consideration to overall agency status and progress on data center optimization efforts.

Sincerely,

Dorothy Aronson
Chief Information Officer

# APPENDIX XVI: COMMENTS FROM THE NUCLEAR REGULATORY COMMISSION

UNITED STATES
NUCLEAR REGULATORY COMMISSION
WASHINGTON, D.C. 20555-0001

January 7, 2019

Ms. Carol C. Harris, Director
Information Technology Acquisition Management Issues
U.S. Government Accountability Office
441 G Street, NW
Washington, D.C. 20548

Dear Ms. Harris:

Thank you for giving the U.S. Nuclear Regulatory Commission (NRC) the opportunity to review and comment on the U.S. Government Accountability Office's (GAO) draft report GAO-19-0241, "Data Center Optimization: Additional Agencies Actions Needed to Meet OMB Goals." The NRC has reviewed the draft report, is in general agreement with it, and does not have any comments.

Sincerely,

Margaret M. Doane
Executive Director
for Operations

# APPENDIX XVII: COMMENTS FROM THE U.S. AGENCY FOR INTERNATIONAL DEVELOPMENT

Carol C. Harris
Director
Information Technology Acquisition Management Issues
U.S. Government Accountability Office
441 G Street, N.W.
Washington, DC 20226

FEB 1 5 2019

Re: DATA CENTER OPTIMIZATION: Additional Agency Actions Needed to Meet OMB Goals (GAO-19-241)

Dear Ms. Harris:

I am pleased to provide the formal response of the U. S. Agency for International Development (USAID) to the draft report produced by the U.S. Government Accountability Office (GAO) entitled, *"DATA CENTER OPTIMIZATION: Additional Agency Actions Needed to Meet OMB Goals"* (GAO-19-241).

USAID is committed to supporting improvements in the efficiency, performance, and the environmental footprint of Federal data centers. The GAO acknowledges this commitment in the text of the draft report by recognizing that USAID is one of only two Federal Departments or Agencies that reported a plan to meet fully their applicable targets under the Data Center Optimization Initiative (DCOI) established by the Office of Management and Budget (OMB) for the end of Fiscal Year 2018. Accordingly, USAID has complied with its DCOI targets, and closed all four of the Agency's data centers. USAID appreciates this opportunity to provide documentation of its compliance with OMB's goals, and our implementation of the one recommendation the GAO issued to USAID in the draft report.

# Data Center Optimization

I am transmitting this letter and the enclosed comments from USAID for inclusion in the GAO's final report. Thank you for the opportunity to respond to the draft report, and for the courtesies extended by your staff while conducting this engagement. We appreciate the opportunity to participate in the complete and thorough evaluation of the management of our responsibilities under the DCOI.

Sincerely,

Angelique M. Crumbly
Acting Assistant Administrator
Bureau for Management

**COMMENTS BY THE U. S. AGENCY FOR INTERNATIONAL DEVELOPMENT ON THE DRAFT REPORT PRODUCED BY THE U. S. GOVERNMENT ACCOUNTABILITY OFFICE (GAO) ENTITLED, *DATA CENTER OPTIMIZATION: Additional Agency Actions Needed to Meet OMB Goals* (GAO-19-241)**

The U.S. Agency for International Development (USAID) would like to thank the U.S. Government Accountability Office (GAO) for the opportunity to respond to this draft report. We appreciate the extensive work of the GAO's engagement team, and the specific finding that will help USAID achieve greater effectiveness in managing our information-technology (IT) resources.

USAID has committed to meet established Federal goals for reducing the number of data centers; lowering the cost of the IT hardware and software for, and the operations of, data centers; increasing the overall IT-security posture of the Federal Government; and shifting IT investments to more efficient computing platforms and technologies.

As noted in the GAO draft report, USAID does not have any tiered data centers. Therefore, the Agency focused on plans to meet the one optimization metric established by the Office of Management and Budget (OMB) applicable to our non-tiered data centers (the utilization of servers, and automated monitoring).

The report contains one recommendation for USAID:

*The Administrator of USAID should take action to meet the data center closure targets established under the Data Center Optimization Initiative (DCOI) by OMB.*

USAID has met OMB's targets for closing data centers established under DCOI. USAID's specific goal under DCOI was to close its four data centers, and the Agency has accordingly done so according to the following schedule:

**Data Center 1:** closed in the Second Quarter of Fiscal Year (FY) 2017;
**Data Center 2:** closed in the Third Quarter of FY 2018;
**Data Center 3:** closed in the Third Quarter of FY 2018; and
**Data Center 4:** closed in the Third Quarter of FY 2018.

USAID is submitting its encrypted DCOI submission for the Fourth Quarter of FY 2018, which indicates and documents the closures of the data centers. USAID has submitted its updated DCOI strategic plan to OMB's IT Dashboard on December 21, 2018 to reflect our compliance with the closure target. USAID requests that GAO close this recommendation upon issuance of the final report.

In: Key Government Reports. Volume 17    ISBN: 978-1-53616-003-1
Editor: Ernest Clark    © 2019 Nova Science Publishers, Inc.

*Chapter 4*

# INFORMATION TECHNOLOGY: EFFECTIVE PRACTICES HAVE IMPROVED AGENCIES' FITARA IMPLEMENTATION[*]

*United States Government Accountability Office*

### ABBREVIATIONS

| | |
|---|---|
| CIO | chief information officer |
| Commerce | Department of Commerce |
| DHS | Department of Homeland Security |
| FITARA | Federal Information Technology Acquisition Reform Act |
| GSA | General Services Administration |
| HHS | Department of Health and Human Services |
| IT | information technology |
| Justice | Department of Justice |
| NASA | National Aeronautics and Space Administration |

---

[*] This is an edited, reformatted and augmented version of United States Government Accountability Office; Report to Congressional Requesters, Publication No. GAO-19-131, dated April 29, 2019.

210      *United States Government Accountability Office*

OMB      Office of Management and Budget
USAID     U.S. Agency for International Development
USDA     Department of Agriculture
VA       Department of Veterans Affairs

# WHY GAO DID THIS STUDY

Congress has long recognized that IT has the potential to enable federal agencies to accomplish their missions more quickly, effectively, and economically. However, fully exploiting this potential has presented challenges to covered agencies, and the federal government's management of IT has produced mixed results.

As part of its effort to reform the government-wide management of IT, in December 2014 Congress enacted FITARA. The law included specific requirements related to enhancing Chief Information Officers' (CIO) authorities, improving the risk management of IT investments, reviewing agencies' portfolio of IT investments, consolidating federal data centers, and purchasing software licenses. GAO has reported numerous times on agencies' effectiveness in implementing the provisions of the law and highlighted agencies that have had success in implementing selected provisions.

In this chapter, GAO identifies practices that agencies have used to effectively implement FITARA. GAO selected five provisions of FITARA to review: (1) CIO authority enhancements; (2) enhanced transparency and improved risk management; (3) portfolio review; (4) data center consolidation; and (5) software purchasing. GAO then selected nine agencies that had success in implementing at least one of the five provisions. GAO compiled practices where at least one agency was better positioned to implement a provision or realized an IT management improvement or cost savings.

# WHAT GAO FOUND

Nine selected agencies (the Departments of Agriculture, Commerce, Health and Human Services, Homeland Security, Justice, and Veterans Affairs; the Agency for International Development; the National Aeronautics and Space Administration; and the General Services Administration) identified 12 practices that helped them to effectively implement one or more Federal Information Technology Acquisition Reform Act provisions (commonly referred to as FITARA). The following figure identifies the 12 practices, including the four overarching ones, considered vital to implementing all provisions.

By applying the overarching practices, covered agencies were better positioned to implement FITARA. In addition, by implementing the practices relative to the five FITARA provisions GAO selected, covered agencies realized information technology (IT) management improvements, such as decommissioning old systems and cost savings.

April 29, 2019
Congressional Requesters:

Congress has long recognized that information technology (IT) has the potential to enable federal agencies to accomplish their missions more quickly, effectively, and economically. However, fully achieving this potential has presented longstanding challenges to agencies. In this regard, the federal government's management of IT has produced mixed results despite a continued increase in federal IT spending, which is planned to be more than $92 billion in fiscal year 2019.

As part of its effort to reform the government-wide management of IT, in December 2014, Congress enacted the Federal Information Technology Acquisition Reform provisions (commonly referred to as FITARA) of the *Carl Levin and Howard P. 'Buck' McKeon National Defense Authorization*

212     *United States Government Accountability Office*

*Act for Fiscal Year 2015.*[1] FITARA holds promise for improving covered agencies' management and acquisitions of IT, facilitating Congress' monitoring of agencies' progress, and holding those agencies accountable for reducing duplication and achieving cost savings.

Since its enactment, we have reported numerous times on agencies' efforts toward implementing FITARA. Our work has highlighted various agencies' successes, as well as challenges, in implementing selected provisions of the act.[2]

This chapter responds to your request that we conduct a review of FITARA implementation practices. Our specific objective was to identify practices that federal agencies have used to effectively implement the provisions of the act.

To address this objective, we first identified the specific provisions of the act to include in our review. To do so, we (1) reviewed our previously issued reports that have examined various aspects of the act;[3] (2) met with relevant officials from the Office of Management and Budget's (OMB) Office of Electronic Government and Information Technology; and (3) reviewed data contained on the IT Dashboard,[4] as well as other relevant

---

[1] *Carl Levin and Howard P. 'Buck' McKeon National Defense Authorization Act for Fiscal Year 2015*, Pub. L. No. 113-291, division A, title VIII, subtitle D, 128 Stat. 3292, 3438-50 (Dec. 19, 2014).

[2] GAO, *Information Technology: Additional OMB and Agency Actions Needed to Ensure Portfolio Savings Are Realized and Effectively Tracked,* GAO-15-296 (Washington, D.C.: Apr. 16, 2015); *IT Dashboard: Agencies Need to Fully Consider Risks When Rating Their Major Investments,* GAO-16-494 (Washington, D.C.: June 2, 2016); *Information Technology Reform: Agencies Need to Increase Their Use of Incremental Development Practices,* GAO-16-469 (Washington, D.C.: Aug. 16, 2016); *Information Technology: Agencies Need to Improve Their Application Inventories to Achieve Additional Savings,* GAO-16-511 (Washington, D.C.: Sept. 29, 2016); *Information Technology Reform: Agencies Need to Improve Certification of Incremental Development,* GAO-18-148 (Washington, D.C.: Nov. 7, 2017); and *Data Center Optimization: Continued Agency Actions Needed to Meet Goals and Address Prior Recommendations*, GAO-18-264 (Washington, D.C.: May 23, 2018).

[3] GAO-15-296, GAO-16-494, GAO-16-469, GAO-16-511, GAO-18-148, GAO-18-264.

[4] The IT Dashboard is OMB's public website that reports performance and supporting data for major IT investments. Major IT investment means a system or an acquisition requiring special management attention because it has significant importance to the mission or function of the government; significant program or policy implications; high executive visibility; high development, operating, or maintenance costs; an unusual funding mechanism; or is defined as major by the agency's capital planning and investment control process.

information supporting the House of Representatives Committee on Oversight and Government Reform's biannual scorecards on the 24 covered agencies' progress in addressing the act's requirements.[5]

As a result of these activities, combined with our professional judgment, we identified five FITARA provisions that were most relevant to enabling agencies' IT management improvements. These provisions were: Chief Information Officer (CIO) authority enhancements, enhanced transparency and improved risk management in IT investments, portfolio review, the federal data center consolidation initiative, and the government-wide software purchasing program.

We then identified nine agencies that had implemented at least one of the five FITARA provisions we included in our review. Our identification of the nine agencies was based on information in our previous reports that indicated each agency had realized an IT management improvement or cost savings with respect to one or more of the five selected FITARA provisions. Additionally, we considered other relevant information supporting the House of Representatives Committee on Oversight and Government Reform's scorecards that indicated an agency had effectively implemented FITARA. These nine agencies were the Departments of Agriculture (USDA), Commerce (Commerce), Health and Human Services (HHS), Homeland Security (DHS), Justice (Justice), and Veterans Affairs (VA); and the Agency for International Development (USAID); the National Aeronautics and Space Administration (NASA); and the General Services Administration (GSA).

---

[5] Beginning in November 2015, the House of Representatives Committee on Oversight and Government Reform released its first FITARA scorecard that assigned letter grades to federal agencies on their implementation of FITARA. Additionally, the term "covered agency" refers to the 24 major agencies listed in the Chief Financial Officers Act of 1990. 31 U.S.C. § 901(b). The agencies are the Departments of Agriculture, Commerce, Defense, Education, Energy, Health and Human Services, Homeland Security, Housing and Urban Development, the Interior, Justice, Labor, State, Transportation, the Treasury, and Veterans Affairs; the Environmental Protection Agency; General Services Administration; National Aeronautics and Space Administration; National Science Foundation; U.S. Nuclear Regulatory Commission; Office of Personnel Management; Small Business Administration; Social Security Administration; and U.S. Agency for International Development.

214 *United States Government Accountability Office*

These nine agencies account for about $27 billion (or about 59 percent) of the $45.8 billion in estimated non-defense IT spending for fiscal year 2019.

To gain additional information on the nine agencies' FITARA implementation, we obtained and reviewed relevant documentation, such as FITARA implementation plans, capital planning and investment control processes, data center optimization plans, and software licensing policies. Additionally, we conducted interviews with relevant officials at these agencies to discuss actions taken to implement the provisions of the act. These officials included a FITARA Program Manager, a Director of FITARA Operations, and staff within department-level CIO offices responsible for implementing the provisions of the act.

We compiled practices where at least one agency had taken action to implement one of the five selected provisions that led to an IT management improvement or cost savings. We then compiled descriptions of the actions that the nine agencies had taken. Additionally, we reviewed actions the agencies have taken in response to our previous recommendations to corroborate the IT management improvements and cost savings. Agencies also identified overarching practices that were not unique to a specific provision but, instead, better positioned agencies to implement one or more of the five provisions. Further, we shared the practices with the nine agencies' Inspectors General to provide additional assurance that the practices were consistent with the agencies' activities to address FITARA. In addition, we solicited comments on a draft of this chapter from the nine agencies included in our review and OMB.

We conducted this performance audit from January 2018 to April 2019 in accordance with generally accepted government auditing standards.

Those standards require that we plan and perform the audit to obtain sufficient, appropriate evidence to provide a reasonable basis for our findings and conclusions based on our audit objectives. We believe that the evidence obtained provides a reasonable basis for our findings and conclusions based on our audit objective.

# BACKGROUND

Although the federal government has undertaken numerous initiatives to better manage the billions of dollars that federal agencies annually invest in IT, these investments too frequently fail or incur cost overruns and schedule slippages, while contributing little to mission-related outcomes. We have previously reported that the federal government has spent billions of dollars on failed IT investments.[6] These investments often suffered from a lack of disciplined and effective management, such as project planning, requirements definition, and program oversight and governance. As a result of these failures, we added *Improving the Management of IT Acquisitions and Operations* to our biennial high-risk list in 2015.[7]

With its enactment in 2014, FITARA was also intended to improve agencies' acquisitions of IT and facilitate Congress' efforts to monitor agencies' progress and hold them accountable for reducing duplication and achieving cost savings.[8] The act included specific provisions related to seven areas, including the five areas selected for our review:[9]

- CIO authority enhancements—Covered agencies' CIOs are required to (1) approve the IT budget requests of their respective agencies, (2) certify that agencies' IT investments are adequately implementing OMB's incremental development guidance, (3) review and approve contracts for IT, and (4) approve the

---

[6] GAO, *Information Technology: OMB and Agencies Need to More Effectively Implement Major Initiatives to Save Billions of Dollars*, GAO-13-796T (Washington, D.C.: July 25, 2013).

[7] See GAO, *High Risk Series: An Update*, GAO-15-290 (Washington, D.C.: Feb. 11, 2015) and subsequent report, GAO, *High-Risk Series: Progress on Many High-Risk Areas, While Substantial Efforts Needed on Others*, GAO-17-317 (Washington, D.C.: Feb. 15, 2017).

[8] FITARA's provisions apply to covered agencies, defined in the statute as the agencies listed in the Chief Financial Officers Act. Pub. L. No. 113-291, § 831, 128 Stat. 3438 (2014), referring to 31 U.S.C. § 901.

[9] The two provisions of FITARA that we did not include in our scope were the expansion of training and use of IT cadres and maximizing the benefit of the federal strategic sourcing initiative.

appointment of other agency employees with the title of CIO (e.g., component agency CIOs).[10]

- Enhanced transparency and improved risk management in IT investments—OMB and covered agencies are to make detailed information on federal IT investments publicly available, and department-level CIOs are to categorize their major IT investments by risk.[11] Additionally, in the case of major investments rated as high risk for 4 consecutive quarters,[12] the act required that the department-level CIO and the investment's program manager conduct a review aimed at identifying and addressing the causes of the risk.

- Portfolio review—OMB and the CIOs of covered agencies are to implement a process to assist agencies in reviewing their portfolios of IT investments. This review process is intended to, among other things, identify or develop opportunities to consolidate the acquisition and management of IT services; identify potential duplication, waste, and cost savings; develop a multi-year strategy to identify and reduce duplication and waste within the agencies' portfolios, including component agency investments, and to identify projected cost savings resulting from such a strategy.

- Federal data center consolidation initiative—Agencies are required to provide OMB with a data center inventory, a strategy for consolidating and optimizing the data centers (to include planned cost savings), and quarterly updates on progress made. The act also requires OMB to develop a goal for how much is to be saved through this initiative, and provide annual reports on cost savings achieved.

---

[10] Federal agencies with component agencies typically have one CIO at the federal agency level (i.e., department-level) and may have an official with the title of CIO within each component agency.

[11] "Major IT investment" means a system or an acquisition requiring special management attention because it has significant importance to the mission or function of the government; significant program or policy implications; high executive visibility; high development, operating, or maintenance costs; an unusual funding mechanism; or is defined as major by the agency's capital planning and investment control process.

[12] The IT Dashboard lists the CIO-reported risk level of all major IT investments at federal agencies on a quarterly basis.

*Information Technology* 217

- Government-wide software purchasing program—GSA is to develop a strategic sourcing initiative to enhance government-wide acquisition and management of software. In doing so, the law states that, to the maximum extent practicable, GSA should allow for the purchase of a software license agreement that is available for use by all executive branch agencies as a single user.[13]

## GAO Has Previously Reported on Agencies' FITARA Implementation and Identified Areas for Improvement

We have issued a number of reports that have identified actions that OMB and federal agencies needed to take to improve their implementation of the FITARA provisions.

### *CIO Authority Enhancements*

In reporting on incremental software development in November 2017, we noted that department-level CIOs certified only 62 percent of major IT software development investments as implementing adequate incremental development in fiscal year 2017.[14] Officials from 21 of the 24 agencies in our review reported that challenges had hindered their CIOs' ability to implement incremental development. These challenges included: (1) inefficient governance processes; (2) procurement delays; and (3) organizational changes associated with transitioning from a traditional software methodology that takes years to deliver a product, to incremental development, which delivers products in shorter time frames. We made recommendations to department-level CIOs to improve reporting accuracy and update or establish certification policies. As of February 2019, agencies had taken steps to address eight of the 19 recommendations.

---

[13] The "Making Electronic Government Accountable By Yielding Tangible Efficiencies Act of 2016" (known as the "MEGABYTE Act") subsequently required OMB to issue a directive to every executive agency CIO to, among other things, establish a comprehensive, regularly updated inventory of software licenses and analyze software usage to make cost-effective decisions.

[14] GAO-18-148.

218        *United States Government Accountability Office*

Additionally, our August 2018 report on department-level CIOs noted that none of the 24 agencies had policies that fully addressed the role of their CIOs consistent with federal laws and guidance, including FITARA.[15] In addition, the majority of the agencies had not fully addressed the roles of their CIOs for any of six key areas that we identified. Although officials from most agencies stated that their CIOs were implementing the responsibilities even when not addressed in policy, the 24 CIOs acknowledged in a survey that they were not always very effective in implementing all of their responsibilities.

Further, the shortcomings in agencies' policies were attributable, at least in part, to incomplete guidance from OMB. We noted that, until OMB improved its guidance to clearly address all CIO responsibilities, and agencies fully addressed the role of CIOs in their policies, CIOs would be limited in effectively managing IT and addressing long-standing management challenges. We made 27 recommendations for agencies to improve the effectiveness of CIOs' implementation of their responsibilities. Most agencies agreed with the recommendations and described actions they planned to take to address them.

### *Enhanced Transparency and Improved Risk Management*

In June 2016, we reported on rating the risk of IT investments and noted that agencies underreported the risk of almost two-thirds of the investments their CIOs reviewed.[16] All 17 selected agencies incorporated at least two of OMB's factors into their risk rating processes and nine used all of the factors, interpreted differently, less often than on a monthly basis. Our assessments generally showed more risk than the associated CIO ratings.

We also issued a series of reports about the IT Dashboard that noted concerns about the accuracy and reliability of the data on the Dashboard. In total, we have made 25 recommendations to OMB and federal agencies

---

[15] GAO, *Federal Chief Information Officers: Critical Actions Needed to Address Shortcomings and Challenges in Implementing Responsibilities,* GAO-18-93 (Washington, D.C.: Aug. 2, 2018).

[16] GAO-16-494.

# Information Technology 219

to help improve the accuracy and reliability of the information on the Dashboard and to increase its availability. Most agencies agreed with the recommendations or had no comments. As of February 2019, 11 of these recommendations remained open.

## *Portfolio Review*

In April 2015, we reported on actions needed by 26 federal agencies to ensure portfolio savings were realized and tracked. We noted that these agencies had decreased their planned PortfolioStat[17] savings by at least 68 percent from what they reported to us in 2013.[18] Specifically, while the agencies initially had planned to save at least $5.8 billion between fiscal years 2013 and 2015, these estimates were decreased to approximately $2 billion. We made recommendations to OMB and the Department of Defense aimed at improving the reporting of achieved savings, documenting how savings are reinvested, and establishing time frames for PortfolioStat action items. As of February 2019, OMB had addressed one of the five recommendations.

Our September 2016 report on application inventories noted that most of the 24 agencies in the review fully met at least three of the four practices we identified to determine if agencies had complete software application inventories.[19] Additionally, six of the agencies relied on their investment management processes and, in some cases, supplemental processes to rationalize their applications to varying degrees. However, five of the six agencies acknowledged that their processes did not always allow for collecting or reviewing the information needed to effectively rationalize all their applications. We made recommendations that 20 agencies improve their inventories and five of the agencies take actions to improve their processes to rationalize their applications more completely. Agencies had addressed four of the 25 recommendations as of February 2019.

---

[17] In March 2012, OMB launched PortfolioStat, which required agencies to conduct annual reviews of their IT investments and make decisions on eliminating duplication, among other things. In March 2013, OMB launched the second iteration of PortfolioStat with the goal of eliminating duplication and achieving savings through specific actions and time frames.

[18] GAO-15-296.

[19] GAO-16-511.

220      *United States Government Accountability Office*

### Federal Data Center Consolidation Initiative

We have reported annually on agencies' efforts to meet FITARA requirements related to the federal data center consolidation initiative. For example, in March 2016 we reported that, as of November 2015, the 24 agencies participating in the initiative had identified a total of 10,584 data centers, of which they reported closing 3,125 through fiscal year 2015.[20] In total, 19 of the 24 agencies reported achieving an estimated $2.8 billion in cost savings and avoidances from fiscal years 2011 to 2015.[21] We recommended that 10 agencies take action to address challenges in establishing, and to complete, planned data center cost savings and avoidance targets. We also recommended that 22 agencies take action to improve optimization progress, including addressing any identified challenges. As of February 2019, agencies had addressed 14 of our 32 recommendations.

Our May 2018 report on data center consolidation noted mixed progress toward achieving OMB's goals for closing data centers by September 2018.[22] Over half of the agencies reported that they had either already met, or planned to meet, all of their OMB-assigned goals by the deadline. This was expected to result in the closure of 7,221 of the 12,062 centers that agencies reported in August 2017. However, four agencies reported that they did not have plans to meet all of their assigned goals and two agencies were working with OMB to establish revised targets. No new recommendations were made to agencies in this chapter because agencies had yet to fully address our previous recommendations.

### Government-Wide Software Purchasing Program

In May 2014, we reported on 24 federal agencies' management of software licenses and the potential for achieving significant savings

---

[20] GAO, *Data Center Consolidation: Agencies Making Progress, but Planned Savings Goals Need to Be Established*, GAO-16-323 (Washington, D.C.: Mar. 3, 2016).

[21] Consistent with OMB Circular A-131, the term cost savings refers to a reduction in actual expenditures below the projected level of costs to achieve a specific objective and the term cost avoidance refers to an action taken in the immediate time frame that will decrease costs in the future.

[22] GAO-18-264.

Information Technology 221

government-wide.[23] Specifically, we found that OMB and the vast majority of the 24 agencies reviewed did not have adequate policies for managing software licenses. We also reported that federal agencies were not adequately managing their software licenses because they generally did not follow leading practices in this area. Consequently, we could not accurately describe the most widely used software applications across the government, including the extent to which they were over and under purchased. We recommended that the 24 agencies improve their policies and practices for managing licenses. Most agencies generally agreed with the recommendations or had no comments.

We then reported in September 2014 that the 24 agencies had either provided a plan to address most of the recommendations we made to them, partially disagreed with the report's prior findings, or did not provide information on their efforts to address the recommendations.[24] As of February 2019, the agencies had addressed 109 of the 136 recommendations.

## SELECTED AGENCIES IDENTIFIED PRACTICES THAT FACILITATED EFFECTIVE IMPLEMENTATION OF FITARA PROVISIONS

The nine selected agencies identified a total of 12 practices that helped them to successfully implement the FITARA provisions considered in our review. Among the practices, a number of the agencies identified four that were overarching—that is, the practices were not unique to a specific provision, but, instead, better positioned agencies to implement the five provisions selected for our review. In addition, agencies identified

---

[23] GAO, *Federal Software Licenses: Better Management Needed to Achieve Significant Savings Government-Wide*, GAO-14-413 (Washington, D.C.: May 22, 2014).

[24] GAO, *Most Agencies Have Reported Planned Actions to Address Our Prior Recommendations on Software License Management*, GAO-14-835R (Washington, D.C.: Sept. 23, 2014).

- one practice that helped ensure effective implementation of CIO authority enhancements,
- one practice that helped ensure enhanced transparency and improved risk management,
- one practice that ensured effective portfolio review,
- four practices that facilitated data center consolidation, and
- one practice that facilitated software purchasing.

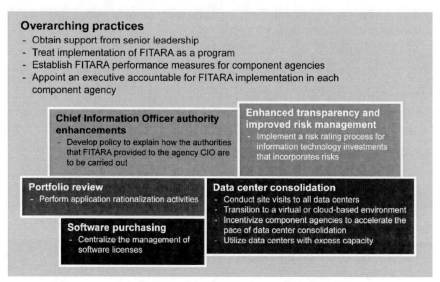

Source: GAO analysis of agency-provided information. | GAO-19-131.

Figure 1. Practices that Selected Agencies Used to Effectively Implement Key Provisions of the Federal Information Technology Acquisition Reform Act (FITARA).

Figure 1 identifies the 12 practices that the nine agencies used to effectively implement the selected FITARA provisions. In addition, the narrative following the figure provides details on how these agencies implemented the provisions and realized associated IT management improvements or cost savings.

## Information Technology

223

## Overarching Practices Vital to Implementing FITARA

Four of the nine agencies that we reviewed—Commerce, HHS, NASA, and USDA—identified one or more overarching practices that have been vital to their efforts in implementing FITARA:

- obtain support from senior leadership,
- treat the implementation of FITARA as a program,
- establish FITARA performance measures for component agencies, and
- appoint an executive accountable for FITARA implementation in each component agency.

As a result of implementing these practices, each of the agencies was better positioned to implement FITARA.

### *Obtain Support from Senior Leadership*

Three of the agencies—USDA, NASA, and Commerce—emphasized that the support of senior leadership was essential to implementing requirements in FITARA. This support was demonstrated, for example, by senior officials highlighting the act's importance during key executive-level meetings and in their key memorandums and other communications to the agencies' workforce. We have previously reported that having senior leadership support is critical to the success of major programs.[25]

According to USDA's Director of FITARA Operations, the agency made a decision to raise the topic of FITARA implementation at each monthly executive leadership meeting that is attended by the Deputy Secretary, Chief Operating Officer, and Assistant Secretary for Administration, in order to keep attention focused on the act's implementation. In addition, the agency's October 2016, Concept of Operations for *The Oversight, Management, and Operations of FITARA*

---

[25] GAO, *Information Technology: Critical Factors Underlying Successful Major Acquisitions*, GAO-12-7 (Washington, D.C.: Oct. 21, 2011).

224      *United States Government Accountability Office*

document, which is the primary document used by the agency to assist with the implementation and execution of the act, was signed by the Deputy Secretary, CIO, and Deputy CIO. The officials reported that obtaining support from senior leadership had helped ensure buy-in to changes resulting from implementing provisions of the act.

NASA officials also highlighted senior leadership support as being essential to their actions to implement FITARA. For example, the NASA Deputy Administrator and Associate Administrator for Mission Support signed and distributed a memorandum in August 2010 that emphasized the agency's commitment to the data center consolidation effort.[26] The memorandum stated that Mission Directorate Associate Administrators and Center Directors shall direct their staff to cooperate fully and openly with NASA's data center consolidation plan. An official in the Office of the CIO stated that the memorandum was evidence of the support the agency had from senior leadership to close data centers.

Further, a Commerce official stated that FITARA implementation activities at the agency have had support from agency leadership, including the Deputy Secretary and the CIO. For example, according to the official, the Deputy Secretary provided each of the component agency FITARA sponsors with a signed memorandum asking for assistance from the components. This action resulted in increased cooperation throughout the agency when components were asked to respond to FITARA-related requests for information.

### *Treat Implementation of FITARA as a Program*

Commerce and USDA reported that treating FITARA implementation as if it were an IT program was important to implementing the requirements of the act. The two agencies demonstrated this practice by assigning staff to manage implementation of FITARA and regularly discussing implementation of the act at meetings with senior-level officials.

---

[26] National Aeronautics and Space Administration, *Implementation of the Federal Data Center Consolidation Initiative*, (Aug. 2, 2010).

*Information Technology* 225

According to a Commerce lessons learned document, the agency has managed FITARA like a program by reporting regularly on its implementation status to internal agency stakeholders. In addition, the agency has assigned a program manager to assist with implementation of the act and to track progress on implementing the act's provisions. As a result, Commerce officials reported that the importance of FITARA has been regularly discussed throughout the agency in bi-weekly meetings within the Office of the Secretary. These meetings led to an increased sense of cooperation between different disciplines (e.g., IT, budget, acquisition, legal, and human resources) and reduced the impression that FITARA was solely focused on the department-level CIO office.

Further, USDA created the position of Executive Director for FITARA Operations within the department-level CIO office. This position has responsibility for, among other things, establishing the processes and procedures to bring the agency into compliance with the act and IT management controls that meet the FITARA requirements. The Director stated that treating the implementation of FITARA as if it were an IT program has led the agency to develop key documentation that has assisted in the implementation of the act, including its *Concept of Operations for the Oversight, Management, and Operations of FITARA and Data Center Closure Process.*

### Establish FITARA Performance Measures for Component Agencies

HHS established internal FITARA performance measures for its component agencies that officials believe have led to increased effectiveness in implementing the act. Specifically, the agency undertook an effort to increase its FITARA scorecard grades—called "A by May"—with a goal to attain an 'A' on the May 2018 FITARA 6.0 scorecard. As part of this effort, HHS created its own internal scorecard for each of its component agencies that mirrored the agency's FITARA scorecard.

According to an HHS lessons learned document, aligning the FITARA metrics to component agency performance resulted in greater transparency between the department-level CIO and component agency CIOs. The effort to establish internal performance measures received support from senior

226 *United States Government Accountability Office*

agency leadership. Specifically, it was endorsed by the Assistant Secretary for Administration and the Principal Deputy for Administration, which agency officials believed was a key factor in the effort's success.

HHS officials also reported that their internal scorecard was helpful because it let component agencies know how well they were doing relative to each other. The officials also believed that establishing FITARA performance measures led to increased cooperation and communication between component agencies and the department-level CIO office. For example, the increased cooperation allowed HHS to more easily collect data required to update the House Committee on Oversight and Government Reform's FITARA scorecard.

At the December 2018 House Committee on Oversight and Government Reform hearing on FITARA, the HHS Acting CIO attributed the agency's increased scorecard grade—from a 'D' on the initial November 2015 scorecard to a 'B+' on the December 2018 scorecard—to the "A by May" initiative. According to this official, the measurement of component agencies' performance had elevated the importance of meeting FITARA objectives and paved the way for agency-wide participation in improvement efforts.

### *Appoint an Executive Accountable for FITARA Implementation in Each Component Agency*

According to a Commerce memorandum, the Assistant Secretary for Administration asked each component agency to identify a FITARA executive sponsor. The sponsors were assigned responsibility for gathering the necessary information on component agencies' efforts to implement FITARA and for alerting the agency's CIO of any issues that needed to be addressed. Once the sponsors were identified, the Commerce Deputy Secretary sent a letter to each sponsor, asking them to help ensure cooperation between their component agencies and the department's CIO office. A Commerce official reported that having a sponsor in component agencies with responsibility for providing the information needed to report on FITARA results to the department's CIO office had increased

*Information Technology* 227

component agencies' responsiveness to information requests and improved cooperation throughout the agency.

## CIO Authority Enhancements

Commerce and DHS developed policies to explain how the specific authorities that FITARA provided to the agency CIO are to be carried out. The agencies identified the policies as essential to their ability to implement the CIO authority enhancements provision in FITARA. Commerce officials stated, for example, that their agency established a policy to ensure that the CIO certified major IT investments as adequately implementing incremental development. Specifically, Commerce's capital planning guidance required component agency CIOs or other accountable officials within the component agencies to certify the adequate implementation of incremental development for these investments. Commerce's guidance described the role of the CIO in the certification process and how the CIOs' certification should be documented. The guidance also included definitions of incremental development and time frames for delivering functionality. Officials in Commerce's Office of the CIO reported that the certification policies assisted them in overseeing the management of IT investments and ensuring the use of incremental development throughout the agency, as called for by FITARA.

Also, Commerce changed its personnel policy to require the department-level CIO to approve all senior level IT positions, which addressed the FITARA requirement for the CIO to approve the appointment of other staff with the title of CIO (e.g., component agency CIOs). Specifically, in February 2016, Commerce developed a new human capital policy to give its department-level CIO input into the hiring of all senior level IT positions, including component CIOs. As a result, a Commerce official reported that the policy ensures that the CIOs' authority has been enhanced to include significant involvement in the hiring of IT leaders throughout the agency.

228     *United States Government Accountability Office*

For its part, DHS established a policy to ensure that the department-level CIO certified major IT investments as adequately implementing incremental development. Specifically, DHS's technical investment review guidance states that the CIO is to conduct a review of each investment using an investment review checklist that includes information provided by project managers as to whether the investments have used incremental development adequately. The CIO is to certify whether the project is implementing incremental delivery at least every 6 months and is to document this certification in the checklist. As a result, officials in DHS's Office of the CIO said that they can now use information from the incremental certification checklist to improve incremental development processes and to make corrections to projects that were not adequately implementing incremental development.

## Enhanced Transparency and Improved Risk Management

Three agencies—Commerce, DHS, and USDA—identified one practice that was key to their effective implementation of the enhanced transparency and improved risk management provision of FITARA. The practice is to implement a risk rating process for IT investments that incorporates risks (e.g., funding cuts or staffing changes).

Commerce's Office of the CIO implemented a process where this office reviewed at least the top three risks for each investment, verified that these risks were specific to the investment and were appropriately managed and mitigated, and verified that the risk register was updated regularly. In addition, DHS implemented a process that included a review of investment risks, ensured that the risks were current, and that risk mitigation plans were in place. Also, in November 2017, USDA updated its risk rating process to incorporate risks. Specifically, it updated its risk management scoring criteria to include an evaluation of the management and risk exposure scores of risks.

The actions that Commerce, DHS, and USDA took to incorporate reviews of risks into their risk rating processes better positioned the

Information Technology 229

agencies to provide more detailed and accurate information on their IT investments to the public.

## Portfolio Review

Four of the agencies—GSA, Justice, DHS, and USAID—identified performing application rationalization activities[27] as vital to their effective implementation of the portfolio review provision of FITARA. Application rationalization activities can include establishing a software application inventory, collecting information on each application, or evaluating an agency's portfolio of IT investments to make decisions on applications (e.g., retire, replace, or eliminate). We have previously reported that the principles of application rationalization are consistent with those used to manage investment portfolios.[28]

GSA and Justice performed application rationalization by engaging in efforts to establish complete and regularly updated application inventories. To do so, component agencies specified basic application attributes in their inventories (e.g., application name, description, owner, and function supported), and regularly updated the inventories. As we have previously reported, by having an application inventory that is complete and regularly updated, agencies such as GSA and Justice are better positioned to realize cost savings and efficiencies through activities such as consolidating redundant applications.

For its part, DHS utilized application rationalization to identify duplicate investments and consolidate systems. Part of the effort included the regular assessment of programs against criteria such as the program's cost, schedule, and performance relative to established targets. According to the agency, this resulted in the consolidation of site services, including help desk operations. DHS reported that this consolidation resulted in savings that cumulatively accrued to $202 million by fiscal year 2015.

---

[27] Application rationalization is the process of streamlining the portfolio of IT investments to improve efficiency, reduce complexity and redundancy, and lower the cost of ownership.

[28] GAO-16-511.

230 *United States Government Accountability Office*

In addition, as an application rationalization activity, USAID reviewed its portfolio of IT investments in order to identify systems to potentially retire or decommission—a requirement of the portfolio review provision of FITARA. Specifically, the agency developed an information system decommissioning plan to retire old systems. The plan described USAID's three-step approach to decommissioning systems: (1) identifying decommissioning candidates, (2) conducting system reviews and decommissioning decisions and (3) decommissioning planning and execution.

As a result of this approach to implementing the portfolio review provision of FITARA, the agency reported in its Information Systems Decommissioning Plan that it has decommissioned 78 old systems and identified additional systems to decommission in future years. Agency officials reported that USAID achieved cost savings of almost $10 million since 2016 as a result of decommissioning systems.

## Data Center Consolidation

GSA, Justice, NASA, USAID, and USDA identified four practices that were essential to their effective implementation of the data center consolidation provision of FITARA and resulted in agencies realizing cost savings or other IT management improvements:

- conduct site visits to all data centers,
- transition to a virtual or cloud-based environment,[29]
- incentivize component agencies to accelerate the pace of data center consolidation, and
- utilize data centers with excess capacity.

---

[29] Cloud technologies can improve the government's operational efficiencies and result in substantial cost savings. Virtualization is a technology that allows multiple, software-based machines with different operating systems, to run in isolation, side-by-side, on the same physical machine.

Information Technology 231

Agencies' actions to implement these practices have led to the retirement of older systems, increased cost savings and future cost avoidance, and a reduction in the number of data centers. In addition, as a result of applying these practices, the agencies were better able to make progress in consolidating and optimizing data centers.

### *Conduct Site Visits to All Data Centers*

USDA and Justice conducted site visits to all of their data centers to more effectively address the data center provision of FITARA. Both agencies stated that the site visits had allowed them to more thoroughly document the inventory of applications and IT hardware in each of the data centers and to validate progress made toward closing data centers.

USDA officials stated that conducting site visits to their data centers played a pivotal role in the successful implementation of data center consolidation by providing more direct communication with data center staff to address concerns and issues that staff had about consolidation of the centers. Additionally, agency officials reported that they were able to obtain more detailed information necessary to meet the FITARA requirements for reporting to OMB on USDA's data center inventory and progress made on data center closures as a result of conducting site visits.

Further, Justice officials stated that site visits conducted by staff in the CIO's office that were responsible for data center consolidation played a key role in the closure of many of the agency's data centers. Specifically, the officials said that conducting site visits in person showed data center staff that data center consolidation was a priority for the agency. The officials added that the site visits also showed data center staff that they were valued as partners in the consolidation effort.

### *Transition to a Virtual or Cloud-Based Environment*

USDA, GSA, NASA, and USAID have taken actions to transition to a virtual or cloud-based environment as a way to effectively implement the data center consolidation provision of the act. The agencies' actions consisted of moving data from agency-owned data centers to cloud-based

232     *United States Government Accountability Office*

environments, which helped the agencies make progress toward meeting the cost savings and data center optimization requirements of FITARA.

USDA officials reported that the agency has been successful in having its components use cloud technology to reduce the number of data centers. For example, the USDA Forest Service developed a migration strategy to move all of the Forest Service production systems and applications from its data centers to USDA's Enterprise Data Center and Cloud Infrastructure as a Service located at the National Information Technology Center in Kansas City, Missouri. As a result of moving its production systems and applications, the Forest Service increased virtualization, resolved many long-term security vulnerabilities, and reduced the number of duplicative and stand-alone applications by 70 percent. The Forest Service reported that it had identified cost savings of up to $6.1 million annually as a result of these efforts.

In addition, GSA developed a data center consolidation strategy which included migrating services from agency-owned data centers to more flexible and optimized cloud computing environments, shared service and co-location centers, and more optimized data centers within their own inventory. For example, the agency migrated numerous systems to provisioned services via cloud computing services. GSA officials reported that their agency has encouraged virtualization and cloud computing as preferred options above new physical implementations. The agency also continues to migrate away from hardware-dependent operating systems and to utilize, build upon, and mature its enterprise service virtualization platform offerings and capabilities. As a result of these actions, the agency has been able to more effectively retire older systems in order to shift them to newer, virtualized technologies.

NASA officials stated that their agency is transitioning to a cloud-based environment to close its data centers. For example, NASA moved all of the data from the Earth Observing System to a new commercial cloud-based model that hosts all the data in one location. The Earth Observing System was designed over a decade ago and its data were held at different partner locations based on science discipline (e.g., land, oceans, and atmosphere) and provided data that were used by the public in various

Information Technology 233

capacities. The agency funded data center hardware at each of the locations and transported data between the locations, as necessary, to create integrated data products. According to NASA officials, transitioning to a cloud-based environment has resulted in easier access to NASA data by the public, elimination of recurring capital investments in data center hardware, and improved IT security.

USAID reported that it saved money and increased efficiency by consolidating all of its data centers into a single data center in 2012 and then transitioning its single data center to a cloud-based environment. USAID completed the migration of its data center to the cloud in June 2018. According to the agency, moving to the cloud is expected to result in $36 million in future cost avoidance for the agency.

## *Incentivize Component Agencies to Accelerate the Pace of Data Center Consolidation*

Data center consolidation activities can be costly, requiring agencies to use resources to, for example, analyze the need for IT equipment (e.g., servers, processors, networking, and other hardware) and to move such equipment between locations. Our May 2018 report on the results of agencies' efforts to consolidate data centers noted mixed progress toward achieving OMB's goals for closing data centers.[30]

Justice incentivized a component agency to accelerate its participation in data center consolidation by providing supplemental funding for costs associated with consolidation. For example, the agency's CIO office provided funding for a component agency to offset the cost to move servers and data center equipment to another location. Justice officials noted that the agency has seen increased cooperation from component agencies as a result of offering supplemental funding to participate in its data center consolidation effort.

---

[30] GAO-18-264.

234 *United States Government Accountability Office*

### *Utilize Data Centers with Excess Capacity*

A part of GSA's strategy for consolidating data centers was to move existing data to other government data centers that had the capacity to store its data. To do so, GSA established shared service agreements with the Environmental Protection Agency's National Computer Center and NASA's Stennis Space Center data centers.[31] As a result of moving its data to other government data centers with excess capacity, GSA was able to consolidate numerous data centers, resulting in increased efficiency and cost savings.

## Software Purchasing

USDA, VA, GSA, NASA, and USAID identified the practice of centralizing the management of software licenses as essential to their effective implementation of the software purchasing provision of FITARA. These five agencies did this by, for example, establishing a software management team, creating contracts with vendors to centrally manage licenses, and establishing governance processes for software license management.

USDA employed a centralized software license management approach by establishing a Category Management Team. This team was responsible for the oversight of all software license enterprise agreements, which included collecting, reviewing, consolidating, and reporting on all software procurements. The agency also created Enterprise IT Category Management guidance that supported the central oversight authority for managing enterprise software license agreements. Further, according to USDA officials, management has been supportive in ensuring that all organizations and components join existing enterprise contracts that are already in place.

USDA's actions to centralize the management of its software licenses have led to effective agency-wide decisions regarding software purchases

---

[31] IT shared service is defined as an IT function that is provided for consumption by multiple organizations within or between federal agencies.

Information Technology | 235

that the agency reported have yielded cost savings. For example, the agency identified instances where multiple software contracts at different price points among component agencies could be consolidated into one contract at the lowest price. This resulted in reducing the cost per license for a software product from $250 to $15.75, saving the agency approximately $85,000 between 2016 and 2017, according to USDA documentation.

VA established an Enterprise Software License Management Team to centralize the management of its efforts to purchase software. According to officials in VA's Office of Information and Technology, this team consisted of knowledgeable staff that had experience with software management and development, and was familiar with software that was deployed across the entire agency. These officials also stated that the Enterprise Software License Management Team conducted weekly meetings with GSA to discuss software licensing and category management to ensure they were aware of other opportunities for cost savings.[32] VA also established an Enterprise Software Asset Management Technical Working Group that was formed to define and document a framework that employed a centralized software license management approach.

By centralizing the management of its software licenses, VA has been able to make effective agency-wide decisions regarding the purchase of software products and reported that it has realized cost savings. Specifically, VA provided documentation showing that it had implemented a solution to analyze agency-wide software license data, including usage and costs. The agency identified approximately $65 million in cost savings between 2017 and 2020 due to analyzing one of their software licenses.

---

[32] Category management is an approach the federal government is applying to buy smarter and more like a single enterprise. Category management enables the government to eliminate redundancies, increase efficiency, and deliver more value and savings from the government's acquisition programs. It involves identifying core areas of spend; collectively developing heightened levels of expertise; leveraging shared best practices; and providing acquisition, supply and demand management solutions.

236        *United States Government Accountability Office*

We previously reported that GSA and USAID had centralized the management of their software licenses.[33] We reported that GSA's server-based and enterprise-wide licenses were managed centrally, whereas non-enterprise-wide workstation software licenses were generally managed regionally. GSA also issued a policy that established procedures for the management of all software licenses, including analyzing software licenses to identify opportunities for consolidation.[34]

Centralizing the management of its purchase of software licenses has led GSA to make effective agency-wide decisions regarding its software licenses and avoid future costs, according to agency documentation. For example, in fiscal year 2015, the agency consolidated licenses for one of its software products, saving the agency over $400,000 and avoiding over $3 million in future costs.

For its part, USAID had a contract in place with a vendor for centrally managing licenses for all of its operating units. Further, according to officials within USAID's Office of the CIO, the agency established a governance process to manage the introduction of new software. As part of this governance process, USAID's Software and Hardware Approval Request Panel was responsible for reviewing requests to procure new software.

USAID's actions on centralizing the management of its software licenses have led to effective agency-wide decisions regarding software purchases that the agency reported have yielded cost savings. For example, USAID identified opportunities to reduce costs on its software licenses through consolidation or elimination of software. This resulted in the agency reporting a cumulative savings from fiscal year 2016 to fiscal year 2018 of over $2.5 million on software licenses.

NASA issued a software license management policy that included the roles and responsibilities for central management of the agency's software licenses.[35] In addition, in May 2017, NASA's Administrator issued a

---

[33] GAO-14-413.

[34] General Services Administration, *GSA Order, CIO 2108.1, Software License Management* (Washington, D.C.: Sept. 22, 2015).

[35] National Aeronautics and Space Administration, *NASA Interim Directive, Software License Management*, NID 7150-13, NPR 7510.2B (July 13, 2017).

# Information Technology 237

memorandum requiring component agencies to use the agency's Enterprise License Management Team to manage software licenses.

By employing a centralized software license management approach, NASA made effective agency-wide decisions on software licenses which the agency reported led to cost avoidance. For example, the agency increased the number of software agreements managed by its enterprise license management team from 24 to 42 in fiscal year 2014, and analyzed its software license data to identify opportunities to reduce costs and make better informed investments moving forward. As a result, NASA reported that it realized cost avoidance of approximately $224 million from fiscal years 2014 through 2018.

In summary, as a result of applying the practices identified in this review, the selected agencies were better positioned to implement FITARA provisions and realized IT management improvements and cost savings.

## AGENCY COMMENTS AND OUR EVALUATION

We requested comments on a draft of this chapter from each of the nine agencies included in our review, as well as from OMB. In response, one agency—USAID—provided written comments, which are reprinted in appendix I. Another agency—DHS—provided technical comments, which we incorporated in the report, as appropriate. The other 7 agencies and OMB did not provide comments on the draft report.

In its comments, USAID described actions that it had taken to enhance the authority of its CIO. Specifically, the agency stated that it had proposed that the CIO report directly to the Administrator and had notified the congressional committees of jurisdiction about this intended action. Further, USAID stated that, as of April 2019, the Administrator would be expected to approve revisions to internal policy to clarify and strengthen the authority of the CIO in line with FITARA and our report.

We are sending copies of this chapter to the appropriate congressional committees, the heads of the Departments of Agriculture, Commerce, Health and Human Services, Homeland Security, Justice, and Veterans

238     *United States Government Accountability Office*

Affairs; the General Services Administration; the National Aeronautics and Space Administration; the U.S. Agency for International Development; the Director of the Office of Management and Budget; and other interested parties.

Carol C. Harris Director
Information Technology Management Issues

## List of Requesters

The Honorable Elijah E. Cummings
Chairman

The Honorable Jim Jordan
Ranking Member
Committee on Oversight and Government Reform
House of Representatives

The Honorable Gerry Connolly
Chairman

The Honorable Mark Meadows
Ranking Member
Subcommittee on Government Operations
Committee on Oversight and Government Reform
House of Representatives

The Honorable Will Hurd
House of Representatives

The Honorable Robin L. Kelly
House of Representatives

# Appendix I: Comments from the US Agency for International Development

APR 0 4 2019

Carol C. Harris
Director, Information-Technology Acquisition-Management Issues
U.S. Government Accountability Office
441 G Street, N.W.
Washington, D.C. 20226

Re: Information Technology: Effective Practices Have Improved Agencies' FITARA Implementation (GAO-19-131)

Dear Ms. Harris:

I am pleased to provide the formal response of the U.S. Agency for International Development (USAID) to the draft report produced by the U.S. Government Accountability Office (GAO) titled, *Information Technology: Effective Practices Have Improved Agencies' Federal Information Technology Acquisitions Reform Act (FITARA) Implementation* (GAO-19-131).

We would like to thank the GAO for including our effective practices in this report. I hope our practices will be beneficial to other Federal Departments and Agencies. In addition to the effective practices documented in the draft report, I am pleased that we have taken a major step forward in our compliance with the FITARA's requirement to enhance the authority of our Chief Information Officer (CIO) by proposing in our Agency Transformation that the CIO report directly to the Administrator. The Congressional Notification for this proposal, submitted in August 2018, is pending with our Committees of jurisdiction.

In addition, this month the Administrator will be approving revisions to Chapter 509 of our Automated Directive System, *Management and Oversight of Information Technology Resources*, to clarify and strengthen the authority of our CIO in line with the GAO's report and FITARA. We hope to make additional improvements to meet - and exceed - the requirements of the aforementioned legislation in a holistic, fulsome, and sustainable way, which USAID will be able to do once Congress lifts its hold on the Notification.

I am transmitting this letter for inclusion in the GAO's final report. Thank you for the opportunity to respond to the draft report, and for the courtesies extended by your staff while conducting this engagement. We appreciate the opportunity to participate in the evaluation of our effective FITARA practices.

We do not have any additional comment on the draft report.

Sincerely,

Angelique M. Crumbly
Acting Assistant Administrator
Bureau for Management

# CONTENTS OF EARLIER VOLUMES

**Key Government Reports. Volume 16: April 2019**

**Finance**

**Chapter 1**   Foreign Asset Reporting: Actions Needed to
Enhance Compliance Efforts, Eliminate
Overlapping Requirements, and Mitigate Burdens
on U.S. Persons Abroad
*United States Government Accountability Office*

**Chapter 2**   Tax Refund Products: Product Mix Has Evolved
and IRS Should Improve Data Quality
Government Operations
*United States Government Accountability Office*

**Chapter 3**   2020 Census: Further Actions Needed to
Reduce Key Risks to a Successful Enumeration
*United States Government Accountability Office*

**Chapter 4**   Data Act: Pilot Effectively Tested Approaches for
Reporting Burden for Grants but Not for Contracts
*United States Government Accountability Office*

242  *Contents of Earlier Volumes*

**Veterans**

| | |
|---|---|
| **Chapter 5** | Military Spouse Employment: Participation in and Efforts to Promote the My Career Advancement Account Program<br>*United States Government Accountability Office* |
| **Chapter 6** | Veterans Health Administration: Past Performance System Recommendations Have Not Been Implemented<br>*United States Government Accountability Office* |
| **Chapter 7** | Veterans Health Care: VA Needs to Address Challenges as It Implements the Veterans Community Care Program<br>*United States Government Accountability Office* |

**Key Government Reports. Volume 15: April 2019**

**Energy**

| | |
|---|---|
| **Chapter 1** | Modernizing the Nuclear Security Enterprise: NNSA Is Taking Action to Manage Increased Workload at Kansas City National Security Campus<br>*United States Government Accountability Office* |
| **Chapter 2** | National Nuclear Security Administration Contracting: Review of the NNSA Report on the Nevada National Security Site Contract Competition (Updated)<br>*United States Government Accountability Office* |

**Science and Technology**

| | |
|---|---|
| **Chapter 3** | Scientific Integrity Policies: Additional Actions Could Strengthen Integrity of Federal Research<br>*United States Government Accountability Office* |

*Contents of Earlier Volumes* 243

**Chapter 4**   Workforce Automation: Better Data Needed to
Assess and Plan for Effects of Advanced
Technologies on Jobs
*United States Government Accountability Office*

**Key Government Reports. Volume 14: March 2019**

**Business**

**Chapter 1**   SBA Veterans Assistance Programs:
An Analysis of Contemporary Issues (Updated)
*Robert Jay Dilger and Sean Lowry*

**Chapter 2**   Small Business Administration Microloan
Program (Updated)
*Robert Jay Dilger*

**Chapter 3**   Small Business Administration:
A Primer on Programs and Funding (Updated)
*Robert Jay Dilger and Sean Lowry*

**Education**

**Chapter 4**   District of Columbia Opportunity
Scholarship Program (DC OSP):
Overview, Implementation, and Issues
*Rebecca R. Skinner*

**Chapter 5**   Laws Affecting Students with Disabilities:
Preschool Through Postsecondary Education
*Kyrie E. Dragoo and JD S. Hsin*

**Finance**

**Chapter 6**   The Debt Limit Since 2011 (Updated)
*D. Andrew Austin*

**Chapter 7**   What's the Difference?—
Comparing U.S. and Chinese Trade Data
*Michael F. Martin*

244                     *Contents of Earlier Volumes*

**Key Government Reports. Volume 13: March 2019**

**Government**

**Chapter 1**     The War Powers Resolution:
                  Concepts and Practice (Updated)
                  *Matthew C. Weed*

**Chapter 2**     Infantry Brigade Combat Team (IBCT) Mobility,
                  Reconnaissance, and Firepower Programs
                  *Andrew Feickert*

**Chapter 3**     Assessing NATO's Value
                  *Paul Belkin*

**Middle East**

**Chapter 4**     Armed Conflict in Syria:
                  Overview and U.S. Response (Updated)
                  *Carla E. Humud, Christopher M. Blanchard
                  and Mary Beth D. Nikitin*

**Chapter 5**     Iraq: Issues in the 116th Congress
                  *Christopher M. Blanchard*

**Key Government Reports. Volume 12: March 2019**

**Employment**

**Chapter 1**     Employment and Training Programs:
                  Department of Labor Should Assess Efforts
                  to Coordinate Services Across Programs
                  *United States Government Accountability Office*

**Housing**

**Chapter 2**     Real Estate Assessment Center: HUD Should
                  Improve Physical Inspection Process and
                  Oversight of Inspectors
                  *United States Government Accountability Office*

# Contents of Earlier Volumes 245

**Human Capital**

**Chapter 3**  Internal Revenue Service: Strategic Human
Capital Management is Needed to Address Serious
Risks to IRS's Mission
*United States Government Accountability Office*

**Key Government Reports. Volume 11: March 2019**

**Education**

**Chapter 1**  Federal Student Aid: Actions Needed to Evaluate
Pell Grant Pilot for Incarcerated Students
*United States Government Accountability Office*

**Chapter 2**  Student and Exchange Visitor Program-DHS
Can Take Additional Steps to Manage Fraud
Risks Related to School Recertification and
Program Oversight
*United States Government Accountability Office*

**Transportation**

**Chapter 3**  Automated Trucking: Federal Agencies Should
Take Additional Steps to Prepare for Potential
Workforce Effects
*United States Government Accountability Office*

**Chapter 4**  Surface Transportation: Action Needed to Guide
Implementation of Build America Bureau and
Improve Application Process
*United States Government Accountability Office*

**Chapter 5**  Transit Workforce Development: Improved
Strategic Planning Practices Could Enhance
FTA Efforts
*United States Government Accountability Office*

# INDEX

## A

agencies, vii, viii, ix, 1, 8, 11, 12, 13, 14, 15, 22, 23, 24, 26, 27, 30, 31, 50, 57, 59, 62, 64, 83, 92, 98, 106, 116, 117, 118, 119, 120, 121, 122, 123, 124, 125, 126, 127, 128, 129, 131, 132, 133, 134, 135, 136, 137, 138, 141, 142, 143, 144, 145, 146, 147, 148, 151, 152, 153, 155, 157, 159, 160, 161, 162, 163, 164, 165, 169, 170, 171, 174, 175, 176, 178, 179, 180, 181, 182, 183, 210, 211, 212, 213, 214, 215, 216, 217, 218, 219, 220, 221, 222, 223, 224, 225, 226, 227, 228, 229, 230, 231, 233, 234, 235, 237

assessment, 18, 36, 38, 40, 57, 75, 76, 79, 80, 81, 82, 84, 85, 88, 89, 90, 91, 94, 95, 96, 150, 182, 229

assessment procedures, 88, 89

avoidance, 27, 121, 135, 161, 180, 220, 231, 233, 237

## B

benefits, 4, 6, 7, 8, 107, 109, 145, 153, 165, 183

business environment, 35, 59, 61, 62, 97

business partners, 9

business processes, 35, 38, 39, 59, 60, 61, 62, 64, 65, 97, 98, 99

## C

categorization, 84, 86, 87, 95

challenges, vii, viii, ix, 1, 2, 4, 5, 10, 11, 16, 17, 18, 22, 30, 34, 38, 47, 61, 65, 77, 82, 107, 131, 133, 152, 155, 156, 210, 211, 212, 217, 218, 220

Chief Information Officers' (CIO), ix, 8, 12, 13, 14, 24, 25, 27, 28, 29, 88, 89, 91, 115, 119, 125, 126, 141, 156, 157, 158, 178, 209, 210, 213, 214, 215, 216, 217, 218, 222, 224, 225, 226, 227, 228, 231, 233, 236, 237

closure, 117, 123, 133, 134, 137, 141, 157, 159, 161, 165, 166, 167, 168, 169, 170, 171, 172, 173, 174, 175, 177, 180, 183, 220, 231

communication, 64, 74, 82, 164, 226, 231

compliance, 25, 48, 56, 88, 92, 225

computer systems, 56

# 248 *Index*

computing, 52, 76, 119, 125, 158, 160, 162, 232

confidentiality, 15, 29, 84, 86, 87

configuration, 19, 79, 84, 85, 87, 89, 92, 102

consolidation, viii, ix, 12, 13, 24, 26, 27, 115, 116, 118, 119, 120, 121, 122, 124, 125, 128, 129, 130, 132, 133, 134, 140, 141, 142, 152, 155, 156, 157, 158, 159, 161, 162, 163, 164, 180, 181, 210, 213, 216, 220, 222, 224, 229, 230, 231, 232, 233, 236

cost saving, viii, ix, 12, 13, 25, 26, 31, 116, 117, 120, 121, 122, 123, 124, 128, 129, 130, 131, 132, 133, 134, 135, 136, 142, 145, 152, 153, 155, 159, 161, 162, 164, 165, 166, 167, 168, 169, 170, 171, 173, 179, 180, 181, 182, 210, 211, 212, 213, 214, 215, 216, 220, 222, 229, 230, 231, 232, 234, 235, 236, 237

cybersecurity, v, vii, viii, 2, 4, 5, 14, 15, 28, 29, 30, 31, 33, 34, 35, 36, 38, 40, 41, 52, 54, 56, 57, 58, 76, 83, 85, 86, 92, 93, 95, 97, 102, 103

cybersecurity risk management, viii, 34, 56

## D

data center, v, viii, ix, 4, 5, 12, 13, 24, 26, 27, 115, 116, 117, 118, 119, 120, 121, 122, 123, 124, 125, 126, 127, 128, 129, 130, 131, 132, 133, 134, 135, 136, 137, 138, 139, 140, 141, 142, 143, 144, 145, 146, 147, 148, 149, 150, 151, 152, 153, 154, 155, 156, 157, 158, 159, 160, 161, 162, 163, 164, 165, 166, 167, 168, 169, 170, 171, 172, 173, 174, 175, 176, 177, 179, 180, 181, 182, 183, 210, 212, 213, 214, 216, 220, 222, 224, 225, 230, 231, 232, 233, 234

data center optimization, v, viii, 5, 26, 27, 115, 117, 118, 119, 120, 121, 122, 123, 126, 127, 130, 132, 133, 136, 143, 144, 146, 147, 148, 149, 151, 152, 154, 159, 166, 167, 168, 171, 172, 173, 174, 175, 176, 179, 180, 181, 182, 212, 214, 232

data collection, 169

data transfer, 77

database, 50

DCOI, viii, 115, 116, 117, 118, 119, 120, 121, 122, 123, 124, 125, 129, 132, 133, 134, 135, 136, 140, 141, 142, 143, 145, 146, 152, 153, 155, 156, 157, 161, 162, 164, 165, 166, 167, 168, 170, 171, 172, 173, 174, 175, 176, 177, 180, 181, 182, 183

Department of Agriculture, 115, 139, 140, 144, 149, 210

Department of Commerce, 115, 123, 139, 144, 149, 209

Department of Defense, 8, 12, 115, 120, 128, 139, 144, 145, 149, 219

Department of Education, 115, 134, 138, 139, 144, 149

Department of Energy, 115, 124, 139, 144, 149, 190

Department of Health and Human Services, 8, 116, 139, 144, 149, 166, 200, 209

Department of Homeland Security, 33, 36, 37, 100, 109, 115, 139, 144, 149, 209

Department of Justice, 116, 139, 144, 149, 209

Department of Labor, 116, 139, 144, 149, 167

Department of the Interior, 116, 139, 144, 149

Department of the Treasury, 12, 116, 139, 144, 149

Department of Transportation, 116, 139, 144, 149

Departments of Agriculture, 12, 120, 123, 133, 152, 180, 183, 211, 213, 237

## Index

District of Columbia Opportunity
Scholarship Program (DC OSP), 243

## E

emergency, 19, 42
emergency response, 42
energy, 15, 118, 124, 125, 127, 131, 136,
146, 147, 242
engineering, 40, 41, 85, 86, 87, 88, 90, 91,
92, 95, 102, 103
environment, viii, 34, 37, 38, 40, 41, 42, 43,
45, 47, 49, 50, 52, 62, 73, 76, 85, 86, 87,
88, 90, 91, 92, 93, 94, 95, 102, 103, 108,
130, 151, 230, 231, 232, 233
Environmental Protection Agency, 12, 115,
120, 123, 139, 144, 149, 152, 180, 183,
202, 213, 234

## F

federal agency, 216
federal data centers, viii, ix, 116, 119, 125,
126, 127, 138, 210
Federal Emergency Management Agency,
33, 35, 37, 44, 45, 46, 48, 51, 54, 61, 69,
80, 82, 85, 89, 97, 104
federal funds, 55
federal government, ix, 10, 15, 37, 50, 52,
98, 106, 119, 124, 210, 211, 215, 235
federal law, 14, 28, 48, 218
financial, 7, 15, 38, 42, 43, 47, 50, 51, 55,
56, 145
financial data, 38, 47
financial reports, 55
financial system, 51, 56
fiscal year, 9, 10, 11, 15, 17, 21, 26, 37, 42,
45, 75, 100, 117, 118, 120, 121, 122,
123, 127, 128, 129, 131, 133, 134, 135,
136, 137, 138, 139, 140, 141, 142, 143,
145, 146, 147, 151, 152, 153, 155, 158,

161, 164, 165, 170, 171, 174, 175, 180,
181, 182, 183, 211, 214, 217, 219, 220,
229, 236, 237
FITARA, v, vii, ix, 2, 3, 4, 5, 12, 13, 14, 23,
24, 25, 27, 28, 30, 116, 119, 120, 128,
129, 132, 133, 141, 142, 146, 183, 209,
210, 211, 212, 213, 214, 215, 217, 218,
220, 221, 222, 223, 224, 225, 226, 227,
228, 229, 230, 231, 232, 234, 237
funding, 9, 13, 19, 25, 80, 99, 100, 106, 145,
212, 216, 228, 233
funds, 152

## G

GMM program, viii, 34, 38, 39, 40, 41, 42,
46, 52, 55, 59, 67, 70, 71, 74, 81, 85, 88,
91, 92, 93, 94, 95, 96, 98, 99, 101, 102
governance, 3, 16, 17, 20, 30, 156, 158, 215,
217, 234, 236
governments, 37, 42, 104
grant programs, 42, 43, 44, 46, 47, 48, 53,
63, 65, 70, 72, 99, 104
grants, vii, viii, 34, 36, 37, 38, 39, 42, 43,
44, 47, 48, 49, 50, 55, 59, 60, 61, 62, 63,
64, 65, 66, 67, 73, 94, 97, 98, 99, 104
grants management, viii, 34, 35, 36, 37, 38,
39, 42, 43, 46, 47, 48, 49, 50, 56, 59, 60,
61, 62, 63, 64, 65, 66, 67, 69, 70, 73, 80,
85, 89, 94, 97, 98, 99, 104
guidance, 9, 13, 14, 20, 26, 27, 28, 36, 38,
40, 49, 52, 56, 57, 77, 85, 87, 88, 90, 91,
93, 95, 96, 98, 102, 106, 121, 129, 130,
131, 132, 137, 140, 142, 156, 158, 170,
171, 173, 174, 175, 176, 177, 181, 215,
218, 227, 228, 234

## H

health, 2, 4, 6, 7, 8, 9, 10, 16, 17, 18, 19, 20,
21, 30

250 *Index*

health care, 6, 7, 8, 9, 10, 16, 17, 18, 19
health care system, 9, 16, 17
health information, 2, 4, 7, 10, 18, 20
higher education, 43
home ownership, 6
homeland security, 48
Housing and Urban Development, 12, 116, 120, 122, 134, 139, 144, 149, 152, 180, 213

## I

improvements, 19, 22, 63, 73, 118, 120, 129, 211, 213, 214, 222, 230, 237
individuals, 29, 43, 56, 86, 89, 164
information security, vii, 1, 4, 5, 14, 15, 28, 29, 33, 47, 57, 87, 89, 102, 119
information sharing, 37, 47
information systems, vii, 1, 2, 4, 7, 14, 16, 18, 28, 29, 40, 44, 56, 57, 83, 87, 102, 230
information technology, 2, 4, 34, 35, 37, 97, 106, 116, 119, 209, 211
infrastructure, 6, 9, 10, 19, 52, 63, 68, 76, 119, 129, 130, 145, 156, 158, 159, 160, 164
integrity, 15, 29, 84, 86, 87, 93
interface, 48, 50, 51
interoperability, 2, 10, 17, 18, 20, 51
isolation, 131, 162, 230
issues, 5, 10, 47, 49, 57, 79, 84, 92, 94, 156, 226, 231
IT acquisitions, vii, 1, 10, 12, 28, 30, 215
IT investments, ix, 3, 10, 12, 13, 23, 25, 27, 98, 106, 121, 125, 180, 181, 210, 212, 213, 215, 216, 218, 219, 227, 228, 229, 230
IT programs, vii, 1, 74, 83, 106, 107
iteration, 54, 108, 219

## L

leadership, 11, 20, 35, 59, 60, 61, 83, 94, 97, 118, 155, 156, 157, 164, 165, 223, 224, 226
local government, 43

## M

major disasters, vii, 34, 42
management, vii, viii, ix, 2, 4, 5, 7, 8, 10, 13, 14, 16, 17, 18, 19, 23, 24, 25, 28, 29, 30, 34, 35, 36, 37, 38, 39, 40, 41, 42, 43, 47, 48, 49, 50, 52, 55, 59, 60, 61, 62, 63, 64, 65, 66, 67, 73, 75, 78, 79, 81, 82, 83, 84, 87, 89, 92, 94, 95, 96, 97, 98, 99, 100,103, 108, 119, 128, 131, 159, 161, 164, 210, 211, 212, 213, 214, 215, 216, 217, 218, 219, 220, 222, 225, 227, 228, 230, 234, 235, 236, 237
medical, 6, 7, 8, 19, 20, 21, 42
medical care, 6
medical history, 19
membership, 61
mental health, 21
methodology, 5, 41, 76, 77, 101, 124, 145, 155, 170, 217
microloan program, 243
migration, 50, 61, 77, 79, 158, 171, 232, 233
mission(s), vii, ix, 1, 2, 4, 6, 7, 10, 13, 37, 41, 42, 53, 60, 63, 70, 89, 121, 141, 165, 210, 211, 212, 215, 216
modernization, vii, 2, 5, 9, 11, 17, 18, 19, 31, 39, 50, 51, 56, 61, 97, 98, 157, 160

## N

National Aeronautics and Space Administration, 12, 116, 120, 140, 144,

149, 152, 168, 180, 187, 209, 211, 213, 224, 236, 238
National Defense Authorization Act, 4, 20, 21, 106, 119, 120, 128, 212
National Institute of Standards and Technology, viii, 15, 34, 40, 58, 89, 102, 119, 158
National Oceanic and Atmospheric Administration, 160
national security, 15, 57, 242
natural disaster, 37
Nuclear Regulatory Commission (NRC), 12, 116, 120, 140, 144, 150, 151, 152, 180, 205, 213

## O

Office of Management and Budget, 13, 106, 116, 117, 119, 127, 144, 147, 148, 149, 154, 210, 212, 238
Office of the Inspector General, 26, 140
officials, 20, 21, 22, 30, 36, 39, 40, 41, 42, 43, 46, 47, 48, 49, 50, 53, 54, 55, 61, 64, 65, 66, 67, 68, 69, 70, 72, 74, 76, 77, 79, 80, 81, 82, 83, 88, 90, 91, 92, 93, 96, 97, 99, 100, 101, 102, 103, 104, 118, 122, 123, 141, 151, 152, 156, 170, 172, 177, 180, 182, 212, 214, 218, 223, 224, 225, 226, 227, 228, 230, 231, 232, 233, 234, 235, 236
operating system, 131, 147, 162, 230, 232
operations, 5, 9, 10, 14, 15, 39, 48, 55, 56, 57, 86, 98, 119, 125, 155, 156, 158, 159, 229
opportunities, 12, 24, 50, 73, 166, 171, 216, 235, 236, 237
optimization, viii, 12, 13, 26, 27, 117, 118, 119, 120, 122, 123, 126, 127, 128, 129, 130, 131, 132, 133, 134, 135, 136, 141, 142, 146, 148, 150, 151, 152, 153, 154, 155, 156, 157, 159, 161, 162, 163, 164,

165, 166, 167, 168, 169, 170, 171, 172, 173, 174, 175, 176, 177, 179, 180, 181, 182, 214, 220, 232
oversight, 24, 52, 55, 56, 61, 74, 135, 156, 215, 234

## P

planned action, 87, 169, 170
planned saving, 121, 133, 134, 136, 143, 171, 181
policy, 9, 13, 14, 24, 27, 28, 29, 55, 65, 89, 132, 156, 160, 162, 163, 172, 174, 176, 177, 212, 216, 218, 227, 228, 236, 237
portfolio, ix, 37, 121, 210, 213, 219, 222, 229, 230
preparedness, 42, 48, 53
private sector, 18, 38, 98
probability, 25
project, 17, 19, 25, 48, 156, 158, 159, 164, 215, 228
public assistance, 48
public health, 37
public interest, 19

## Q

quality control, 39, 41, 100, 103

## R

real estate, 124, 125, 161
real time, 19, 81
recognition, 6
recommendations, vii, 2, 3, 4, 5, 11, 16, 23, 24, 25, 26, 27, 28, 29, 34, 49, 84, 90, 95, 96, 117, 134, 135, 136, 140, 151, 165, 169, 170, 171, 173, 174, 175, 176, 178, 214, 217, 218, 219, 220, 221

252 *Index*

reengineering, viii, 34, 35, 38, 59, 60, 61, 62, 64, 65, 94, 97, 98

Reform, viii, ix, 3, 4, 5, 106, 116, 119, 128, 179, 209, 210, 211, 212, 213, 222, 226, 238

regulations, 63

reliability, viii, 21, 34, 38, 39, 40, 41, 97, 100, 101, 103, 121, 122, 123, 180, 181, 182, 218

requirements, vii, viii, ix, 2, 7, 9, 12, 14, 19, 24, 25, 27, 34, 35, 38, 39, 43, 49, 52, 55, 57, 59, 60, 61, 66, 67, 68, 69, 71, 72, 74, 90, 93, 94, 95, 97, 98, 99, 100, 107, 108, 109, 119, 120, 125, 128, 135, 136, 142, 159, 160, 163, 172, 174, 176, 177, 210, 213, 215, 220, 223, 224, 225, 227, 230, 231, 232

resources, 9, 14, 21, 30, 52, 76, 78, 80, 82, 92, 119, 131, 152, 157, 158, 160, 161, 171, 172, 233

response, vii, 2, 3, 5, 23, 44, 49, 71, 72, 82, 84, 87, 89, 91, 92, 94, 96, 121, 145, 214, 237

risk, viii, ix, 3, 4, 5, 10, 11, 12, 13, 15, 23, 24, 25, 29, 30, 34, 36, 40, 47, 56, 57, 61, 66, 69, 76, 78, 79, 81, 82, 83, 85, 86, 87, 87, 89, 90, 91, 92, 94, 95, 102, 107, 131, 159, 210, 213, 215, 216, 218, 222, 228

## S

savings, viii, 3, 13, 24, 26, 27, 117, 120, 121, 122, 123, 125, 129, 131, 133, 134, 135, 136, 137, 142, 143, 144, 145, 153, 161, 165, 166, 171, 174, 179, 180, 181, 183, 214, 216, 219, 220, 229, 235, 236

Secretary of Agriculture, 166

Secretary of Commerce, 166

Secretary of Defense, 166

Secretary of Homeland Security, 96

security, 4, 14, 15, 29, 36, 41, 47, 57, 58, 70, 83, 84, 85, 86, 87, 88, 89, 90, 91, 92, 93, 95, 96, 102, 103, 119, 125, 129, 130, 131, 161, 232, 233

servers, 76, 119, 124, 125, 130, 147, 158, 161, 162, 163, 233

service organization, 42

service provider, 8, 52, 76, 92, 137, 159

services, 6, 7, 8, 12, 15, 21, 52, 106, 119, 121, 130, 131, 137, 155, 158, 159, 160, 161, 171, 181, 216, 229, 232

Social Security, 12, 116, 120, 123, 126, 138, 140, 145, 150, 152, 180, 183, 213

Social Security Administration, 12, 116, 120, 123, 126, 138, 140, 145, 150, 152, 180, 183, 213

software, ix, 3, 12, 13, 23, 24, 25, 39, 51, 52, 54, 66, 68, 71, 76, 81, 98, 101, 106, 107, 108, 124, 125, 131, 147, 156, 158, 161, 162, 163, 210, 213, 214, 217, 219, 220, 222, 229, 230, 234, 235, 236, 237

Software Engineering Institute, viii, 34, 38, 59, 66, 71, 73, 97

spending, 25, 37, 121, 142, 156, 158, 211, 214

## T

target, 35, 58, 59, 61, 62, 63, 64, 77, 80, 82, 97, 98, 118, 127, 131, 135, 138, 140, 142, 143, 144, 145, 146, 147, 153, 157, 158, 173, 174, 175, 182

technical comments, 96, 169, 173, 176, 237

techniques, 78, 81, 163, 164

terrorist attacks, 37, 42, 104

testing, 19, 52, 76, 83, 84, 87, 92, 93, 106, 158

time frame, 11, 23, 27, 53, 54, 65, 66, 69, 70, 77, 82, 83, 94, 95, 121, 141, 142, 164, 180, 217, 219, 220, 227

## Index 253

transparency, ix, 12, 13, 210, 213, 216, 222, 225, 228

## U

United States, v, 1, 8, 33, 44, 115, 178, 179, 209, 242, 243

## V

virtualization, 118, 131, 136, 146, 155, 161, 162, 232

## W

web, 37, 48, 160, 162, 164
web pages, 162
websites, 121, 160, 181
work activities, 78
workflow, 62
workforce, 4, 30, 223
workload, 3, 21
workstation, 236